D0771438

CONTENTS

To all the men and women who made the ultimate
sacrifice in times of war.
Our freedom stands squarely upon their shoulders.

PREFACE

"The Greatest Generation." And maybe they were. Swarms of men enlisted after the attack on Pearl Harbor, and as the war dragged on, young boys barely old enough to shave joined up, often lying about their age to do so. The women worked in factories as riveters, on the front lines as nurses, and in the armed forces as WACs, WAVES, or WASPs.* Civilians throughout the country rationed food and supplies, bought war bonds, and mourned the thousands of casualties the United States suffered every month.

And unlike the conflicts that have followed, few could question the absolute necessity of a war in which our enemies were a Japanese empire that was brutally attempting to conquer every parcel of land in the Pacific and a Nazi regime that was perhaps even more brutal in its attempt to reign over Europe and exterminate the vast multitude they so casually considered "inferior."

But we look back on those days through the rose-colored glasses of nostalgia. Ask one of the Tuskegee Airmen how it felt to be prohibited from eating with the white bomber crews they so valiantly protected. Ask a black military policeman how it felt to be forced to eat in the kitchen of a restaurant in Alabama, while the German POW he was guarding was allowed to eat in the dining room. Ask a Japanese-American soldier of the 442nd Regimental Combat Team how it felt to be bleeding in France while his family members, citizens of the United States, were corralled in an internment camp in Utah. No, life wasn't as perfect back then as we'd like to believe. And the war wasn't any more sanitary, nor the combatants any more honorable or

---

* WAC: Women's Army Corps
  WASP: Women's Airforce Service Pilots
  WAVES: Women Accepted for Volunteer Emergency Service (officially known as
     U.S. Naval Women's Reserve)

resilient, than those who came before or since. In spite of the noble efforts of great films like *Saving Private Ryan* and *The Best Years of Our Lives*, and powerful television programs like *Band of Brothers*, we are still imbued with the more archaic Hollywood portrayal of World War II: nearly bloodless combat being carried out by men of impeccable moral standards, unflinching even in the face of an evil enemy committing despicable acts, and returning home with hardly a trace of the horrors they witnessed and the hardships they endured.

But that's not quite how it was, and that is one reason I am compelled to share the story of Murray Jacobs. He and many men like him were irreversibly damaged by their experience during the war. And many, if not most, took their own ugly truths silently and stoically to their graves. When we judge soldiers simply by their actions, without understanding the profound impact violent conflict has on the human psyche, we are unfairly considering them from the narrow focus of our own point of view, safe and sound in the comfort of our own homes. Moreover, our judgment is influenced by the incorrect notion that the soldier of yesteryear—particularly of the Second World War—was more righteous or more virtuous. Make no mistake— I am in no way condoning the torture or mistreatment of prisoners or the desecration of the bodies of fallen combatants. I am suggesting that we take pause before we judge these, and other actions, too harshly, or without the realistic expectation that if we put a young person into an irrational situation, their behavior is likely to become at least equally irrational.

Murray himself kept his own account secret for over sixty-five years, never telling a soul about it until he agreed to divulge the details to me, and he did so with the absolute caveat that his story would not be published until after his death. His revelation proved to be an arduous process for both of us. Murray dredged up memories and images that he spent the greater part of his life trying to forget.

For me, what started as a simple attempt to document the historical contributions of a Navy veteran—as told in his own words—quickly metamorphosed into a journey of understanding. At first, an endeavor to understand the effect of war on an otherwise peaceful man's behavior. Later, an astonishing descent into a troubled man's mind in strenuous pursuit of the truth—a quest that required multiple layers of analysis and validation. In today's world, we have video and photographic images that document nearly every action of every soldier. The further we delve back in time, the cloudier the picture becomes, and the more elusive the truth. And anyway, what is the truth? Ten people can share a common experience and later provide eleven different accounts of the events. But there are facts, and then there is fiction. And in the end, the facts are worth pursuing, whatever the cost. In the words of James A. Garfield, twentieth president of the United States, "The truth will set you free, but first it will make you miserable."

CHAPTER 1

GENESIS OF A PROJECT

Utah.

If you had told me in 1985 that in twenty years I'd be practicing medicine in Utah, I'd have said you were nuts. After all, I had just graduated from Downstate Medical Center in Brooklyn, and as I was about to begin a pediatric residency in New Jersey, the move across the Hudson River felt as adventurous to me as the journey up the Missouri River must have felt to Lewis and Clark. But after three years of residency, I settled down nicely in central New Jersey, opened up my own office, and started the Pediatric Emergency Medicine program at Robert Wood Johnson Medical School in New Brunswick.

My introduction to Utah came in 1994 when I took a ski trip to Park City with my good friend Bruce Quinn. I fell in love with the state almost instantly. In 1996, I convinced my wife, Julie, that we should invest in a condominium, and for the next five years we vacationed in Utah at least twice every winter and once every summer. With each passing trip, Utah felt more and more like our home-away-from-home. By 1998, I was growing dissatisfied with the increasingly mundane practice of general pediatrics and frustrated by the obtuse politics involved in running a pediatric emergency department. Trying to revitalize my enthusiasm for the practice of medicine, I decided to learn medical acupuncture and enrolled in a course offered at UCLA. That proved to be one of the best decisions I have ever made, and the most satisfying, enriching educational experience I have ever had. I immediately started to incorporate acupuncture into my practice, specifically concentrating on children with Attention-Deficit Disorder, and also into my work in the ER, treating patients with acute trauma and headaches.

By 2001, Julie and I decided we needed a change of scenery, and while visiting two friends who had recently moved from New

Jersey to Salt Lake City, we were surprised to see how seamlessly they had adapted to life in Utah. After careful consideration, Julie and I decided to relocate. We were both determined to make the move, although we needed to alter the courses of our careers in order to do so. Julie started a fellowship in Bone Marrow Transplant (she already had been appointed assistant professor of Pediatric Hematology and Oncology in New Jersey), and I took a job as the medical director of a chain of locally owned pediatric urgent care clinics.

Julie completed her fellowship and eventually made a transition entirely into the world of adult medicine, becoming assistant director of the Intermountain Blood & Marrow Transplant Program at LDS Hospital. My road was not quite as smooth. The individuals who owned the clinics I was working for turned out to be a coalition of liars, thieves, and sociopaths, and within nine months the whole organization was bankrupt. Since Julie's career was flourishing, I decided to take the opportunity of unemployment to immerse myself further into the world of Chinese medicine, and I started a practice devoted exclusively to medical acupuncture, focusing my attention primarily on adults with chronic pain problems.

Ever since I first learned the science of acupuncture, I had imagined a practice model in which patients were treated in their own homes, allowing for a comfortable and serene environment as well as affording me the liberty of spending ample time with each patient, free from the constraints of traditional office overhead expenses. In 2003, I sent out a bulk mailing advertisement in an effort to grow my practice, and shortly thereafter I received a call from a woman named Catherine Jacobs-Washburn, a forty-eight-year-old thyroid cancer survivor with chronic arthritis and migraine headaches. When I took her on as a patient and began treating her in her Midvale, Utah home, I realized that I was about as far from being a pediatrician in New Jersey as I could possibly be.

Catherine proved to be an excellent patient. She tolerated acupuncture well and had a good clinical response to the treatments. She taught elementary school and maintained a hectic lifestyle, and her home environment wasn't what I had envisioned as serene. There was her husband, Bob Washburn, a rather intense attorney dividing his time between their home in Utah and his practice in Cincinnati, Ohio. Also residing in the house were her two adolescent sons, her seven-year-old daughter, a Jack Russell terrier, two cats, a rabbit, several tropical fish, and a large boa constrictor. The whole scene became exponentially more chaotic in 2005, when Catherine's father became too ill to continue living on his own, and the family decided that he should move in with them. And that, my friends, is the conclusion of the circuitous, improbable journey that brought my life into direct juxtaposition with the life of Murray Jacobs.

The first several times I interacted with Murray were rather unremarkable. Most of his time was spent sitting in an armchair in the front room of the house, watching TV and napping. He had a full head of gray hair, small, closely set eyes, and a rather bulbous nose that divulged his enthusiasm for alcohol in his younger days. Although he required oxygen and moved around cautiously with the aid of a walker, he seemed relatively sturdy and in fairly good physical condition, particularly for a man of his advanced age. (He was eighty-nine when I met him.) I knew from Catherine that he was generally belligerent, even more so now that he had his loss of independence to be bitter about. Both his older daughters refused to take him in, but Catherine, nurturing angel of mercy that she is, couldn't let her father spend the winter of his life in a nursing home. In spite of her kindness to him, Murray was unnecessarily harsh, disagreeable, and demanding toward Catherine. Having a vitriolic father of my own, I was very familiar with this type of behavior, and although comfortable around it, I did not approve of it, particularly as his caustic demeanor caused Catherine considerable stress and adversely affected her health. So typically, when I came into the house I would give him a polite "Hello," ask how he was doing, and quickly get down to the task at hand.

At some point along the way, Catherine mentioned to me that her father was a veteran of World War II and served in the Pacific Theatre. She didn't know any details about his service because throughout his life he refused to discuss it. Now, I have had a soft spot in my heart for veterans for as long as I can remember. Quite frankly, I think it stems in part from feelings of guilt that I harbor, having never served in the military. When the war in Vietnam ended I was only thirteen, and at the time Operation Desert Storm was taking place, I was deeply involved in getting my medical career off the ground. I hold veterans in great esteem, and I have always been extremely appreciative of their sacrifices and their contributions to our society. So that day as I left, I paused for a moment and thanked Murray for his service in the military. After a few seconds of silence, he turned toward me with a piercing glare and growled, "Well, you're not speaking Japanese, are you?" I was a little taken aback but responded gently, "No, I'm not. And it's thanks to guys like you. And I want you to know that I appreciate you." Well, that took some of the bluster out of him as he softened his gaze, lowered his voice, and simply responded, "You're welcome." I think it was after that encounter that I started referring to Murray (behind his back, of course) as "Captain Cantankerous."

My relationship with Murray changed in 2010, after I watched the HBO series *The Pacific*. Having seen that depiction of the horrors our Marines endured, I became curious as to what sort of experiences Murray might have had, and why he refused to talk about his service for all these years. He agreed to meet with me, and we chatted for over two hours. I learned he was in the Navy and served as a member of the Seabees. He explained that prior to the war he worked at a copper mine as a heavy equipment operator, and that was how he came to enlist in that particular branch of the military. Up until that point, I knew very little about the Seabees; only what I remembered from watching the 1944 John Wayne film *The Fighting Seabees* many years before. I have since learned that the Seabees were developed in early 1942, at the behest of Rear Admiral Ben Moreell.[1]

Moreell was born in 1892, in Salt Lake City, Utah, and had served in the Navy during World War I. In 1937, Moreell was appointed by President Franklin Delano Roosevelt to be chief of civil engineers of the Navy, as well as chief of the Bureau of Yards and Docks. Shortly after the attack on Pearl Harbor, Rear Admiral Moreell, in what could only be described as a brilliant moment of foresight, recognized that there would be an urgent need for skilled construction crews who were militarized and prepared to exchange their tools for weapons at any moment. He was granted authority to recruit men from the construction trades for assignment to naval construction battalions, or 'CBs,' hence the name Seabees. Throughout the Second World War, the Seabees completed innumerable vital construction assignments in both the Atlantic and Pacific Theaters of Operation.

Murray went on to tell me that he was involved in amphibious landings on three islands during the course of his nearly two years of service. He explained that on each occasion, the Marines landed first, followed only minutes later by the Seabees. He described the brutal combat he experienced and vividly recalled how the ocean turned red with the blood of his fallen comrades. He confided in me that he still had nightmares about the terrible things he had seen and done, and that he was still being treated at the local VA hospital for Post-Traumatic Stress Disorder (PTSD), or what was referred to during World War II as "battle fatigue." While I knew that more probing questions might prove upsetting for Murray, my curiosity compelled me to ask him about the things he had done that were still haunting him. There was a long pause, and I could see by the troubled look on his face that he was dredging up images that he would have rather forgotten, while at the same time he was trying to decide whether or not to share those particular memories with me. After the uncomfortable silence, he looked at me with the icy gaze that was becoming all too familiar and sternly said, "Things like cuttin' a Jap in half with a knife. Now I don't want to talk about it anymore."

I was surprised by his answer, and from that moment onward, I saw Murray in a different light. Here was this old man, tethered to his oxygen tank, every breath a challenge, every step an adventure, but in his day . . . boy, in his day, he must have been hell on wheels. In my imagination, I could suddenly see him as a young man: rugged, tough, working at a copper mine one day, then killing Japanese soldiers with his bare hands the next. In his mind, his response made him a barbarian, but it my mind it made him altogether human.

It's so easy to minimize old folks—to simply take them at face value. But with the elderly, what you see is not what you get. Behind every weathered, wrinkled face there's a whole life that was lived. Sometimes a simple life, sometimes complex, sometimes a mundane existence, but other times a fascinating journey that is decelerating to its inevitable conclusion.

I remember very clearly the first time I ever had this revelation about the elderly. I was a third-year medical student, doing an internal medicine rotation at Long Island College Hospital in Brooklyn. I was sent in to draw blood from an old guy with some sort of cancer that had metastasized to his liver. I approached his bedside, and I saw this small, withered man, his skin canary yellow from jaundice. He barely had the energy to acknowledge my presence. I introduced myself, explained what I needed to do, and proceeded to attempt to obtain a sample of blood. This proved to be a formidable task. His veins had been ravaged by the combination of age, chemotherapy, and the countless attempts at phlebotomy by the students who preceded me. As I continued to poke at his nearly fluorescent skin, I noticed that his arms were adorned by a variety of tattoos, not nearly as common a sight in 1983 as they have since become. He moaned in discomfort as I tried many times to get that specimen, but he couldn't even muster the strength to offer the least bit of resistance. When I finally accomplished my goal, I left his room and went to his chart to complete the paperwork that was needed to accompany his blood to the lab. And that's when it hit me. Right there at the top of his initial history. His occupation was listed as "stevedore." Suddenly I pictured him as a young man, in his tattooed glory, unloading cargo from ships on the docks of New York, maybe even at the old Brooklyn Navy Yard, which was right nearby the hospital. And I thought to myself, "Man, in his day, this guy could've kicked my ass ten times over if I even looked at him funny, and now he can't even put up a struggle." I was overcome at that moment by a feeling of sadness. Sadness for a man whose power and vitality had been drained by time and by disease. I was so overcome by this sorrow that I nearly wept. And I wondered if that is indeed the fate that awaits us all. We think we're strong, we think we're invincible, but in the end, we all have two things waiting for us: a hospital bed and a casket. I think that encounter, as much as anything else, steered me away from a medical career involving the care of the elderly. As my friend and classmate Mark DiBenedetto once told me, "Zuck, practicing internal medicine is a constant reminder of your own mortality." And that's probably one good reason I became a pediatrician.

After that first substantial conversation with Murray, I think he saw me differently as well. He could tell that I was genuinely interested in him and his story, and more importantly, he realized that I wasn't judging him but simply accepting him. After that encounter, we greeted each other much more warmly, having rather quickly established a unique, unspoken connection. The following year, 2011, found me staring down the barrel of my fiftieth birthday, and in a bit of a conundrum regarding how exactly to spend it. The year before, we went to Hawaii to celebrate Julie's fiftieth, and I wanted to do something for myself that would be equally memorable. Any semblance of rational thought was temporarily suspended when I received an advertisement from the National World War II Museum for one of their travel programs. It was a tour of Europe, retracing the steps of the men who fought in the Battle of the Bulge, continuing on to the site of Dachau Concentration Camp, and concluding at Hitler's Eagle's Nest in Berchtesgaden, Germany. World War II combat veterans would accompany the tour, and at Dachau, there would be Holocaust survivors who would share their memories. I knew it immediately. That would be the perfect way to celebrate my special birthday: a tour of blood-soaked battlefields, a notorious concentration camp, and Adolph Hitler's mountaintop teahouse.

In all fairness to my apparent fascination with the macabre, I have for many years, certainly since seeing *Schindler's List* and probably long before, felt a deeply ingrained sense that those concentration camps are the hallowed ground of my ancestors. Unlike most Jews, who consider Israel the Holy Land and spend the better part of their lives trying to get there, I hold a much greater spiritual devotion to the synagogues, ghettos, and death camps where my people were robbed, tortured, and slaughtered. Perhaps it's because my family originated in those same countries of Eastern Europe where the Nazi sociopaths practiced their special brand of racial hygiene—places like Romania, Poland, and Lithuania. Maybe it's because the ancient history of Jews in Israel is just that—ancient, and therefore less meaningful to me than events that took place during my grandparents' lifetime. For whatever reason, I am drawn to those places and feel very strongly that someday I need to stand on that soil, see with my own eyes the remnants of the evils that were perpetrated upon my antecedents, and in doing so, try to feel the suffering and the anguish that they felt. So, for me, spending my fiftieth birthday at Dachau was just as logical as someone else spending theirs in Jerusalem.

Unfortunately, the trip was not to be, as lucid thought prevailed and it became clear that Julie and I could neither afford the expense nor the nearly three weeks away from our work that such a journey would require. After several weeks of feeling sorry for myself, having been deprived of such a magnificent experience, Julie came up with the idea that we could visit the World War II Museum itself, located in one of our favorite cities:

New Orleans. We had been there twice before, but in the inter-
vening years the museum had expanded, and anyway, Julie
and I had been wanting to go back to New Orleans ever since
the city was devastated by Hurricane Katrina to support their
economy with some of our tourist dollars and enjoy some of our
favorite food. After all, there really isn't anything, anywhere,
quite like a debris po'boy at Mother's on the corner of Poydras
and Tchopitoulas. So, we planned the trip, and made sure to be
at the museum on June 6, knowing that there would be some
special events to commemorate the sixty-seventh anniversary of
the D-Day invasion at Normandy.

The keynote speaker was Dr. Harold Baumgarten, a highly
decorated veteran who had landed on Omaha Beach and was
wounded five times in just a little over twenty-four hours. His
description of the events of that day and the carnage around
him was vivid and poignant. He described standing neck-deep
in bloody red water, the beach strewn with the body parts of his
fallen comrades, men being blown to bits immediately to his left
and to his right. A true American hero, Dr. Baumgarten's ability
to recall even the most minor details made his discourse especially riveting. He made a particular point to mention the names
and the hometowns of the men with whom he served, many
of who did not survive. He explained that as he pondered the
question of why he was allowed to survive while so many others
perished, he realized that it was his responsibility to tell the stories of those who could no longer speak. That resonated with me
and got me thinking about Murray, who was involved in not one
but three amphibious assaults and undoubtedly experienced a
lot more than twenty-four hours of combat. I came to the realization that his story, whatever it was that he experienced, was
valuable and deserved to be told. Otherwise, once he's dead, the
events and the history die with him, as though they had never
happened. Although at the time I was in the midst of writing a
book (my autobiography), given Murray's advanced age, I knew
that I had to put that project on the back burner and try to
document the details of Murray's life.

As soon as I returned home to Utah, I ran the idea past
Catherine, who was thrilled but at the same time skeptical,
since her father had always steadfastly refused to discuss his
war experiences with anyone. When I asked Murray about it,
about sitting down with him and getting all the details of his life

and, in particular, dredging up everything that happened during the war, he responded in his typically gruff fashion: "Well why do you want to know all of that?"

"Because you've lived a long life, and you've experienced some things that are historically important. And once you die, your eyewitness account of those events will be gone if they aren't preserved."

"Well, maybe some things are better left forgotten."

"I don't agree with that. Anything that has happened, for better or for worse, is worth remembering. Especially anything that happened during World War II, which you could argue was the most important event of the twentieth century, an event that shaped our current society, and an event that, as more and more of you old veterans die off, people are just going to stop remembering. Not to mention the fact that over the course of your life you've seen countless other important events, like the Great Depression, various assassinations, and mankind landing on the moon. And I think it would be interesting to know how you experienced those events and how they affected your life." I was giving him the hard sell, and he was thinking about it.

"Well I suppose I could talk to you, but there are two conditions. First, you can't use my real name. Second, you can't write anything until after I'm gone. I don't want my family to know some of the things I've done while I'm still around. And I have to tell you, by the time we're done, I think you'll hate me."

I reassured Murray that I would change his name and the names of his children, so that he could not be identified. And I promised him that I would not divulge any of the details of our conversations to his family until after his death. But I also gave him a stipulation of my own: I was going to ask him whatever questions I could think of, no matter how difficult or distressing, and I expected him to answer candidly and honestly. We shook hands and agreed to have our first meeting about a month later, allowing me to clear some time in my schedule. As I was leaving, excited about the task I was about to undertake, Murray said, in a quieter voice than usual, "I just hope you don't hate me when we're through." As I persuaded him that my feelings toward him wouldn't change, no matter what he told me, I have to admit that I privately questioned whether I was actually telling him the truth.

CHAPTER 2

THE FIRST TIME I SAW COMBAT

When Murray and I finally sat down for our first real interview, I positioned a small tape recorder between us, so I could capture everything he said, exactly as he said it. True to my word I dove right in.

"Tell me about the very first time you saw combat."

He looked a little surprised, but I think he appreciated my straightforward approach. "Oh, so you want to go right into it?"

"Well, that's what we agreed upon."

"The first time I saw combat was on a small island called Majuro that the government decided we had to take to build an airstrip on. I wasn't nervous as we approached Majuro. I don't know why, but I just wasn't. I had heard all the horrible stories of the previous island invasions, and we knew we weren't all going to come back. But we had just completed a relatively quiet eight-day voyage from Hawaii, and intelligence informed us that only a few hundred Japanese were expected to be defending the island. Now, by 'relatively quiet,' I mean we had just one encounter with the enemy, an attack by a type of torpedo bomber that was called a 'Kate.' He had come in behind us at low altitude, which made it harder to pick him up on radar. As soon as the plane was spotted, a General Quarters alarm was sounded, and the crew took to their battle stations. As a member of the 100th Naval Construction Battalion, I was just a passenger on board, but I had a front-row seat for the action. I was standing right next to one of the ship's 30mm anti-aircraft cannons, which was being manned by a young sailor with an equally young officer by his side. As the bomber approached, the sailor kept asking the officer, 'Should I shoot? Should I shoot?' But the officer was frozen and didn't respond. As I was looking over his shoulder, right down the barrel of the gun, I could see the plane getting closer and closer, until I couldn't stand it anymore and shouted, 'Shoot that son-of-a-bitch already!' Maybe the sailor thought the officer gave him the command, and he finally opened fire and blew that bomber out of the sky. I don't know whether he hit an engine, or a propeller, or what, but the plane went right down into the ocean. Our ship never even stopped. We just kept right on a-goin'. Outside of that, it was a wonderful trip to Majuro. The water was crystal clear and pretty calm. I can still see the flying fish jumping between the waves.

"We landed in LSTs [Landing Ship, Tank]. We had five minutes after the Marines went in ahead of us. I don't know what their strategy was. Five minutes didn't give them much of a hold on the island."

Murray was painting a dramatic picture, and I was fascinated.

"Were you taking fire right away?"

"Yes, we were taking fire—there was resistance from the Japs that were on the island. They were shooting at us while we were still in the boat; bullets were hitting the boat, and there were bombs of some kind being dropped around us. Some guys got killed right in my boat. You get your head up too high and you get it shot off. It scared the shit out of us. Some men got hit and fell before they ever got ashore. It was utter confusion. Chaos. Once we were up on the beach nobody knew what to do, and everybody was just trying to stay as low as they could. There wasn't somebody who said, 'You go here and you go there.' Everybody was just trying to protect their own butt. There were Japs shooting at us from up in the palm trees—what was left of them. Our planes had been over the island days before and bombed it all to hell. But when we landed, you wouldn't think they had bombed it at all. There were Japs all over; like flies! You wanted to dig a hole to crawl into, but the island was nothing but coral, and if you tried to dig a foxhole the water just seeped right through. Our casualties weren't real heavy, but as far as I was concerned one casualty was enough—that one casualty could've been me!

"I had two friends who were killed right on that first day. One was Doyle Smith from Texas. He was tall and lanky, good-natured, and a real good friend. The other guy was named Ross. I don't remember his last name; I don't know if I ever knew it. He was from somewhere back east, and I don't even know why he was there. He had five kids."

Thinking back to what Dr. Baumgarten had said, how important it is to pay tribute to the men who had sacrificed for our freedom, and thinking that Murray might be the last living person who knows what happened to these particular individuals, I probed for more details: "Do you remember what happened to them?"

"Ross got shot in the boat, before we ever landed. He stuck his head up, and boom. The bullet went right through his helmet. Doyle made it to the island, but a mortar dropped right close by him and blew him into little pieces."

"What was going through your mind at that time?"

"I remember thinking, 'What the hell am I doing here? How can I get down low enough, how can I hide?' I was yelling at the others, 'Get down! Get down!' We all had little collapsible shovels, but it was almost impossible to dig a hole. You'd dig a little into the coral, but it'd fill up with water."

At that point, Murray paused for what seemed like several minutes. We were in his bedroom, he was sitting in his easy chair, and he just stared down at his feet. It was quiet, except for the flow of his oxygen and the ticking of the large clock on his wall. After a while, he looked up at me, and in a somber voice that I had not previously heard from him he muttered, "And that water . . . was red. The guys who got shot on the beach bled right into the ocean. And the water in the ocean turned red. But when the bullets started getting heavy you'd dig down in there, and the water would come in, but you didn't give a damn. You just got down lower, right into the water, even though it was red with the blood of your buddies."

I could see that Murray was shaken, almost to the brink of tears. And I was not really sure what to say. He gathered himself and a bit more boldly said, "You know, it's awfully hard to think about this, and even harder to talk about it."

Something in my brain switched at that moment, transforming me from a hard-boiled investigative reporter back into the tenderhearted pediatrician that is always lurking at my core. And, at least in my eyes, Murray transformed from the battle-tested combat veteran back into the frail old man whose mind was filled with painful memories. I took a moment to retreat.

"I really appreciate how honest you're being. Do you want to talk about something else for a while?"

"No, I want to go to the bathroom." And with that, he abruptly got up out of his chair. He grabbed hold of his walker, gingerly making his way to the bathroom, which was in the hallway just outside of his bedroom. When he had made it about halfway, he turned to me and said, "If we had to go to the bathroom, we just went, right in our pants. What the hell difference did it make? We figured we were all going to die anyway." And then he looked down at the ground, turned around, and continued on his way.

When he returned and got himself settled back into his chair, I thought it would be best to have a change of subject.

"Did you encounter any civilians during your time on Majuro?"

"There were maybe a few dozen people that lived there, and that's all. And Majuro was the only island where we saw any native people. Here, look at this."

Murray took a small album out of the drawer of his nightstand. It was weathered but in pretty good condition. The pictures were held onto the pages with old-fashioned adhesive corners. The photos were taken on Majuro, and the vast majority of the images were of native women, all of whom were topless.

"The women on Majuro all went around like that," Murray said as he looked wistfully through the photos. "They thought nothing of it. So, the Navy says we should give them T-shirts to wear. So, we issued them all T-shirts. And guess what they did? Within a couple of days, they had cut holes in the shirts so their breasts were still exposed!"

The way Murray was looking at his photos—it seemed like he was conjuring up some fond memories.

"You know, looking at these pictures reminds me of an old joke about an elderly woman who wanted to commit suicide. She asked her doctor how to do it, and he told her, 'Point a gun two inches below your left nipple and pull the trigger.' She came back to see him the next day, and she had shot herself in the knee. He says, 'Why'd you shoot yourself in the knee?' And she says, 'Well, you said to aim two inches below my nipple!'"

I was surprised by Murray's humorous interlude, and I couldn't help but chuckle.

"You're a funny man, Murray." I could tell he was proud to have gotten a laugh out of me. But I wanted to get back on

track. There were also some interesting shots of the construction work being done on the island.

"So, you said that the reason for landing on Majuro was to build an airstrip. I think not too many people would know how you guys built a runway on an island in the middle of nowhere, so I'd like you to tell me how it was done."

"Well, first we had to clean the whole island out, which didn't happen overnight. Guys were getting shot all the time. Then we got our equipment off the LST: a couple of dragline cranes, big generators, and a machine to transform salt water into fresh water to drink . . ."

I was surprised to learn that such technology was available in 1944. One of my professors at Downstate Medical School had been involved in quite a bit of pioneering research using direct osmosis to desalinate seawater in the 1970s.

"You had a desalinator on Majuro?"

"Yes, a big one that ran twenty-four hours a day, and a big canvas tank that we'd dip our canteens into to get our water. And that water tasted like hell because of the canvas. It didn't taste worth a damn, and about made me throw up, but you had to have some anyway. After a while I'd get most of my water from coconuts. You had to use the green coconuts off the trees. That water was hard to get—you had to get the husk off, and that wasn't easy—but it was worth it because that water tasted good. The natives had a trick to it: they'd put a sharp stick in the ground and have that husk off in a minute. But we'd use a machete and whack it open.

"Anyway, we got all our equipment onto the island, and every man was assigned to a particular machine. There were truck drivers, plumbers, electricians, surveyors . . . at least, we had them to start with. Some of them got eliminated. Then others took over, but they might not be as good. Once we got established we started knocking down coconut trees immediately. We used a bulldozer—we had *one*—and then cranes would pick up the trees, put them in trucks, and the trucks would haul them away. These were ten-wheeler trucks. We had a lot of them. Those trees were not easy to get out; coconut trees are in the ground pretty tight. After the trees were knocked down we started to tear the ground up and level it, as good as we could. We used an attachment on the back of a bulldozer called a sheepsfoot roller compactor. By the time we were on that island eight days,

The B-25 "Luscious Lucy" shortly after its fortuitous landing on Majuro.

we had moved quite a few trees and had the ground dug up and leveled pretty good. And it's a good thing we did, because it was on that eighth day that the first plane landed on the island.

"It was a Billy Mitchell Bomber that had one wheel shot off and one engine knocked out. [Author's note: Murray is referring to the B-25 Mitchell bomber, named after General Billy Mitchell.] We had just enough of a strip cleared for him to make a bumpy landing on the dirt. We hadn't even compacted the ground or put down any coral yet. When they landed, they didn't even know if there were enemy or friends on the island. They got out of the plane, and they were all shaking like leaves. As I recall, I think there were six of them in the crew: pilot, co-pilot, bombardier, navigator, and a couple of machine gunners. They were so happy to see us, you can't imagine. They were happy, happy, happy. They got out and hugged us, they thanked us; they were as happy as a cat with three tails. The pilot gave each of us that welcomed him a .50-cal shell as a souvenir. Not everybody in the whole outfit didn't swarm around them—there were just a few of us there. You didn't go running hither and tither wherever you wanted; you were busy doing your job. I just happened to be in that area when they landed. I never seen them anymore after that, and what happened to the bomber afterwards, I have no idea. That's the end of that story."

"So, after that bomber landed, it sounds like you still had some work to do to make a proper landing strip."

The grateful crew.

"Oh hell, we hadn't even got started. We didn't have the length done, nor the full width. That bomber barely had room enough to land. Of course, with the tire shot off he wasn't going to go as far anyhow, and once he hit that soft dirt it stopped him from going too far also. As quick as we could we started compacting the soil using a large roller that ran on a diesel engine. We worked 'round the clock. At night, we worked with minimal light, of course, and whenever an enemy plane came over we'd turn off all the lights. After we got the ground properly compacted and leveled, we started hauling coral, dumping it, spreading it out, and rolling it. Once we rolled the coral it was just like concrete."

"So, is that what you were doing with the dragline? Moving coral?"

"Yeah, I was digging coral out of the ocean, putting it in the trucks, and the trucks would haul it, dump it, and come back for another load. It was maybe a quarter mile from where I was working to where they were building the airstrip. You know, I was remembering something just the other day. Those trucks had no cover over where the driver would sit. They were regular dump trucks, but where the driver was sitting was just wide open. And those drivers never did get out of those trucks. The dragline bucket would come over the truck and dump the load of coral, and then off he'd go back to the airstrip. Everything had to be coordinated. One time I got pissed off at a driver, so I got a really sloppy load of coral and water, got the bucket over the truck, and gave it a little flip, and it gave that driver a real good bath."

"What were you pissed off at him about? Do you remember?"

"He was supposed to come in with his truck a certain way, and he just wouldn't do it. He was a young kid. He came in the right way from then on.

"There was a lot of coral that went into that airstrip. The dragline was going twenty-four hours a day. When I got through, it got serviced and fueled up, and another crew took over. I had an oiler that greased the machine up before we started to work, and I broke him in to where he could run it himself. He was a kid from Mississippi, and he was good. In fact, that's what we called him, 'Mississippi.' I don't know what his real name was. The machines were brand new, so they didn't need much repair, but if a cable broke, he helped me replace it. That was a two-man job. A couple of times a jeep-load of officers would come by. I don't know what they were doing—just looking around. One time one of them said to me, 'How come you're not running that thing? You're supposed to be running it, and every time we come by here he's running it.' He was a young officer, so I didn't swear at him, I just said, real nice, 'How many trucks you see there by that dragline?' And he says, 'One.' And I said, 'Do you see any trucks there waiting?' 'No.' So, I say, 'You know what, I did you a big favor. If I get killed you've got yourself a dragline operator.' The other officers in the jeep kind of snickered a little. Because what I said was true. That's why I broke the kid in, and he took to it real fast. There are things like that—that you can tell somebody, but they can't learn it until they've been there and done it. It's like when you're fighting the enemy. You can tell somebody that's never been there how you did it, but they don't really realize it until they've done it themselves."

"So about how long did it take you guys to finish that airstrip?"

"It took about a month and a half to get to where we could call it a proper airstrip. Don't forget, at the same time we were setting up our living quarters too. The latrines were set up pretty fast, but it took longer to get showers set up. After about a week, I remember one night I just felt like I had to get washed off. So, about midnight, it was dark, and I crept down to the beach over on the far side of the island, away from where we had landed. I slipped off my pants and shirt, and I sat down in the water. That water was so warm you could hardly tell you were in it. I didn't have any soap, but I needed to get washed off anyhow, so I used sand instead—I was tough in my day. I scrubbed myself down with that sand, and it felt good. It's good I got out when I did, though. Right after I got my clothes back on two Japs came by, circling around behind us."

"Was there anyone there with you?"

"I was by myself! I had my rifle leaning against a coconut tree, right handy. I grabbed that 30-ought-6 and never even raised it to my shoulder. I just shot. And those Japs never did make it. I got them both.

"Anyway, after we got the airstrip finished, there was maintenance that had to be done. Where the planes would land would get washboardy, and we'd have to get I don't know how many loads of coral to repack it. There was always maintenance work going on. But there was also a lot of waiting time in between. After a couple of months, I got pissed off at sitting around. We had terminology for that: 'I got the red ass.' So, while we were waiting they asked for volunteers to go to another island, and I volunteered, which is something you never do."

"So, you volunteered for the next landing just because you were sitting around and bored?"

"That's right."

"What was the name of that island?"

"As far as I knew it didn't have a name. It was a small island, not even big enough for an airstrip. They sent us over there to get rid of some Japs, and that's exactly what we did. There were two hundred of us that went, and we had a lot of casualties on that one."

Murray's voice abruptly became a little softer and his speech more deliberate.

"A lot of casualties. I don't think more than fifty of us came back. We went over with the Marines, and they suffered a lot of losses too. We worked very close with the Marines, and you know, the Marines like the Seabees very well, even today. The Marines went in first with flamethrowers, and behind them were the guys with guns. They shot everything that got in their way. Everything. And then we went in right behind the Marines."

I could sense that Murray was getting tired and that the act of recalling all these memories was wearing him out. I knew we should leave the details of that second island for another time, but I couldn't resist asking one more question before I left.

"How many Japanese soldiers do you think you killed?"

"Oh, I wish you hadn't asked me that."

"Well, I told you before we started I was going to ask difficult questions."

Murray took a deep breath and sighed before he answered.

"It got to where you and your close buddies, if you had any left, would make a bet which of you could knock off the most that day. We made a game of it."

Another sigh, another long pause, with Murray looking at the floor.

"A helluva game . . . one hell of a game." He paused again, this time for only a second, turned his head to look me square in the eye, and solemnly said, "I personally killed fourteen and a half Japs. There was one that two of us were shooting at, and I don't know which of us killed him. It didn't make any difference . . . dead was dead."

With that, Murray shrunk down into his easy chair, exhausted, and almost in tears. He muttered in a trembling voice, "I can't go on."

I thanked him and reiterated how much I appreciated him sharing his difficult memories with me. When I left his room, I was surprised to see how much time had passed; that day had become night in what felt like only an hour or two. I said goodbye to Catherine, and true to my word, I revealed nothing about what Murray and I had discussed. But I told her that the session had been a little rough for him and that she should be watchful and give him a little extra TLC that evening.

While our meeting proved grueling for Murray, it was energizing for me. I was bursting with excitement during my drive home, and my mind was racing. I felt like I was fortunate enough to have a front row seat for a declaration of history, and in fact, for a history that no one before me had the privilege to know. I was now in the unique position to reveal it to the world. Murray was a gold mine of information, and we had only begun to scratch the surface. I couldn't wait to get started writing. Having never heard of Majuro, as soon as I returned home, I immediately started doing research about that island. Not being particularly sophisticated with the use of computer technology, it took me a while, but eventually I found a couple of websites that were quite informative.[2]

I learned that Majuro Atoll is part of the Marshall Islands, approximately 2,000 miles to the southwest of Pearl Harbor. An atoll is a group of small coral islands forming a circle or semi-circle, surrounding a shallow lagoon. Majuro Atoll, at the western edge of the Marshalls, consists of fifty-six islands, of which Majuro Island is the largest. At the onset of the campaign in the Marshall Islands, Admiral Chester W. Nimitz had determined that a naval base should be established on Majuro. Prior to the amphibious assault, there were two months of bombing

by carrier-based B-24 Liberator Bombers and several hours of naval bombardment. Pre-invasion intelligence suggested that the Japanese garrison numbered only about three hundred men. Army assault forces landed on the island on January 31, 1944, followed by a Marine defense battalion and the 100th Naval Construction Battalion on February 1.

Strangely, every source I found stated that there was no combat on Majuro. The Japanese had abandoned the atoll almost a year before. In fact, when the assault forces landed, they found only a single member of the Japanese military, who had been left behind as a caretaker of the island and was subsequently taken prisoner. I even found a source that cited his name: Warrant Officer Nagata of the Imperial Japanese Navy.[3] I found corroborating evidence of nearly all the other details that Murray had disclosed, right down to the emergency landing by the Mitchell bomber on the eighth day and the giant desalinator that produced 50,000 gallons of fresh water a day stored in four 12,000-gallon canvas tanks. My references went on to state that Majuro became one of the major forward bases in the Pacific and an essential fleet anchorage that also provided facilities for numerous bomber and fighter squadrons. The tiny island of Majuro actually played a substantial role in the Pacific campaigns that followed, although the capture of Majuro seemed rather uneventful. [Author's note: The capture of Majuro was codenamed 'Sundance' by the US Navy.[4] I found this a rather odd coincidence, considering decades later Robert Redford would establish both Sundance Ski Resort and the Sundance Film Festival here in Murray's home state of Utah.]

That's when I first realized the intrinsic difficulty in trying to reconstruct distant history, particularly when your primary resource is the memory of a ninety-five-year-old man. And not just any ninety-five-year-old man, but one whose combat experience was so terrifying that he was still being treated for PTSD sixty-eight years later. Perhaps the entirety of his combat had blended in his mind into one long, horrific nightmare. Maybe after all these years he was unable to distinguish one island from another, one firefight from the next. And why should that have surprised me? The same thing occasionally happens to me when I try to conjure up memories from only a few years ago—memories that aren't even disturbing. Like remembering an incident involving a patient I took care of in medical school, only to recall later that the event actually took place during my residency. (Now, just for clarification, both medical school and residency were moderately traumatic, but there was only one incident involving gunfire, and my life was only in danger a couple of times, so my recollection should not be clouded by PTSD.)

Anyway, this revelation led me to change the manner in which this story is being told. Murray was so lucid and such a great storyteller that my original plan was to write this book in the first person as an autobiography that I was just ghostwriting. But if Murray's memory was not accurate, and we were dealing with historic events that have been previously documented, then I could not in good faith simply put down on paper whatever he told me. I needed to investigate the facts, to authenticate the where and when of his experiences. As a scientist by nature I could not endorse that which could easily be proven incorrect. The result is the product you see before you: Murray's story, but with an added layer of scrutiny and verification.

The more I thought about this whole situation, all the things that Murray told me, all the evidence that refuted any battle taking place on Majuro, one thing actually began to make much more sense. I didn't really understand why on earth Murray would have volunteered to go to another island after having such an awful experience during his first landing. The whole "red ass" business, sitting around and being bored, was one thing. But, after being in such a terrible circumstance, why would an otherwise rational man put his life in jeopardy again, *voluntarily*, simply to escape the monotony of maintaining an airfield? Now I knew why: Because he hadn't actually experienced the horror of warfare at that point, and he, like so many other men of that era, was anxious to get into combat to get started "killin' Japs." That's why he volunteered. He didn't actually know what he was getting himself into. And what he got himself into was exactly what I wanted to find out. I could hardly wait for our next session so I could uncover what happened on that next island. But like Murray, I wasn't quite prepared for what I was going to experience next.

CHAPTER 3

BEDLAM

"Tell me about that second landing you participated in."

"Well, we took an LST to that next island, and it wasn't a long trip. It only took us two days to get there, and we stayed there about a week and a half. And we didn't go there to build anything."

"Then what did you go for?"

"To kill Japs! We had to clear out these small islands so we could take the big ones. The Navy didn't anticipate the force on those little islands because Japan would bring men in overnight on boats as reinforcements. The war in the Pacific was all about manpower. Manpower. That's all."

"What kind of supplies did you have when you hit the beach?"

"When we got off the LST we had our rifle. We had a canteen hooked onto our belt, along with a small shovel. And I had a knife with a five-inch blade that I had brought from home."

"What kind of a knife was it?"

"It was a killing knife! Twasn't to pick my fingernails with! Like I said, I had brought it with me from home, and back then I could do that, legally. The Navy gave me a knife, too, but shit, that thing wouldn't cut butter. My knife had been given to me by a guy who worked at the Midvale smelter. He made it by hand out of the hardest steel you could get at that time, and he put a real nice handle on it. I carried a little whetstone with me, and I kept that knife sharp. I used that knife to shave with, it was that sharp. Yeah, I kept that knife in good shape, and it's a good thing I did."

I could tell that talking about that knife had started to dredge up some unpleasant memories.

"You know, what I get into next is going to be heavy, and you're gonna hate my guts. I hate myself. But I was there. I had a reason. And I was young.

"I'm starting to touch on stuff that bothers me. We didn't go through these islands like it was a cakewalk. We paid a heavy price. The combat was very violent. The Japs didn't have big guns, but they had fortified the island pretty good and had a lot of machine guns and mortars. As soon as we landed there was bullets flying, there was bombs going off, there was screaming. It was regular bedlam. Utter turmoil. I can't even describe to you the chaos . . . the confusion . . . the smell . . . of this whole thing. You could write a thousand books, but you could never get the feeling that was there. Shells going off, flamethrowers constantly going, young boys, maybe eighteen years old, lying on the ground screaming. It was noise, noise, noise—all kinds of noise. And everybody looking at everybody else and wondering what the hell you're supposed to do. Nobody gave orders for anything. Everybody was just looking out for their own ass. When I say it was utter confusion . . . it was.

"That's where you separated the men from the boys. There were some of them, particularly the younger ones, you couldn't get to move, no matter what. These kids just laid on the ground— screaming, squirming, refusing to shoot. You couldn't waste much time on them, but eventually most everybody got to where they'd do what they were supposed to do, and a semblance of order came about. Since we outnumbered the Japs, then we were finally able to start moving forward. But as we advanced forward, what some of those Japs had done, they had dug tunnels and they'd be waiting down in these holes that they had camouflaged. After we went by them, they came at us from the back, usually at night. They'd sneak in with knives or bayonets and cut somebody's throat. And you'd never know if you'd be next. That's why nobody moved around at night. Everybody just stayed put after darkness fell.

"One night, one of those Japs came at me, and I don't know why, but I happened to turn around and I saw him coming. He came at me with a bayonet, and I couldn't get to my rifle, but luckily, I had my knife right there. I hit his rifle with my left arm with an upward motion, and with my right hand I went in with the knife. I cut him from his navel clean up to his chin."

"Was that the only time you were in hand-to-hand combat?"

"Yeah. I don't like hand-to-hand. Too close. I'd rather just shoot them and know they ain't there no more."

"Do you still have that knife?"

"No, I gave it to my grandson Jason. As far as I know he still has it. And he knows the history behind it, too.

"Anyhow, as we kept pushing forward, we came upon some Marines that had gone through—at least, they tried to. They didn't make it."

Murray looked down and paused for a long time. His grip on the arms of his chair seemed to tighten. When he finally continued, his voice trembled.

"Their cocks were cut off and shoved in their mouth."

After another long, pensive pause, Murray took a deep breath, looked me square in the eye, and scowled as some sixty-eight-year-old anger erupted to the surface.

"Monkey see, monkey do!"

I just looked at him, having no idea what to say, and realizing that I might not want to hear what he was about to tell me.

"By this time, thank goodness, I had been hardened a little bit, as we called it. So, while it bothered me some, I just said in my mind, 'Fine, you want to play dirty, we'll play dirty.' And so I did. And so did others. And there were a few heads cut off.

"Now, when we first discovered this cutting-off business, we were pinned down by machine-gun fire. Then we broke loose, and we got a hold of a couple of those bandy-legged sons-of-bitches."

Murray's voice started to quiver, and he began speaking more and more quietly.

"We cut them off . . . one of the guys took his helmet off . . . and we made a fire."

At this point, Murray was barely audible.

"We . . . cooked them . . . and . . . ate them. And then we cut their throats."

I was in utter disbelief, not fully able to comprehend what was just said to me. I hesitated but eventually stammered out my query.

"What . . . what are you saying to me? Are you telling me that you ate an enemy soldier? That you cooked him and you ate him?"

"No! We cut off their penises, boiled them in a helmet, and made them eat them."

"Oh. You made them eat their own penises." I felt a little relieved by this revelation, as if this were somehow better than learning our own troops had cannibalized their prisoners.

"Yes."

"And then you killed them."

"Yes. You see, our initial orders were to take no prisoners. After we got control of the island, the officers eventually decided they did want some prisoners. So, we grabbed some and threw them in a ten-wheeler truck and sent them down to a ship in the harbor that was waiting to take them I don't know where. We got a call on the radio asking where the prisoners were. We told them, 'Well, we sent you a truckload of them.' It turns out that as soon as the truck got out of sight the Marines unloaded the sons-of-bitches and shot every one of them. You know, whoever said that war is hell didn't know what he was talking about. It was worse than hell. You got to the point where things that were once revolting to you became old hat."

There was a long period of silence between us. I was trying to digest everything that Murray had just told me, and I think Murray was trying to put those horrible memories back into the recesses of his mind where he had hidden them for the past six decades.

Eventually I decided to keep probing.

"I've heard that men fighting in the Pacific took souvenirs from the Japanese after they killed them."

"We were given strict instructions that if we were caught with a souvenir we would be court-martialed."

"So nobody in your battalion took any souvenirs?"

"Well, nobody that I knew. But I didn't pay attention to a lot of things."

"And you didn't take any souvenirs?"

"I didn't take a souvenir. I took other things, but I didn't take anything you could bring home."

"What do you mean?"

"I took things there."

"What do you mean? What things?"

By now Murray had become frustrated by my persistence. He desperately wanted me to let sleeping dogs lie, but I was tenacious in my quest for the truth. He gave me that piercing look of his and barked, "I took a couple of heads! That was my souvenir. And now, even though I left them on the island, they're staying too close to me. I can still see them at night when I'm trying to get to sleep. I fight with them every night I get in that bed. Every damned night I get into that bed."

"Were those men alive when you did that? When you took their heads off? I'm just asking you; I'm not judging you."

"No, I didn't do that. I never got down to that level. You know, I'm telling you things that I've never told my psychiatrist. For ten years—ten long years—I woke up at one o'clock every morning, sweat pouring off my face, heart going a hundred miles an hour, shaking like a leaf. My wife had to calm me down. That was a regular nightly occurrence. You have no idea. You're like the other civilians. They knew it was bad, but words can't even begin to describe it. Let me show you something."

Murray reached down into the bottom drawer of his dresser and carefully pulled out a small envelope that had been hidden way in the back, under a pile of his other belongings. In the envelope were about two-dozen old black-and-white photographs.

"Look at these pictures," Murray said. "A friend of mine in the outfit was a professional photographer in civilian life, and he took these on the sly. That's what it looked like . . . that's what I had to live through. You see these sorts of things, and maybe you can begin to understand why it's hard for me to go to sleep at night."

The photographs are poignant and riveting. We looked at them together, and Murray offered me a description of each, along with whatever details he could remember.

"This first picture (below) is of Majuro. Every day, PBYs would go out on patrol and make sure no submarines were around. This photo must have been taken by one of those PBY pilots."

[Author's note: The PBY, or "Patrol Bomber," was a type of seaplane that was used extensively during World War II, particularly in the Pacific.]

"You know, I just remembered that one day when I didn't have anything else to do I talked one of those PBY pilots into letting me fly around with him. That water was so clear you could see down into it a hundred feet. Beautiful. I remember I could see whales.

"This next picture is of one of the LSTs that shuttled us to the islands."

"And here's a picture of one of those big desalinators I was telling you about."

"Now, these next few pictures might give you some idea of the sort of bedlam I was trying to describe when we hit the beach. There are really no words to express it."

"This picture shows a few of the guys with a big pile of supplies and crates of K-rations."

"Each box of rations was about the size of a Crackerjack box. In that box was a fruit bar of some type, three or four crackers, a chocolate bar, and four cigarettes. And there was also a little can of meat of some kind. It was probably nutritious, but it tasted like hell. I've often wondered about that meat—how they managed to package it to keep it from spoiling. Sometimes you might get a little can of cheese. I smoked back then, and I liked most of the cigarettes in those K-rations, except when they were Lucky Strikes. Not every box was the same. They had Camels, Lucky Strikes, or Chesterfields, and I just didn't care for Lucky Strikes. The guys, naturally, if you left them alone, they'd screw themselves up . . . they got to where they were taking out the cigarettes and throwing the rations away.

"These pictures will give you an idea of what we found as we advanced."

"It's hard for me to try to convey to you the feelings I had when I was living through that. Here are some photographs of dead remains. And if you think they're all Japs, you're mistaken."

"The odor is something I will never forget. Never. Thousands of bodies laid out there in that hot sun."

"This is one of the flamethrowers I was telling you about."

"And here's a Jap who was 'barbecued,' as we called it."

"Things like this don't sit very well. You don't forget things like this overnight."

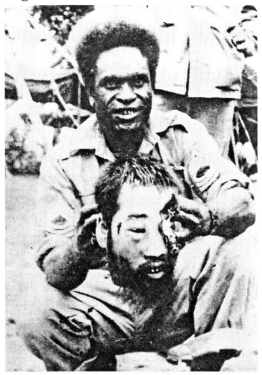

"The Japs had taught us some tricks of the trade, and we picked them up pretty fast and threw those tricks right back at them. There were no rules, no guidelines. It was kill or be killed."

For most of this time, I was silently absorbing the images I was seeing. While listening to Murray's narrative, I was studying the grotesquely deformed corpses, and at the same time, I was mesmerized by the clarity of the photos—how eloquently they captured the men who were still alive. Finally, I interjected with a question.

"When you look at these photographs, do you feel differently about it now than you felt about it then?"

"Yes. Back then I was hardened. I had become a different person. If you didn't, you couldn't survive there. You had to be there to understand the impact of it. It's been very hard for me to dig up the past. These are things that I've spent my life trying to bury.

"Now, that's me right there on the side of that hill. You can't recognize me, of course, but the guy who took the picture told me it was me."

"And this last picture was . . . I guess you could call it a funeral. We all got together to honor the dead."

I commented, "You know, seeing how intense the violence was, it's amazing that you weren't wounded in that battle."

Murray thought about it for a moment then responded. "Well . . . I did take a bullet here in my knee. It was superficial, really just under the skin. It went in here and came out over here."

"Did it hurt? I've never been shot."

"It hurt a little bit, yeah, but it didn't stop me. I just kept right on going. A medic bandaged it, and that was it."

"Why didn't you get the Purple Heart?"

"Well, the ranking officer just wouldn't acknowledge that I was wounded. He says, 'I guess you want a Purple Heart for that scratch.' So I said, 'Well it's not a scratch. It's not my guts hanging out in my hands, but you'd have to OK the Purple Heart.' And he says, 'No, I won't do that . . . not for that.' I didn't argue with him over it. I just let it go. I figured that if he wouldn't acknowledge it . . . well, I just said 'Fuck it.' I got pissed off then let it go. That's it. I had some run-ins with him a couple of times before, back in Hawaii. Little things that didn't amount to a hill of beans. But now all he was doing was throwing his weight around; he knew that since he was an officer, his word was the word of God."

We sat quietly together for a few minutes. Murray closed his eyes for a while, and when he opened them he turned toward me with a look that was resolute yet melancholy.

"I think that's more than enough for today."

I could sense his sadness, and I felt the need to express my gratitude: "You know, I appreciate what you went through so that we could all live our lives."

"Well, I went through a lot that I didn't need to go through. But at the time, it seemed right. Under the same circumstances, I don't know what I would do. I just don't know. It's hard for me to fathom. But right now, it happened . . . and it's over and done. And I can't take it away. Even the things I'm not proud of."

"Well, I appreciate you, and I especially appreciate you talking to me. I'll see you next week."

"All right. Next time let's talk about something else for a change."

CHAPTER 4

AN UNUSUAL GUY

By the time I got home from that session my head was spinning. I knew the Japanese had committed atrocities, and certainly suspected that there may have been similar actions taken by our military given the circumstances, but I never imagined the depths of depravity that Murray had just described. The brutality he witnessed, and even participated in, was not something I had previously considered within the context of World War II. So I started investigating, researching subjects I never imagined would become part of this project. Subjects like beheading, genital mutilation of fallen soldiers, and the execution of prisoners. And what I found turned out to be just as shocking as the events Murray had described.

Back when I was in school, doing research was straightforward. You looked things up in an encyclopedia or a textbook and generally accepted at face-value that what was printed there was accurate. Of course, that was never really true, because while there are names and dates and places that may be irrefutable, much of history is open to interpretation. That has been one of the great revelations of my adult life: The history I learned in my youth was woefully inaccurate, either by deliberate omission of details or by outright distortion of facts. That being said, back in the old days, all one could do was use whatever resources were available and assume, or at least hope, that the material contained therein was factual.

Nowadays, there's a world of information right at our fingertips, accessible with just the touch of a button or the click of a mouse. But while modern technology has given us access to an infinitely greater breadth and depth of knowledge, that same glut of data has made it vastly more difficult to separate that which resembles truth from that which is merely propaganda. For every website that discusses the firebombing of Dresden in

1945—an incident that is rarely mentioned in American history classes but is considered an egregious assault on civilians
by most modern-day historians—there are a hundred websites
that vehemently deny that the Holocaust ever happened. This
poses a great challenge for a scientific researcher of history:
How to separate fact from fiction, the real from the artificial.
Moreover, the events we are discussing happened decades ago,
in a time and situation when strict documentation was neither
essential nor practical. Just using my example of the Dresden
firebombing by Allied forces, even the most reputable sources
are unable to accurately and consistently report how many civilians were killed, with estimates ranging anywhere from 35,000
to over 200,000. These challenges were not obvious to me until
I became immersed in this project. Dammit, I'm a doctor, not
a historian! Most everything I've ever needed to know about
anatomy I was able to dissect and hold in my hand. Anything
I've learned about pharmacology has been developed using data
from randomized, placebo-controlled, double-blinded studies.
Not much room for ambiguity there. But history, it would seem,
is an inexact science at best, and so into the abyss I dove.

One of the first incidents I stumbled upon was the so-called
"Dachau Massacre." The Dachau Concentration Camp was lib-
erated by the American infantry on April 29, 1945. Upon seeing
boxcars filled with decaying corpses nearby, the piles of dead
bodies within the camp, and the horrible condition of the surviving inmates, American soldiers personally executed many
of the camp's guards after they had been taken prisoner and
turned a blind eye while inmates took care of some surrendered
guards themselves. [Author's note: For a fascinating timeline
of this incident, I recommend the website www.humanitas-
international.org, which includes a sequence of chilling photographs.] I found several things to be surprising, not the least
of which was that I had never heard of this episode before. I
consider myself to be fairly knowledgeable about World War II
and the Holocaust and could hardly believe that an event of this
notoriety somehow stayed below my radar. But then I searched
for the incident on a website I felt would be accurate beyond re-
proach: that of the United States Holocaust Memorial Museum.
After all, a museum of that magnitude, with all their resources
and all the scholars at their disposal, should be the final word
on all things regarding the Holocaust. But, strangely, within

their vast archive, I found . . . nothing. Dachau is discussed, as is the liberation by American forces, including a photograph of soldiers looking at corpses in the woods near the camp. There are even films of the trial of members of the SS [Schutzstaffel] accused of executing American soldiers at Malmedy in December 1944—a trial that took place in the city of Dachau in 1946. But not a single reference to a single guard executed during the liberation of the Dachau Concentration Camp. I found this to be rather interesting in and of itself—perhaps a convenient shaping of history retrospectively through intentional omission of certain details.

I was also surprised by the ambiguity of the details of the incident. The Humanitas International website referenced the eyewitness account of retired US Army Colonel Howard Buechner, who specifically described, in great detail, 520 German guards being executed in one way or another. However, the personal account of US Army Brigadier General Felix Sparks was altogether different. In the *Stars and Stripes* publication, "The Story of the 45th Infantry Division," General Sparks, who was in command and intervened when guards who had surrendered were being executed by machine-gun fire, reported: "The total number of Germans killed at Dachau that day most certainly did not exceed fifty, with thirty probably being a more accurate figure." How could two men who witnessed the same event at the same moment in time provide two body counts that differed by a factor of ten?

Of further interest to me was that the report of the incident, which was initially presented to General George Patton (who promptly destroyed the original copy), remained secret for forty-six years, only being declassified by the US Army in 1991. So, it would seem that even at the very time at which history is taking place, there are those who would attempt to change it, disguise it, or erase it altogether. This truth stuff is rather elusive indeed. Now, make no mistake—I am neither condoning nor condemning those soldiers or their actions. In an ideal world, should they have behaved differently? Probably. Did the German guards meet the fate they deserved? Maybe, maybe not. If I, after months of combat, and particularly as a Jew, had seen firsthand the atrocities that were perpetrated against the prisoners of the camp, would I have had the restraint to conduct myself differently than they did? Doubtful. And if I'm being brutally honest, the answer is no. The purpose here is not to judge, but to understand. And to understand why something happened you first have to know what it is that actually transpired. That's where the truth comes in.

But I digress. This is another problem with the Internet. I started looking for atrocities committed in the Pacific, and three hours later I'm consumed by an event that took place in a concentration camp in Germany; three hours after that I've somehow, through a series of connections that seemed to make sense at the time, segued into a search for Ted Williams' batting average in 1946. (Just for the record it was .342.)

The brutality of the Japanese military has been well-documented and does not need to be rehashed here. Suffice to say that I found ample evidence, albeit largely anecdotal, of torture, beheadings, and genital mutilation perpetrated by members of the Imperial Japanese Army. One can find several eyewitness accounts of the castration of US servicemen, often while still alive, and frequently with their penises and testicles stuffed into their mouths. Perhaps the most well-known of these accounts came from Corporal Eugene Sledge, in his 1981 memoir, *With the Old Breed*, which chronicled his service in the United States Marine Corps on Peleliu and Okinawa.

In the course of my investigation, I found that one has little choice but to rely on the statements of individuals who were eyewitnesses. It would seem that the Japanese were less interested in photographing their atrocities, and thereby preserving them for posterity, than were their Nazi counterparts. I also found it of interest that for one reason or another, the war crimes committed by the Japanese were not made public to the same extent as those that were perpetrated by the Germans, despite the fact that during the war there was generally a much greater degree of American racism against the Japanese. For example, the 1946 International Military Tribunal for the Far East, in which several high-ranking Japanese officers were tried and convicted as war criminals, was far less publicized than the comparable Nuremberg Trials, and remains less well known today. And while the medical experiments conducted by Dr. Josef Mengele at Auschwitz are common knowledge, far fewer people today have heard of Unit 731 in Pingfang, China, where Dr. Shiro Ishii conducted equally gruesome experiments on human victims. Remarkably, Ishii received immunity from General

Douglas MacArthur in exchange for full disclosure of the data from all his human experimentation. He was never prosecuted for any war crimes, allowing him to die peacefully in Tokyo at the age of sixty-seven.[5] It would seem that the more one delves into history seeking answers, the more questions about deceit and manipulation arise.

One particularly disturbing and grotesque subject I came upon unexpectedly was that of cannibalism. I found several anecdotal reports of cannibalism perpetrated by the Japanese military, not only against Americans but against the Chinese, Koreans, and other groups as well. In some instances, the acts of cannibalism may have been due to the circumstance of profound hunger caused by dwindling supplies as the war progressed. But in other cases, it would seem that the cannibalistic acts were a depraved form of victory celebration in which the victors ingested the flesh and viscera of their defeated enemy. While it remains difficult to determine the veracity of these accounts, one would—at the very least—be compelled to accept the testimony of those Japanese who confessed to acts of cannibalism themselves. On October 2, 1946, the *Knoxville News Sentinel* reported that a US military commission on Guam convicted seven members of the Japanese military of beheading and subsequently eating the flesh of American airmen who had been captured on the island of Chichi Jima. While the commanding officer, General Yoshio Tachibana, denied the charges, Major Sueo Matoba described several episodes in which the flesh of murdered prisoners was consumed, particularly by officers.[6] And on August 28, 1948, the *Sydney Morning Herald* reported that a US military tribunal at Yokohama sentenced five Japanese to be executed for vivisecting captured American fliers during the war and eating their flesh at Kyushu Imperial University. Strangely, because military and international law had no precedent for the heinous crime of cannibalism, some of the perpetrators were actually convicted of offenses such as "prevention of honorable burial" or "violating the laws and customs of war."

Now, I feel compelled to share with you an experience I had in performing this research. While I was visiting one website after another, searching for reputable sources and doing my best to construct sentences that have some semblance of grammatical structure while at the same time being interesting, everything seemed fine. Then my day came to an abrupt end when I had to go meet Julie and some friends for a concert at our beautiful Red Butte Garden here in Salt Lake City. By the time I got in my car and started driving, I found myself becoming increasingly unsettled, almost to the point of being physically ill. The cause became clear to me right away—I had just spent eight hours staring at a computer screen, looking at images and reading descriptions of some of the most disgusting acts imaginable. Pictures of beheadings, vivid accounts of castrations, photos of Japanese soldiers using live prisoners for bayonet practice, page after page discussing the vile experiments of Dr. Ishii, detailed stories of men consuming the livers of other men. By the time I arrived at the concert, Julie and our friends, Nicole and Leslie, could tell there was something wrong with me. It took a couple of glasses of wine and the virtuoso guitar work of Rodrigo y Gabriela, but in a few hours, I was almost back to myself. Almost. There were some images I had come upon that I still had trouble clearing from my mind.

Why am I telling you this? Consider my background: I have never been in combat, but the first thing I did when I got to medical school was dissect a human corpse, and in my twelve years working in an emergency department, I saw firsthand cases of dead children, flesh torn open, hideous child abuse, and at one time or another found myself splattered with blood, pus, phlegm, vomit, urine, and feces. I am no neophyte. But after a day of just sitting safely at home, looking at and reading about these repulsive crimes, I was that strongly affected. I'm not sure why. Was it the thought of the terror and pain those poor men went through, or was it recognizing the absolute perversion that drove the perpetrators to commit those sickening acts of hatred? In any event, I had an unexpected and profound visceral reaction.

Now consider the teenage boy from a farm, or the twenty-year-old soda jerk, or the high school graduate who hasn't experienced a damned thing in his life. Suddenly dropped right into the middle of hell itself, seeing those repugnant acts up close and personal—not to mention the "routine" horrors of war and the fact that at any moment their own life could be snuffed out. What would you expect their reaction to be? I would suspect it would be infinitely worse, and vastly more persistent, than my own. Like me, they might become so immersed in the situation

that they wouldn't even recognize that they were feeling anything. But then, once removed from the horrible circumstance,
that temporary numbness might be replaced with confusion,
disgust, and even shame. Shell Shock. Battle Fatigue. PTSD.
Whatever you want to call it, the depths of immorality created
in times of war are the ultimate mind-fuck for the unfortunate
participants. I got a little, tiny, fleeting taste of it for a few hours.
Imagine the effect on the men who spent months, even years,
submerged in it. Just keep that in mind as the story unfolds.

My next order of business was to see what sort of evidence I
could find regarding similar barbaric acts committed by American personnel against their Japanese counterparts. I found
plenty. The taking of Japanese body parts as trophies seemed
particularly common, although just how prevalent this practice
was is almost impossible to ascertain. Teeth and ears were the
most popular items, with accounts of Marines collecting these
souvenirs as early as Guadalcanal in August 1942.[7] While it is
likely that only a small percentage of American troops actually
participated in this sort of grisly behavior, it was apparently
common enough that in September 1942, Admiral Chester Nimitz, commander of the Pacific Fleet, issued an order stating that
no part of an enemy body was to be used as a souvenir, under
the threat of "stern disciplinary action."[8]

Perhaps the most surprising and notorious of the human
souvenirs were the skulls of Japanese combatants. In spite of
the official prohibition of such mementos, it would appear that
the procurement and preservation of Japanese skulls was not
an uncommon practice.[9] US troops concocted a variety of in-
novative techniques for sanitizing their gruesome memorabilia,
including boiling, removing the flesh with lye, or, in the case of
sailors, dragging the heads in a net behind their vessels and letting the salt water do the work. In the May 22, 1944, issue of *Life*
magazine, the full-page "Picture of the Week" on page thirty-five
depicted a young blonde American woman gazing dreamily at
a Japanese skull that had been sent to her by her boyfriend, a
lieutenant in the Navy. Photographer Ralph Crane dramatically,
and perhaps unintentionally, captured the irony of a pretty and
well-dressed girl, identified as twenty-year-old Natalie Nicker-
son from Phoenix, Arizona, writing a thank-you note for the depraved gift that would have been considered obscene were it not
for the ongoing war and the associated torrent of anti-Japanese

racist sentiment throughout the United States. The skull itself was autographed by the boyfriend and inscribed: "This is a good Jap—a dead one we picked up on the New Guinea Beach." Even President Franklin D. Roosevelt was not above the frenzy. Columnist Drew Pearson reported in the June 13, 1944, edition of the *Washington Merry-Go-Round* that Congressman Francis Walter of Pennsylvania "presented the President with an odd gift . . . a letter opener made from the forearm of a Jap soldier."[10] Roosevelt responded, "This is the sort of gift I like to get," and it wasn't until several weeks later, and after considerable pressure from civilian groups and religious leaders, that the president ordered the gift to be returned, with the explanation that "he did not wish to have such an object in his possession."[11]

In the course of my research I found that this sort of desecration of dead soldiers, while uncommon in Europe, was ubiquitous throughout the Pacific. There were examples documented in almost every campaign, even as late as the battles of Iwo Jima and Okinawa in 1945. Somewhere along the path of my circuitous journey through the vast expanse of the Internet I accidentally stumbled upon something I didn't expect. On the website larryshomeport.com, I found several of the old pictures that Murray had taken out of his drawer to show me. I was surprised, but retrospectively I shouldn't have been—why would I have presumed that Murray was in possession of the only surviving copies of those historic photos? Lawrence "Larry" Smith is a Navy veteran who served as a submariner from December 1971 until January 1983. He started as a gun fire control technician and ultimately advanced to the rank of chief petty officer. On his website, Larry identified the photos as having been taken on the island of Peleliu in 1944. When I contacted Larry to inquire about the origin of the pictures, all he could tell me was that they were sent to him by "a lady who has been involved with some of the survivors of Peleliu."

So, is it possible that the "small" island on which Murray landed was actually Peleliu, site of one of the bloodiest, most violent battles of the entire war? As I explored additional sources that seemed reputable, I found more images of Peleliu that appeared strikingly similar, and sometimes identical, to the photos that Murray had shown me. Clearly, I needed more concrete information to adequately continue my investigation. I needed to find out exactly where Murray had served throughout the duration of his enlistment. I contacted Catherine to see if she was in possession of any of Murray's records, but the only relevant document she had was his Notice of Separation from the US Naval Service (NAVPERS-553). While the information on that certificate was limited, it did provide me with some interesting insights. Murray entered the service on May 5, 1943, and was discharged on April 13, 1945. He had indeed served in the 100th Naval Construction battalion. He received an honorable discharge, but his discharge was based on the recommendation of the Board of Medical Survey. When I asked Catherine what sort of medical condition might have led to her father's discharge from the military, she told me that she thought it had something to do with his PTSD, but she wasn't really sure.

In an effort to gather more data, I looked into the history of the 100th Naval Construction Battalion (NCB).[15] I was able to find the official itinerary of the 100th NCB, dated June 19, 1945. The 100th Battalion was commissioned on July 1, 1943, and left for Pearl Harbor on November 21. They landed at Majuro in the Marshall Islands on February 1, 1944, and then returned to Hawaii on July 5. On July 25, 1944, one officer and seventeen men were sent on temporary duty with a pontoon detachment for the invasion of Angaur in the Palau Islands, with that group of men rejoining the Battalion at Pearl Harbor on November 13. In March 1945, the 100th NCB left Pearl Harbor, and four weeks later landed at Samar Island in the Philippines, where they remained for the duration of the war.

I had never heard of Angaur, so of course further investigation was necessary.[18] Angaur is a small limestone island, part of the Palau Island group, located about five hundred miles east of the Philippines. The invasion at Angaur took place on September 17, 1944—just two days after the Marines had landed on Peleliu, located only six miles to the north. The Battle of Angaur lasted over a month, and resulted in fairly heavy casualties, but only a fraction of the losses our forces suffered on the far more heavily defended Peleliu. Once the combat on Angaur was over and the island was secure, members of the 81st Infantry Division were sent from Angaur to Peleliu to relieve the 1st Marine Division, who had suffered massive casualties. That conflict lasted a month longer, the island finally being declared secure on November 27.

Now my curiosity was really heightened. Was it possible that Murray was one of the seventeen men who detached from the main battalion to invade Angaur and that he subsequently made his way over to Peleliu to aid in the battle there? Was that where he saw the terrible combat he described and where he obtained those pictures he kept sequestered in his dresser drawer? As a matter of extreme coincidence, just a few days after I had this revelation, my good friend Mike Lucas came to visit us from New Jersey, and he brought with him a gift that couldn't have possibly been more timely. It was a boxed set of twenty-four DVDs entitled *WWII A Filmed History from the National Archives*. As I looked through the table of contents, I couldn't believe my eyes when I got to DVD eighteen and noticed that the second film on the disc was "Action at Angaur," a documentary produced by the Army Signal Corps in 1945. Unbelievable! A tiny island I had never heard of, and now within a matter of days, I find out that I know someone who may have fought there and I come into possession of a film that actually documents the combat that took place there. Well, Mike is just as much of a history buff as I am, so we immediately put that disc into the DVD player to see what it might reveal.

The film is riveting. It chronicles the 81st "Wildcat" Division from their days in Hawaii, through their journey across the Pacific, and ultimately to the violent combat they encountered on Angaur. Unapologetically propagandized, the film nonetheless serves as visual evidence of events that would otherwise be forgotten. Men, many of whom would most certainly be killed or wounded in the days to come, can be seen clowning around aboard the transport ship, preparing their weapons, praying, and training at Guadalcanal for their impending amphibious assault. Stunning footage of the bombardment of Angaur that preceded the invasion and equally compelling footage of the landing itself. The camera vividly captures the expressions on the soldiers' faces: First as they anticipated what they were about to encounter, then as they became enveloped in enemy fire, and finally as those who were wounded were tended to at a makeshift field hospital. Pictures that are indeed worth a thousand words, maybe more. The combat sequences and images of dead Japanese soldiers are chilling, and the anti-Japanese racism espoused by the narrator, while typical in 1945, feels abrasive to the conscience today. Then, to my further amazement, precisely thirteen minutes and twenty-six seconds into the film, I saw a fleeting glimpse of a man who was digging a foxhole . . . a man who was eerily similar in appearance to Murray!

I paused the DVD on his image, and the more I studied it, the more I was able to convince myself that the man could actually be Murray Jacobs. I grabbed a photo of Murray that Catherine had given me, and along with Mike, I carefully examined it and compared it to the likeness on the screen, which was grainy and from an altogether different angle. I couldn't go so far as to say that it was certain, but Mike said, "There are an awful lot of similarities between the man in the photo and that man in the film." I'll let the pictures speak for themselves.

So now, not only had I uncovered the possibility that the site of Murray's second landing may have been in the Palau Islands, but I may have fortuitously discovered a rare motion picture that actually shows him in the midst of battle. But another, altogether different question had arisen: What was the nature of the condition that led the Board of Medical Survey to issue Murray an honorable discharge? My next course of action was clear. I needed to see Murray and have a frank discussion about everything I had learned, and I needed to obtain his consent to retrieve whatever military documents were available from the National Personnel Records Archive in St. Louis.

I went to see Murray just a few days later, and I wasted no time getting right down to business.

"You know, Catherine showed me your discharge papers, and it seems that there was some medical reason for your discharge. Do you know anything about that?"

"Well . . . they called it shell shock during World War I, then they changed it to battle fatigue, and later on they came up with PTSD."

"Do you know why they made that diagnosis?"

"No, I really don't. When I first went to the hospital, I went there with sinus problems. I had problems with my sinuses even way back in high school. Then the battalion doctor who was taking care of me sent me back on a hospital ship. I never knew why . . . they never told you anything. I ate when they said eat. I slept when they said sleep. My ass belonged to them. So, when they said, 'You're going home,' I went home. I didn't ask him, and he didn't tell me, so I just don't know. Maybe it was my mood, maybe it was my actions. I don't know what to tell you."

"I'd like to be able to look at your official file and see exactly what it was that led to your discharge. But I need your permission, and your signature, to obtain all your records."

Murray thought about it for just a moment and responded, "That's all right with me. I don't care. But I don't know whether you're going to find anything."

I had already obtained the necessary documents and quickly gave them to Murray for him to sign before he had a chance to change his mind.

"I'll have the records sent directly to me, so if there's anything in there that you don't want your family to see, they won't see it."

"There's not going to be anything in there that I would object to them seeing. I don't know of anything—not one thing."

"Aren't you the least bit curious to know what was written in your records? Wouldn't you like to know why it was that you were sent home?"

"I wouldn't be interested. Not at all. It wouldn't make a damned bit of difference in my life. You know, I can tell by the way I feel . . . I'm not too far from the end. I know that. Just how far—of course, it'd be ridiculous for me to say that I know, because I don't. But it can't be a long ways off."

Every now and again, Murray, like many older folks, would go off on one of these "the end is near" tangents. Usually I just listened sympathetically. But today I had a lot of questions to get through, so I abruptly changed the subject.

"Those are some outstanding photographs you showed me last time."

"Well, the guy was a photographer in civilian life."

"Can you tell me anything more about him? Do you remember his name?"

"No, I don't really remember his name. He wasn't a tall guy, maybe 5'9" at the most. But he was built rugged, had really good arms on him. He and another guy, every once in a while, they'd get into a wrestling match. This was after an island had been secured, of course, and we were just laying around. They'd go at it hard—not mean, just real hard—and the rest of us would get a real kick out of watching them. Anyhow, he took those pictures, illegally, and then after things died down he developed the film, and all the guys in our tent got copies."

"Well . . . as I was doing some research on the Internet, I found copies of some of those pictures. And as best as I could determine, it would seem that they were taken on Peleliu."

"Peleliu? No . . . we were never there. What makes you think they were from Peleliu?"

"Well, I happened upon those pictures on one particular website, where they were identified as having been taken on Peleliu. Then, I found some official military photos that were taken on Peleliu, and there are several . . . they aren't the exact same picture, but I'd swear they were taken at the exact same place at a slightly different time. Now, remember you told me that after Majuro you volunteered for another mission, but you didn't know the name of that island? I looked up the history of your battalion, and as it turns out, a bunch of you guys volunteered and went over to an island called Angaur, which is right next to Peleliu. In fact, I found a video that the government made of the combat at Angaur, and I think I may have even found one shot of you in the film!"

"Well, to the best of my knowledge I was never at Peleliu. Not that I recall. But that was too many years ago."

"Would you at least be open to the possibility that what I'm saying is true? That the second island you landed at was called Angaur, and from there you may have gone over to Peleliu to help in the battle there?"

Reluctantly, Murray admitted, "It's possible. But remember, I've been trying to put all this out of my memory for a number of years. I've been trying to forget it. That's the only way I've been able to live with myself. That's the only way I've been able to live with some of the things I've done. It's been seventy years, and I've still got this damned PTSD."

"Do you think talking to me has made it better, or worse, or no difference?"

Murray thought silently about my question for a minute, maybe longer, and when he finally spoke, his answer was very deliberate.

"I don't know. There are certain aspects of it that haven't bothered me, and there are others that have brought back intense feelings. There have been a few nights when I woke up reliving what I went through."

"I think there are a lot of guys, like yourself, who saw some things—and did some things—that were horrible, and that they have not been able to face for all these years. I think it's probably very lonely being like that, feeling like maybe you're the only one. I'm hoping that even one man who's in a position like yours reads this, and for the first time realizes that he wasn't the only one who had to live through all that. I don't want to put words in your mouth, but I would think that if I were you, carrying this burden for all these years, of things that you did, that as you sit here today you're not proud of . . . I think I would feel better knowing that somebody understands how I could get to the point that I would do those terrible things."

Murray offered further explanation: "Well, you have to understand that as each day went on, life became insignificant, really. You didn't know from minute to minute whether you were going to get shot, or bombed, or what. And as you would see things, the more you saw the less it affected you . . . it became just an everyday happening. The first guy got shot and yelled for the medic and everybody ran to him. The last guy you seen with his guts blown out, you didn't pay any attention to it at all."

"I'd like to ask you about a few of the things you told me the last time we met. In the course of my investigation I've found that beheadings were quite a bit more common than most people realize. And I read that some of the guys would actually boil the Japanese heads and send the skulls back home. Did you know anybody who did that?"

"No. But guys did all kinds of things."

"Well, I want to ask you about something else you told me the last time we met. I've been thinking about it a lot, and I've got to ask you about it, because I haven't come across anybody who has said anything about this particular situation. You told me how you had come across your own guys who had been killed and some of them had their dicks cut off and put in their mouths. And you said it didn't take you guys long to do the same thing back to the enemy. But then you told me about cutting a prisoner's penis off, cooking it, and feeding it to the guy."

"Yeah, we boiled it."

"Now, I realize that must be a difficult memory, but I have to ask you about it. It's interesting because in all the research I've done that story is very unique . . . I've never seen anything about somebody doing that, and I've never heard anyone talk about it. I mean, you have a prisoner, a live individual, and you cut his dick off with a knife, and the guy's still alive. I would imagine that's an extremely painful thing to have done to you, so the guy's got to be screaming bloody murder. Then you boil his dick in a helmet, make him eat it, and then you kill him. Is that right?"

There was a very long silence before Murray answered, and he sighed deeply. When he spoke, he was barely able to muster, in a muffled voice, "Yeah."

When I look back on this particular line of questioning, I clearly was not functioning at the height of my empathetic capacity, apparently channeling my inner Edward R. Murrow, not my inner Florence Nightingale.

"I know this isn't an easy topic for you, but I'm just trying to get myself into the mindset of somebody thinking of doing that to another person, and then actually doing it. It's just not something that I would think of doing. I'm not being critical of it, because I know you saw atrocities that they had committed to our guys, but I'm just trying to understand."

Murray sat silently with his eyes closed for several minutes. A couple of times I asked him if he was OK, and on each occasion, he nodded affirmatively. After a while his respirations became a bit labored, and I needed to make sure that I hadn't inadvertently plunged him into some sort of a death spiral: "You look like you're either falling asleep, or you're having trouble breathing, or you're hoping I forget about what I just asked you."

With that, Murray lifted his head, looked me square in the eyes, and answered, "No. My mind is racing, and I'm trying to get the images out of my head. As far as cutting their dicks off, they taught us that. You do strange things. At the time it seemed all right, but now it seems bizarre . . . cannibalistic."

"You know, I found evidence that some of the Japanese soldiers actually cannibalized our men."

Murray became obviously agitated, and he abruptly barked, "Yes . . . yes! I didn't want to go into that because I don't like to think about it. We came upon guys that had that done to them. The Japs only had been eating a handful of rice. They'd cut off a chunk of leg, or butt, and they'd eat it! You're pulling things out of me that I didn't intend for you to."

"But that explains a lot. I think it makes what you did more understandable. If I came upon one of my own guys, and somebody had killed him and had been eating him, then when I come face-to-face with the enemy—I don't care if it's the same guy who did it—maybe I'd say, 'How would you like to eat your own flesh?' In that absurd circumstance, it actually becomes almost reasonable, don't you think?"

"I don't like to talk about this. I haven't talked to anybody about this for seventy years. The biggest reason I haven't talked about it is because you could talk about it to someone and they wouldn't understand the first thing about what you were telling them. You become a different person entirely. Nothing is banned. The door is wide open and you do whatever comes to your mind. And things come to your mind that normally you would never think of. I think you can put whatever you want into a book and whoever wants to can read it. But you will *never*, in God's world, really understand it, unless you're sitting in a little hole with bullets flying all around you. You know, I've never asked you—and I think I know the answer—but I've never asked you why you're doing this."

"Well, the reason why I'm doing this has changed since I started talking to you, and quite frankly, I've struggled with that myself. When I first started talking to you, all I wanted to do was document your story, a story that nobody had ever heard, and a story that seemed like it would be interesting. But now that I've heard the things you've seen and done, and all that you've been through, I think the purpose of what I'm doing has a much bigger place in our society than just telling your story. There are a lot of men like you. I think everyone who goes through combat is like you, to a certain extent. They've seen things, they've done things, they've become a person that is not at all like the person they were before. And a lot of those men are struggling, in part because they are judged by people who have never seen combat. And the problem with that is we look at the guys from your generation and we say, 'Oh, it's like in all the John Wayne movies: guys get shot but nobody bleeds. Our guys are the good guys and never do anything bad.' And the soldiers in Iraq and Afghanistan are judged by that standard, which isn't real. That standard doesn't exist and it's never existed. And it's unfair to today's soldiers, kids like your grandson, that their actions are being judged, and it's all being videotaped. They all have cameras on their helmets or on their shoulders."

[AUTHOR'S NOTE: Catherine's oldest son, Louis, has been in the Marines for almost ten years. While he has been deployed overseas on several occasions, he has not been in combat.]

"So, we can all see everything they do, and we're scrutinizing them, but when it's all said and done, we don't have enough information to judge them fairly. We look at a Marine in Afghanistan and we watch a video—because we have video today, we didn't have video of everybody doing everything back in your day—and we see that Marine urinating on a dead Taliban fighter. And everybody says, 'Oh that's terrible,' and some woman in Long Island, who doesn't know shit from Shinola, looks at that video and says, 'Well the Greatest Generation would never have done something like that.' And I don't think it's fair to that Marine."

Murray started laughing out loud as soon as I brought up that incident, which took place in 2011 and resulted in international outrage.

"I seen that. And I thought to myself, what a small item that is . . . what a small incident. But what a big thing they made of it."

I had just connected with Murray in a way that I hadn't before.

"Right . . . and I think there are three reasons why that became such a big deal today. Number one, because like I said, everything today is recorded. As we've gone along in history there's been more and more documentation. So now we can actually see the images of one of our soldiers urinating on a corpse, and in Vietnam we saw the film of one guy holding a gun to a prisoner's head and blowing his brains out. That probably happened a thousand times during World War II—one of our guys executing a prisoner—but nobody was photographing it back then, so the incidents were never brought to the public's attention.

"Number two is that the people doing the judging . . . they don't know shit about it. When you came home from the war, most men, and even a lot of women, had been in the military. Millions of men shared that experience. Today, something like half a percent of the population is in the service. So even if you were being judged back in your day, a lot of people would understand what you had gone through. Today nobody knows anything about it. And the third reason that incident became a big story was because people think that the Marine who urinated on a dead body invented that sort of behavior . . . that the guys of your generation would never have thought of doing something like that to the enemy. What people don't realize is that for as long as there's been war, there's been guys doing shit that they never would have done if they didn't go to war."

I could tell that what I was saying was really resonating with Murray.

"That's right. A lot of the stuff we'd see, we'd just go by it and think nothing of it. Of course, it meant something to you when one of your own group got killed, but eventually you became hardened even to that, to a certain extent. If I had never been to war, and I just spent my life working at the copper mine, I never would have thought in a million years of doing the things I did. These are the type of feelings you just can't get out of reading a book."

"So, is your implication that it's not even worth trying to explain it; that the book isn't even worth writing?"

"Well, I wouldn't say that. But a certain number of people out there will read this—maybe—and some of them won't care about it, and some of them will think it's a bunch of bullshit."

"You know, before, when you asked me why I was doing this project, you said that you thought you knew the answer. Now that I've given you my response, I wonder how that fits in with what you thought I was going to say."

"Well, I think you are very interested in history, and particularly, in the history of World War II. And I think you want to find out if what you have read is all there was to it."

"And after everything I just told you, what do you think of me doing this project with you?"

Murray thought about my question for a moment, then looked at me and said, very deliberately, "Big trees from little acorns grow."

Every now and then Murray would say something so obtuse that I'd have no idea what the fuck he was talking about.

"What does that mean?"

"Something starts out as two guys just sitting and talking together, and the next thing you know it becomes a big issue. And I don't know whether that's good or bad. I don't know whether anyone will give a damn."

I'm not sure why, but I think the fact that Murray was challenging the worth of our project triggered a need in me to seek out some sort of personal validation from him.

"What do you think of me, anyway? Do you like talking to me?"

Murray gave my question careful consideration before he answered. "Well . . . I think you're an unusual guy, number one. You are unusual. After all, how many doctors do you see going around doing house calls in this day and age? You're not lackadaisical or laid-back, that's for sure. I also think you are inquisitive and a very precise individual. You have an air of authority about you. In my book, you're the type of guy who would do exactly what you're doing: sitting here talking to me. And I do like you and I like talking to you . . . I'm flattered that you're taking the time to talk to me. Have you ever written any other book?"

"No."

"Well you picked a helluva one to start with. You're just not a normal guy."

I laughed out loud and couldn't argue with anything Murray had said. I thought maybe we should leave things on that upbeat note.

"Well, is there anything else you want to talk about today?"

"Not really. I've talked too much. About certain things that I didn't want to talk about. One thing leads to another. It's pretty hard to cut open a watermelon and only eat one slice."

"I'll come back and see you again next week. You know, Murray, you're a good man."

"Yes, but there's no market for them though."

"Yeah, tell me about it . . . I'm lucky I found my wife and she puts up with me; otherwise I'd be up a creek."

CHAPTER 5

A WONDERFUL PLACE TO GROW UP

I realized that in order to properly tell Murray's life story, I needed to learn about his childhood and all the years leading up to his military service. I also recognized that these sessions focusing on his combat experience were taking a toll on him. So, I decided to spend our next visit getting as many details as I could about his life before the war. As a gesture of friendship, I started the visit by bringing him some pizza for lunch. Now, pizza was one of those things that you could take for granted growing up in Brooklyn—every neighborhood had a good pizzeria, and any place that was substandard wouldn't stay in business for more than a week. But here in Utah, pizza is tricky. Places serve all sorts of dreck and try to pass it off as pizza when it's barely even edible. For the closest approximation of authentic New York pizza in Utah you have to go to a place called Este in a neighborhood called Sugarhouse. No, it's not John's on Bleecker Street in Greenwich Village, but it's pretty damned good and quite a bit closer. So, I brought over a pie, and the two of us got to talking. Mostly I just listened and let Murray tell me whatever he could remember. I started by asking him about his earliest recollections of childhood.

"I was born in Roosevelt, Utah, on August 28, 1916. My very first memory is when I was three years old; my father and mother were going to visit his parents and they weren't going to take me. I really wanted to go and I remember I started to cry, and I kept right on crying until they finally agreed to take me with them. My grandparents lived in Roosevelt, just a few miles away, and incidentally we went in a wagon pulled by horses. That was our mode of transportation back then. My father's mother was born in Sweden, and his father was born here in Utah. My mother's family originally came from England, but both her parents were born in Utah. I don't have the slightest idea why the families settled in Utah . . . there's a lot of questions I'd like to ask them today if they were still around."

"What were your folks' names, and do you know how they met?"

"My father's name was Guy and my mother's name was Edna. One day my dad was going by my mother's house in a wagon, and she was sitting out on the porch, and he saw her and said, 'That's the woman I'm going to marry, right there.' Eventually they did get married, and for a while, they lived on the farm with my dad's folks. They had a few years of real good crops, but then the soil turned bad and they couldn't grow a damned thing on it. My granddad, and just about all the rest of them in that area, all lost their farms. That's when my father went to work for a company called Newton Brothers in Vernal, and that's where he learned the leather trade. They made saddles, boots, chaps, and harnesses.

"When I was five years old we moved into a nice brick house in Lehi. It had running water and a toilet in it. We were in hog-heaven! Back in Roosevelt we had no inside water, so we had to use an outhouse, which as I recall, wasn't much fun in the winter. My dad opened up a leather shop there in Lehi, and for a while he did a helluva business. But then the situation got pretty bad for the farmers in that area because of a horrible drought. They couldn't afford to pay my dad the money they owed him, so he had to declare bankruptcy, and that followed him for quite a few years. He got into construction and eventually worked his way back to where he had good credit again. His first construction job was in Nevada working on a tunnel for the railroad. After that he went to work at the copper mine in Bingham, building the bridges for the trains that ran there. He did a lot of the heavy timberwork on the trestles that the trains took to haul the ore out of the mine. When the trains ran over the trestles, the bolts would get loosened, so they'd work all night tightening up the bolts and removing any timbers that were rotten and replacing them with new ones. My dad worked long hours.

"In 1924, when I was eight years old, we moved to Bingham. You know, the whole town of Bingham disappeared by the 1950s . . . the copper mine just kept getting bigger and bigger until nothing was left of the town. Anyhow, we only lived in Bingham a couple of years, and then we moved to Copperton. What a

The man standing in the center of the photograph is Guy Jacobs, Murray's father. Taken circa 1923 while Guy was working on a railroad tunnel in Clover Creek, Nevada. Shortly after this photo was taken the tunnel collapsed, and Guy suffered a broken leg.

wonderful place to grow up! My childhood was great. I had a wonderful childhood. Copperton had a nice big park, with a ball field and grass, which was unheard of at the time. There were swings, teeter-totters, slippery slides. By then most everybody owned a car, but nobody drove very much. I could've gone out and went to sleep in the middle of the road and never worried about a car hitting me. The Boy Scouts was a big thing in Copperton. We met once a week, and I always looked forward to that. When we first lived in Copperton I had to ride the bus every day to Bingham to get to school. One year, I don't know what happened to the school bus, but we had to ride in the truck that was bringing the mail from Salt Lake City to Bingham. We'd get into this mail truck and sit right on top of the mail. Twice a month the truck would carry money from Salt Lake to a bank in Bingham. We kids would sit right in the back of the truck with the money, and behind us there'd be a car with guards with shotguns! I remember that clearly, and back then, nobody thought a thing of it. Of course, that'd never happen today. Everybody would be up in arms about it. I don't remember too much about my school years, but I remember I really enjoyed using crayons. I thought it was cool how you could put one color down on another color, and you'd get a different color. I thought that was really cool. You know, this pizza has a really nice flavor."

"Good. I'm glad you're enjoying it. Do you have any siblings?"

"I had three sisters. One died when she was a baby—of whooping cough. That was before I was born. Her name was Sylvia, and I named my one daughter after her. Then there was my sister Marell; she was five years older than me and died when she was ninety. And my sister Evelyn is three years younger than me, and we get along real well.

"You know, I had whooping cough as an adult when I was living in California. I caught it from my middle daughter. I didn't even know you could catch it as a grown man; I thought you'd be immune to it. I could see how it could kill you though, that sticky stuff getting stuck in your throat. I got so I knew how to handle it: I'd start coughing at night and I'd get up and go spit that phlegm out in the backyard. It could have very easily killed me. That would have been the damnedest thing: living through fighting in the Pacific, then dying of whooping cough.

"My father was a good provider, but he wasn't a 'buddy' type of guy, at least not to me. Everybody else loved him . . . he was real friendly to everybody else. He wasn't distant or cold to anyone but me. We just didn't do things together very much. We did fight occasionally, although I didn't talk back too much to my dad. He probably was closer to my sisters than he was to me. You know, when he was dying of a brain tumor, and I took care of him the last six years of his life, he once said to me, 'How come we never got closer than what we did?' I didn't have the heart to tell him, 'Well it was because you didn't get closer to me, that's all.' And he never did until the day he died. He was eighty-four years old.

"I remember when I was about ten years old, my father bought me a violin. Not because I asked for it. He wanted a violin when he was a kid, and his father wouldn't buy him one. So, my dad wanted me to play the violin, which I did, but he never took the time to listen to me, anyhow. I got pretty good at it, too, even though I wouldn't practice like I was supposed to. I played in the school orchestra, but he never did ask me about it, and he never once came to hear me play. Actually, I wish I played the guitar.

"I loved the guitar. It sure is a wonderful instrument. Back then not many people played the guitar, but we had a radio and a phonograph and we'd listen to the weekly programs on the radio and we'd play whatever records were out. There was a place in Salt Lake called Woolworth's Five and Ten Cent Store, and that's where we could go and buy records and all sorts of other stuff. You could go in there and for a nickel you could get a hot dog covered in sauerkraut. And that was a great thing. At that time, we had a green Oldsmobile, one where the doors came together in the middle of the car, and I can remember my mother driving us to Woolworth's in that car. There was a vase where you could put flowers in that car, but we never did—although I do remember that on the Fourth of July my father would put little American flags in there."

"Tell me about your mother. Did you have a better relationship with your mom than with your dad?"

"I wasn't particularly close to her. My mother was a very good wife, though. She had the meal there on the table when my dad got home from work. He'd take a bath, and then we all sat down and ate our family dinner together. My mom was an excellent cook. She did a lot of baking. She'd bake bread five loaves at a time, and there was always a pie for dessert. She cooked everything—lots of vegetables and, of course, lots of potatoes. One night a week we'd have spaghetti. And on Sunday we'd always have roast beef—yeah, you could count on roast beef every Sunday. My mother was eighty-two when she died of a stroke.

"Maybe it was my fault that I wasn't closer to my folks . . . maybe I didn't work at it. I don't know. I wasn't the best of boys—far from it. I goofed off an awful lot. I look back now on things that I should have done and I didn't do. Like when I was about twelve years old and we were living in Copperton, we had a coal stove. Every morning my father had to be at work by seven a.m., and

Murray Jacobs, circa 1929 (age 13) at his home in Copperton.

before he left he had to go down to the coal room, load some coal in a bucket, cut some kindling, and haul it upstairs to get the fire started. And of course, that would take him some time early in the morning. I could've very easily gotten that coal and wood the night before, so all he'd have had to do was put it in the stove and light the fire. But I didn't do it, and I don't know why; maybe it was some kind of rebellion. But I never did get that coal and kindling for him. Of course, he never did take the time to go with me to that nice park we had there in Copperton. But I can't make excuses for myself.

"I liked to have fun. I played tennis, and I was pretty good too. I won the junior championship in high school, and then I damned near won the senior. I remember one winter they flooded one of the tennis courts so it would freeze, and we ice-skated on it. I liked to roller skate. I liked to play basketball. What a place to grow up in!"

"The time period you're discussing now is right in the middle of the Great Depression. How did that affect your family?"

"During the Depression, my father was working at the copper mine, and the work at the mine wasn't affected at all. He'd come home on payday with a check for a hundred dollars for two weeks work, and that was amazing back then. So, we always had food on the table. I don't ever remember having to go hungry. Of course, when I finished high school in 1934, I went to work up there at the mine, also. Everybody who worked there had to start out on what they called the 'track gang.' It took a lot of men to take care of all the track for all the trains. Three dollars a day. That's what I made. Most of my work there was done from six o'clock at night until three o'clock in the morning. I didn't mind, because you could learn to do things better and quicker on night shift than you could in the daytime. And I wanted to learn how to run a shovel. Back then, to be a man, you also had to learn how to stand at the bar and drink a beer. So, I tried to learn that too, as quick as I could. Yeah, my biggest worry after I got out of school was I wanted to go to work and be one of the guys.

"You know, I'm LDS. [Author's note: "LDS" refers to a member of the Church of Jesus Christ of Latter-day Saints.] I didn't grow up close to the church at all, since my parents were not particularly religious, although my father was neither a drinker nor a smoker. Where I grew up, you were considered 'one of the boys' if you would smoke and drink and swear and play with the women. I tried them all. I smoked two packs of unfiltered Camels a day. I chewed tobacco on the job, and I smoked cigars at night. And I was a pretty hard drinker—I drank a lot of Budweiser. I did everything in the world to tear my body down when I was young."

Murray struck a chord with me. My grandfather also smoked two packs a day of filterless Camels, from the age of thirteen until he died in his seventies.

"You're one tough old son-of-a-bitch to have lived to ninety-five after everything you did to yourself."

"Yeah, and I'm still in pretty good shape. There must've been some damned good genes in my family. I'd like to be forty years old again. That'd be great. It lets you look ahead a little bit. As it is right now, everything is in my past. In 1936, I met my wife on a blind date and I fell madly in love with her. Phyllis lived in Salt Lake City, and at the time I was living in Bingham. She was working for the telephone company. Our first date was at the Old Mill—it was a real popular spot back then for dinner and dancing. It was originally a real paper mill that was run by the *Deseret News*, but in 1927 it was turned into a sort of nightclub. It was right near here, at the mouth of Big Cottonwood Canyon, but it's since burned down and been condemned. I was twenty-one when we got married in 1937, and I was still making three dollars a day. Now that was a good job, but it wasn't luxury. Three dollars a day would feed you, and clothe you, and house you. But you had to be very careful how you handled that money. For example, a whole sack of potatoes sold

No that's not Betty Grable. It's Phyllis Jacobs, Murray's wife, circa 1943.

for twenty-five cents. And you'd put those potatoes—along with onions, carrots, and squash—down in the cellar, and you could eat them all winter long.

"My wife was a beautiful woman and an excellent cook. She was 'A-number-1' all the way. She wound up being the glue that held me together. Through all my trials and tribulations, she hung on. We went to a lot of movies together, and we went out to eat a lot. She particularly liked to go get Mexican food. She was a very frugal woman, and from time to time she would go to work somewhere, usually selling ladies' apparel. She was very conservative and didn't drink or smoke—I suppose I did enough for the both of us. Phyllis did like to shop, and I never once said to her, 'You shouldn't buy that.' When she went shopping she could buy whatever she wanted. On December 1, 1937, my first daughter, Rae, was born, and my daughter Sylvia was born on May 22, 1940."

"Do you remember where you were and what you were doing when the attack on Pearl Harbor happened?"

"I was living in Sandy by then, still working at the copper mine. I can't tell you exactly where I was or anything like that."

"How did you feel when you heard about it?"

"At that particular time, it didn't bother me much. It didn't sink in. I don't know. I was a kid that never did grow up. Things like that didn't bother me near as much as it might other people. I didn't realize the extent of the damage that they had done. I really didn't. I didn't know how many men had been killed."

"Well, before Pearl Harbor there was a big controversy as to whether we should get involved in the war or not. Do you remember how you felt about that?"

"I didn't really think about that, either. They couldn't draft me. I had a job deferment because the work at the copper mine was considered to be essential to the military. I had a nice little family. I wasn't worried about politics back then. I had nothing in my head. I was just going through life; sun comes up, sun goes down."

Murray paused for quite a while, and he looked at a photograph of his wife that was in a nice frame on top of his dresser. He turned back toward me and continued: "You know, I cheated on my wife, and it bothers the hell out of me now. It didn't bother me a damned bit back then, but it really bothers me now. At that time, I just didn't seem to care about anything. I don't know why. I can't explain why I cheated on my wife with so many different women. Looking back, all women are practically the same anyway. The best explanation of it I ever heard was: 'when a man marries a woman, he wants a lady during the daytime, but at night he wants a whore.' My wife wasn't like that. She was a lady all the time. A wonderful woman."

There was another long pause as Murray looked back at the photo of his wife.

"I should turn her picture around so she can't hear me. Oh my, the misery I caused her."

I was more than a little surprised, not only by the details of what Murray had just told me, but by the very fact that he had confessed such an intimate matter to me in the first place. My response was rather awkward and insensitive: "Well, if you believe in an afterlife, it has nothing to do with the picture. Wherever she is she probably can hear you anyway."

"Well, she probably knew about it already. She couldn't have helped but know. I'm sure she did."

"Do you think you were a good father?"

Murray responded to my blunt question in an unflinching fashion: "No. I was not a good husband; therefore, I was not a good father. I was very good to my children; I took them places and provided for them. So, in that way I was a good father. But I still cheated on my wife."

"Tell me why you enlisted in 1943."

"I was pissed off with life. Period. The life I was leading, anyway. I was drinking a lot. I was screwing around with all kinds of women. I had heard about the Seabees, and I thought that would be a good way to serve my country."

"But a lot of guys enlisted right after Pearl Harbor, and you didn't. Why not?"

"I don't know. I couldn't tell you."

"So, when you enlisted, you had a six-year-old daughter and a three-year-old daughter. Did your wife give you a hard time about going into the military?"

"Not really. She was probably glad to get rid of me. Back then I did whatever I wanted to do; I didn't think about the consequences. It never entered my mind. It didn't bother me to leave my family. It didn't make a damned bit of difference to me. What a damned fool I was."

"Tell me about the process of being inducted into the Seabees."

"Well, first we went through a pretty thorough physical exam and were given our vaccinations. You know, you'd think I could remember this all very clearly, but I have to admit it's a little foggy to me. I recall getting onto a train in downtown Salt Lake City, and I was carrying a little satchel and wearing a nice Western-style hat. And I remember that everybody on the train looked at me and snickered a little bit. You see, I had never been on a train before and I didn't know that it was a custom that you took your hat off when you were on a train. Not another soul on that train was wearing a hat, and right then, I felt like hell. Well, we got to where we were going, which was Camp Peary in Virginia. And as soon as we got off that train they took everything we owned . . . we kept nothing."

"But you told me you brought a knife with you from home."

"Not then. I got home once more before we went overseas and that's when I picked up my knife. But boy, when everything was laid on the ground, you should have seen the knives, and the straight razors, and the blackjacks. Most of them came from . . . well, back then we called them colored men. We didn't call them black men or African-American."

"Did you ever witness any discrimination against the black men in the military?"

"Back then, they lived in separate tents and their duties were strictly to cook. They didn't intermingle with us, not at all. And I never gave that any thought."

"Have you given it any thought now?"

"I've thought about it a little. They were emancipated, but they still weren't treated as equals. In our battalion, the black men were never on the line fighting. They saw no combat. None. It's just the way things were."

"Did you face any discrimination because you were LDS?"

"I didn't wear garments, and I wasn't close to my religion, so it didn't make any difference."

"Were there any Jewish guys?"

"Just one, from back in New York. And he fought right along with the rest of us. There might have been other Jewish men, but back then I wouldn't have known, and I wouldn't have cared. Anyway, after we arrived at Camp Peary, we were assigned into our barracks, and that night, some of those young boys, some of them were barely eighteen years old, and it was the first time they'd ever been away from home and I could hear them crying. I tried to console them a little bit, and eventually most of them did just fine. The next morning, we got up and showered and shaved, and it took practically the whole day to get all our government-issued stuff. They gave us a big white bag and all our stuff went in there—pants, shirts, blanket.

"After that, we were divided up into platoons, and I remember we did a helluva lot of marching. They kept us damned busy with that marching—the same routine over and over again. We did calisthenics too, but I don't remember exactly what kind. I can remember the damned marching though. We did that constantly. And the food . . . it was just slightly better than you might feed your dog. We stayed there for six weeks. I understand that later in the war Camp Peary was used as a sort of detention center for German POWs.

"After six weeks of boot camp we were transferred to another base in Gulfport, Mississippi. It was in Gulfport that our proper training started. We'd go out to the rifle range and practice shooting. We were taught hand-to-hand combat and the different ways to kill somebody. We would practice on one another: different holds and different ways to immobilize the enemy. Like to jab somebody with your fingers right in the throat. I could kill you like that. Of course, we didn't go through the whole process; we would just get up to a certain point and stop. Otherwise that would've been very bad for morale—actually killing each other. That wouldn't have been good at all.

"We stayed at Gulfport for about another six weeks, and then from there we went by train to California, to a place called Point Mugu. It's right near Port Hueneme, which is where the Navy Seabee Museum is today. By now it was October or November, and we were staying in Quonset huts. And at night it would get cold. The wind would come in off the ocean and just about freeze us to death. I had everything on me that I could put on me. I'd go to bed with all my clothes on, then I'd wrap myself up in two blankets, and I'd still freeze my ass off all night. And believe it or not, we did our guard duty on horseback! Some of the guys in the battalion had never seen a horse, let alone ride one. Fortunately, I was used to riding horses, so I knew how to handle one. I had forgotten about that—doing guard duty on the back of a horse! It seems weird to me now. You know, that pizza left a really good taste in my mouth."

"I'm glad you enjoyed your lunch. But you know, what seems weird to me is why did they have guard duty in California? What were they guarding against?"

"They were looking for Japanese subs or anything else along the coast. By that time, we had been issued rifles. We were taught how to assemble and disassemble the rifles, and to keep them clean, and how to shoot them straight. Now, I had been used to guns since I was fourteen, so it came pretty easy to me. I hunted rabbits with my dad, and sometimes pheasants. Cottontails are good to eat. I skinned them, and Mom cooked them up and we ate them. So, I was already comfortable with a rifle. And I had been home and got my knife. I took my ten days leave before we left Gulfport. I wanted to get home real bad, so I took my leave then, but I wish I had waited until we got to California . . . then I wouldn't have been on the train so damned long.

"I got along pretty good with all the guys in our company. There was only one guy that I didn't like. Because he was . . . well, I really don't know how to describe Ross. He was the clown of the outfit, always pulling jokes on somebody. He made at least one guy's life miserable. A little short, heavy-set guy—I can't remember his name, but he slept in the bunk right next to me. Anyhow, Ross needled this guy so much, finally he couldn't take it anymore, and he started chasing Ross around the barracks, calling him a few choice names, and shouting, 'If I catch you, I'm going to kill you!' Ross was pretty fast though—and he was laughing like hell while this guy was chasing him. But he didn't have to kill Ross. Ross got killed during that very first landing. He never even made it out of the damned boat. Why they took Ross . . . I will never know. He had a wife and five kids. He should've never been there.

"You know, that little short guy had a buddy who he'd always go on liberty with once we got to Honolulu. He was a real slow-talking guy who was a little older, and I remember that he knew everything there was to know about movies. Now, I didn't see this particular incident, but word got around the company that the two of them went into town one night and a guy propositioned them to give them both oral sex. And they took him up on it."

"A guy? Gave them each a blowjob? Back then? That's crazy!"

"Well, the world was crazy then. And as far as we knew, he didn't charge them for it. I don't know what his reason was for doing it . . . I guess that's how he got his jollies. I didn't really give it much thought. Anyhow, while I was in California at Point Mugu, after a while, they let us have liberty. And my wife came down and I remember she rented a place where we could stay and it was on a chicken farm. The people who owned it had set up two apartments, and we stayed in one and there was another couple in the other. He was in the Navy also, a cook, and he brought these big juicy steaks and boy, we ate good. I had almost forgotten about that. It was nice that he shared those steaks with us.

"After about six weeks in California, we finally headed off to Honolulu. We boarded what was called a Liberty Ship, and it was the first time I had ever been on the ocean. I remember going up on deck, seeing the beach in the distance, and wondering if it was the last time I would ever see the United States. I can tell you, going from California to Hawaii was the worst ride that I have ever experienced in a ship. The first night out a storm came in and there were waves fifteen to twenty feet high. It was a bad, bad storm. We had a destroyer escort, and they were being tossed around like toys. Our ship got hit by one big wave and damned near turned over. There were men on that ship that were so sick I don't know how they didn't die . . . guys laying on the floor, urine and puke everywhere. It was a mess! I don't know why, but I never had seasickness—thank God for that. I didn't throw up at all. There was one guy, a big tough brute who was always chewing cigars. He stayed in his bunk the whole time that storm was going on. He must've been scared to death we were going to sink. I can't say that I blame him . . . those Liberty Ships were the worst ships on the water.

"One night, after the storm passed, a few of us went to sleep on the deck. Ross had just gotten a brand-new pair of shoes—roughouts—and he took his shoes off to sleep, naturally. This particular night the ship's cook was baking bread, and oh, it smelled good. So, me and this other guy said, 'I'll bet we could trade a nice new pair of shoes for a loaf of that bread.' So, I stole Ross's shoes, gave them to the other guy, and he took them down to where the cook was at and traded them for a loaf of bread. He brought it back, we opened up a can of Spam, and ate the Spam with the bread, and boy it tasted good."

"Did you at least share that bread with Ross?"

"No. We went to sleep and when we all got up the next morning Ross started looking for his shoes, but of course he couldn't find them. We never did tell him what happened, and he had to get another pair of shoes from the quartermaster.

"Well, eventually we made it to Honolulu. That was around December 1, 1943. And a few weeks after we arrived, while we were getting ready to go to Majuro, I got to see FDR."

"You met Franklin Roosevelt?"

"No, I never met him, but I did see him right up close. He came to Hawaii—for what reason I don't know, of course—and there was a big parade. I was standing on the street, and for some reason or another, I happened to be in a spot where there weren't many people. He went by in his car, waving to everybody of course, and I got a good, good look at him. And then there was a fly-over by all different kinds of planes . . . bombers, fighters . . . so many planes that the ground just shook. That was quite a sight."

"Did you like FDR?"

"Yes, and I'll tell you why. When he took over, you could walk down the street and pass a hundred men, and not one of them would have a dime in his pocket—they were broke! He started that CCC business, and a lot of men went up in the mountains and were able to earn a dollar for a day's work. And they earned their food and shelter, and they were able to send some money back to their families. Those men built bridges,

The men of company 'C' in a deuce-and-a-half (2 1/2-ton truck) on the island of Oahu, December 1943. Murray is just behind the driver, holding a couple of coconuts.

buildings, and trails, and a lot of stuff like that. That program did a lot of good."

[Author's Note: Murray is referring to the Civilian Conservation Corps, a public work program founded by President Franklin Delano Roosevelt in 1933.]

"So, do you think Roosevelt was the best president of the United States that you've seen in your lifetime?"

Murray spoke rather assuredly: "No, I think Harry Truman was the best president. I liked him because he ran the country his way, and he didn't take no bullshit from nobody. If he had something to say, he said it, to no matter who. I just liked the way he did things."

"Tell me more about your time in Hawaii."

"When I was in Honolulu . . . well, of course our training continued there. You know, it takes a lot of planning for a battalion to move out. We got up before daylight, and we went until about four o'clock in the afternoon. Looking back, I think fifty percent of our training was a waste of time. Maybe it was necessary for the guys over in Europe—I don't know. But for us it was a different war. They didn't tell us what to expect on the islands because I don't think they knew anything themselves. We had to find out for ourselves when we got there. You know, a lot of Seabees were sent up to Alaska. I was happy I didn't get sent there. But of course, I wasn't real happy I got sent to the South Pacific, either."

Horsing around in Honolulu. Murray is second from right.

"Now, some of the more memorable times in Hawaii were when we were given liberty. We'd go into town and there were two lines . . . one of them went to the beer joint and the other went upstairs to the girls. That was where I went, pretty much every time. I don't know, maybe I had the feeling like I was going to get killed anyway. I can't remember now. Things I did back then didn't bother me at all. Not one bit. Now it bothers me."

"When you went on liberty, did you go by yourself or did you have any particular friends that you went with?"

Murray looked back at me with a kind of a sentimental, sorrowful expression. He spoke slowly and softly.

"My real close buddy. If you'd have asked anybody in the battalion if they knew Doyle Smith . . . 'no.' But if you'd have said 'Yardbird,' they all knew him. Doyle Smith. Doyle K. Smith. From Texas. He was six-foot-four, and he was slender. Worked welding pipe. A real good guy. Everybody had a buddy. He looked out for me, I looked out for him."

"Why'd you call him Yardbird?"

"I can't tell you. I don't know. And back then, I didn't care. Things I saw or did, that was it, no thought about it. Me and Yardbird were buddies for a long time. I lost Yardbird on our very first day of combat. We were going up the side of a hill, and a bomb hit and wiped him right out."

A single tear trickled down Murray's cheek.

"It must've hit him square. There was just pieces of him left. It felt like the world collapsed. I wanted to go and slaughter every one of those Jap bastards. Let's not talk about this anymore, huh?"

"What's your favorite story about Yardbird?"

Murray's mood brightened as he started to conjure up some more pleasant memories.

"He was a helluva good guy. A lot of fun. And Yardbird was a well-endowed guy, if you know what I mean. You know how sometimes you wake up in the morning with a piss hard-on? Or at least I used to in my younger days."

"Yes, I am quite familiar with that situation."

"OK, well we had two-deck beds, and Yardbird slept underneath. And when he woke up in the morning, it looked like he was sleeping under a little tent!"

I was laughing out loud as Murray was motioning with his hands to illustrate the size of the "tent" he was describing.

"Now don't tell me it was so big that you could feel it in the upper bunk!"

By now Murray's tears had also turned to laughter: "Ha ha . . . no, then I would have asked to switch bunks! But until I met Yardbird I didn't think that a man could ever have a piece of meat hung on him like that. One time back in Gulfport, Mississippi, we went on liberty and we met a couple of gals. There was always women out looking for servicemen to buy them drinks and have a good time. Anyhow, the place was really crowded, and the four of us were sitting at a table, telling jokes and laughing and drinking, and everybody in the place was laughing right along with us. And you know, I can't remember leaving that tavern. I have no memory of what happened the rest of that night. But I can remember the next morning as clear as day. I was having coffee with my girl and Yardbird's girl came out of the room the two of them had stayed in, and she had a kind of a dazed look on her face. She told the girl I was with, 'That guy made bells ring that have never been rung before and that'll never be rung again.' As long as I live I will never forget that statement!"

"Sounds like he was a good guy to go chasing women with."

"Ha ha ha! Well, you know when we went looking for women he didn't have it hanging out! Oh boy, I recall one time we picked up a couple of girls in Honolulu. These girls were from back in the States and they had come to Hawaii to find work. They packed parachutes on an assembly line. The woman I was with was part Chinese, and she was a nymphomaniac! I could lay on top of her all night long and she didn't even want me to pull it out the next morning. Of course, by that time it had shrunk, and I didn't have to pull very far."

I was laughing my ass off at that very descriptive visual, picturing Murray as a horny young stud rather than the creaky old man who sat before me. He took a long drink of water and continued, his mood having become abruptly more serious.

"I wish I had been a different man. But I grew up in a rough town, and after I entered the service I got a little rougher. By the time I got to Hawaii, all sense of decency left me entirely. I pretty much behaved like a wild animal. I wrote letters back to my wife, but not often enough. She sent letters to me pretty regular, and I'd get letters from my mother too. I did miss them. But I really didn't think I would come back, and I didn't ever worry about the people back home. I had the life insurance that the government had issued us, and I thought that was enough."

Murray and I sat together quietly for a few minutes, each of us contemplating the memories he had just shared. Eventually, he continued.

"I remember one incident when me and Yardbird were loading equipment onto the ship getting ready to go to Majuro. There was this one big refrigerator, and we had put cables around it like we were supposed to. We were lowering it into the hold, and I don't know how, but a cable slipped off and the whole thing dropped. And this one officer, a real son-of-a-bitch, starts screaming at us, 'Hey you guys are expendable . . . that cargo is not!' Turns out the refrigerator had all the officers' whiskey in it. He was so pissed off I thought he was going to shit his pants. He was in charge of our company, Company C, and after that, he wouldn't give anyone in the whole company liberty. Yeah, we learned to hate that guy real good.

"Once we boarded the ship and headed to Majuro, he tried to buddy up to all of us. There were a few guys maybe that got friendly with him, I don't know. I wasn't one of them. One time, after we had that airstrip built, we put a couple of stakes in the ground, with a rope across, right outside his tent. You see, whenever a Jap plane flew nearby, an alarm went off, and everybody would run out of their tents and jump into foxholes that we had dug and secured with sandbags. Well, this particular night, that alarm sounded, and he ran out of his tent, tripped on that rope, and broke his leg."

"Did he get sent home?"

"No, and he made it back to the battalion in time to go with us to that next island I landed on. In fact, he was the SOB I told you wouldn't approve me for the Purple Heart after I got shot."

"What ever happened to him? Did he survive the war?"

Murray looked back at me with the sort of piercing glare that I hadn't seen from him in quite some time.

"Well . . . he survived those first two landings. But there were others."

"You know, the very first time I spoke with you about the war you told me you were involved in three landings. What was the name of the third island you landed on?"

"You've heard of Iwo Jima, haven't you?"

"Of course I've heard of Iwo Jima. You landed on Iwo Jima?"

"I landed on Iwo Jima. That was the last place I was before they sent me home. You know that picture with the men putting the flag in the ground? I watched that happen. You know, it's about time for my dinner, so let's continue another day. But that pizza you brought me was very good. Thank you."

Dinner? Murray drops this bombshell in my lap and now he wants to have dinner? And anyway, how the fuck could it be dinnertime? I brought him his lunch and that was only a couple of hours ago! Then I looked out the window and noticed it was pitch black outside. Our conversation was so engrossing that five hours had passed—day had become night—and I hadn't even noticed. I had a hundred questions I wanted to ask, but Murray had already gotten out of his chair and was headed toward the kitchen. I blurted out the first thing that came to my mind: "So are you saying that officer was killed on Iwo Jima?"

Murray glanced back at me over his shoulder. There was that look again.

"I never seen him."

"Well, what was the guy's name anyway?"

Murray was clearly getting annoyed.

"Here . . . I'll show you his picture."

And with that, Murray started rummaging around in his closet until he found an old leather-bound book entitled *Century . . . 100th U.S. Naval Construction Battalion*. He carried it out into the dining room and opened it on the table in the center of the room. Catherine and her daughter Andrea had left. Murray and I were alone in the house. The book was filled with photographs documenting the activities of the battalion during all phases of their training as well as on Majuro. Murray turned to the page with photos of all the officers, and he jabbed his finger right onto the picture of M. S. Blair, a lieutenant from Terre Haute, Indiana.

"That's the SOB right there. And the way he looks in the picture, that's just how he was."

Murray wasn't kidding. While most of the officers were smiling in their photos, this guy Blair had a kind of an arrogant smirk on his face. I could tell Murray was getting agitated, and that he had probably had enough for one day. I put on my jacket, gathered my stuff, and got ready to leave. As I headed toward the door, Murray was still standing at the table, staring at the same photograph. I said goodbye, and Murray grumbled, "So long," but there he stood, leaning on the table and looking at the picture. I was almost at the front door, but I felt uncomfortable just leaving him like that.

"So that guy landed with you at Iwo Jima?"

With that, Murray pushed himself up from the table and started to walk over to the kitchen counter, where he usually ate his meals. He spoke slowly, without looking at me, and he chose his words carefully: "Yeah, he landed. He landed good. Hard. He made a dent in the ground."

I took a step back into the room.

"Was he shot?"

"Yeah. He was shot. I made sure of that. Now do you want to know what's been bothering me all these years?" Murray gingerly sat down on a stool at the kitchen counter. I took another step closer.

"Are you telling me you shot him?"

There was a prolonged silence as Murray looked down at the counter and I just stood there, motionless, staring at him. He muttered under his breath, "I didn't say that . . . you did."

I was a little flustered.

"I just asked."

Another lengthy silence. Finally, Murray looked up at me.

"Well . . . he just didn't go any farther. Now if you'll excuse me, I'd like to eat my dinner."

CHAPTER 6

THE MAN IN THE GLASS

As I was on my way to see Murray the next week, my thoughts drifted back to a discussion I had with a friend many months before. It was just as I was about to embark on this project, and Julie and I were having dinner with our good friends, Bridget and Jasen Lee. Jasen is a journalist, and our conversation naturally turned to the very exciting prospect of interviewing a veteran who had never before shared the details of his combat experience. Bridget insightfully asked me how I would respond if he told me things—bad things—that I didn't expect to hear. Would I be able to remain impartial and non-judgmental if he admitted to atrocities and war crimes? At the time, I pondered her question and answered that I felt that I would, indeed, be able to take in such information while maintaining my objectivity. After all, by then, I had already considered the possibility that Murray might admit to me such incidents as the torture and execution of prisoners, acts of cowardice, or conceivably even the rape of local women. I had prepared myself for such disclosures and believed that I would be able to remain detached and professional.

Now, as I walked up the driveway to enter the house, I was firmly convinced of two things: that I had succeeded in remaining unbiased so far and that my most strenuous test was awaiting me on the other side of the door. Everything Murray had confided in me, all the sins he had finally confessed, and I had not judged him. In fact, I had been sympathetic and supportive, maybe even to a fault. But killing an officer? A fellow member of the United States Navy? This was something altogether different, something that I hadn't imagined. "Fragging," killing an officer usually by means of a fragmentation grenade, hence the term, was commonly reported during the Vietnam War, but I have never heard of such an incident occurring during World

War II. This was an admission that I could not possibly have anticipated—if it was an admission at all. Murray was sufficiently vague and mumbly to allow at least some doubt in my mind as to what exactly he had told me. So, my mission of the day was to clarify the events, get more details, and at the same time, try to avoid making Murray angry or sending him into a downward emotional spiral, all while remaining calm and cool.

Yeah, right.

When I arrived, Murray was alone in the house, sitting in his chair, and talking on the phone. As soon as I sat down, he curtailed his conversation and turned his attention toward me.

"That was my sister, Evelyn. She's just getting over pneumonia. She's ninety-three. We're the only two left. We've always been close."

Murray sighed deeply.

"If I had to do it all over again, knowing what I know now, I'd sure as hell do things a lot different. I wouldn't have enlisted in the military."

Now, that's not something you hear from many veterans of World War II. I pressed Murray on it a little: "Yet, when you talk to people you tell them that it's partly because of you that they're not speaking Japanese. You've said that to me a dozen times. So I think there's a part of you that's proud you served in the military."

Murray conceded, albeit reluctantly: "I guess that's true. I wish I hadn't, but I'm proud that I did. But that's something I ought to stop doing—'Well you're not speaking Japanese, are you?' When the occasion comes up and I think it fits, I say that to somebody, and I don't think that I should. That's one of the things I'm trying to quit doing before I leave this world."

I was anxious to segue into my task at hand.

"Are you angry that you didn't receive the Purple Heart that you earned?"

"No. I can't see that it would make any difference in my life. It might make a difference in my pension, but that's all. But I was angry about it at the time."

"You were pretty pissed off at that officer."

"Well . . . that's putting it very, very mildly. The way I felt about him . . . I still . . . I can remember as clear as day just what he looked like. I hated that guy. I had good reason for hating him. And I avoided him as much as possible."

Murray paused for a minute or two. I could see the decades-old anger bubbling up to the surface.

"You know, the Seabees were notorious for having lax commanders. Because they were all construction men, not military men. Most of the officers were very ineffective. Some of them knew what they were doing. Others didn't. 'An officer and a gentleman.' That always grabbed me. What the hell am I, chopped liver?"

"Well that guy Blair sounds like he was a real piece of work."

"He didn't need to be such a son-of-a-bitch. He could've been a decent guy. You know some of the officers were real good guys. And there were lots of enlisted men that would've made real good officers. Guys that not only knew what they were doing, but that were likable fellows, too. Things happened so fast during World War II, there wasn't time to scrutinize everybody that came in the service. A good officer had to think fast, and from his training and experience, figure out what to do."

"Explain to me how you came to be on Iwo Jima. When I looked up the history of the 100th Naval Construction Battalion, there was no mention that the battalion ever went to Iwo Jima."

"That's because the battalion as a whole didn't go. There was just some of us that went. We were attached to another battalion, but I don't remember which one. And I volunteered for that, too. I was a damned fool the whole way through."

"What I'd like to talk about today is . . . I want you to walk me through exactly what happened on Iwo Jima. I really want to get to the heart of the matter. If you're willing to tell me."

"Well, I think when the Japs got to Iwo Jima, they knew there was no way off of there. They went there on a suicide mission and were told to kill as many Americans as they could kill. For our part, we were told to kill the Japs as fast as we could and not to bother taking any prisoners. It was a bloody mess. We didn't land in the initial wave; we were sent in as reinforcements. The battle had been going on for a couple of days when we got there. Battleships were lobbing big shells onto the island for days, but there were so damned many Japs, and they were dug in so deep in caves and tunnels. They were dug in there like rats. After all that bombardment, the Japs were still throwing firepower at us. We came in on a small landing craft that held about twenty-four men. The LSTs came in later with the equipment. They bombed some of those landing crafts right out of the ocean before they ever got to shore.

"The landing itself was very difficult. We expected the usual banzai charge, like they had done on the other islands. But the Japs didn't charge at us at all. They were holed up in their caves on the side of the mountain. They had gun emplacements all around, and they just stayed there. The Japs were a brutal enemy and they fought very hard. They stayed and fought just about to the last man. When I think about it now, the Japanese were pretty good soldiers, really. I had much more of a dislike for the Japanese back then than I do now. I see no reason to hold a grudge against them now . . . the people there today had nothing to do with it, and in all these years, they haven't shown any signs of retaliation. I think now they just want to live and let live, which is the way it should be. But during the war, they were vicious about it. The only way to get them out of their bunkers was with flamethrowers, and we had plenty of them. Those flamethrowers were filled with napalm, and by the time we were through, there was burnt bodies laying all over the place. A few Japs came out and tried to surrender. No good. We didn't want to take them as prisoners. We were pissed off, and we had plenty of ammo. There were 22,000 Japs on that island, and by the time we got through with them, I think only a couple hundred of them survived. But of course, as we killed them, they killed us, too. Chaos. A bloody bastard. And all for a damned island that was nothing but a pile of volcanic ash.

"Then after a few days the war correspondents started coming in, and they started to report on what was going on. And they had that flag raised on top of Mount Suribachi and the photograph swept through the United States. But that didn't just happen . . . it was planned. I witnessed that flag going up, from a lower elevation. There was still a fierce battle going on . . . we could hardly make any progress."

"What about Blair? Did he do his job in combat?"

Murray gave me a sort of a shrewd look that let me know he was about to be intentionally cryptic: "I don't know. I didn't see much of him. Then he just wasn't around no more. That's all."

Time for some gentle pressure.

"The last time I was here you told me that he 'landed hard' when he hit the beach at Iwo Jima."

Murray answered sarcastically: "Gee, I wonder what I meant by that." He was being intentionally obtuse.

More forceful pressure was indicated.

"Well, to be honest, you implied that you shot him."

"Well, he just disappeared. He ceased to be with us. That's all."

At this point I wasn't interested in any more of Murray's obscure answers. I wanted—no, I needed—to hear the truth. I applied a full-court press.

"You're being very mysterious. Tell me what happened."

Murray gave me a kind of a sheepish look, and he was almost pleading with me as he replied; "Now, you don't want me to do this. You don't want me to leave myself wide open for a hanging."

"Nobody's going to hear any of this until after you're dead. Remember? We have that arrangement."

"I know that. But I'd like to be thought of kindly by my family after I'm gone."

"Well, I can't force you to tell me, but . . . the truth is what it is, and it can't be changed. And sometimes the truth can be liberating."

Murray thought about it for quite a while, as we just sat together in silence, the clock ticking in the background. I could see that he was ambivalent; on the one hand wanting to reveal the facts, but on the other hand not wanting to incriminate himself, especially after keeping such a closely guarded secret for so many years. Finally, he got a little gleam in his eye, as if a light bulb had just lit up in his head and he figured out a way to confess, without really confessing at all. He spoke very deliberately.

"I accidentally stumbled. And my gun went off, accidentally. And I accidentally shot him. And I accidentally hollered, 'Hoorah, you son-of-a-bitch!' Things were rough back then! It was a different world entirely! And that's why I've got PTSD to this day. And that's why I have dreams right here in this bed every night. That's why I have nightmares that I just can't get rid of."

When I was first faced with the possibility that Murray had actually killed his superior officer, in spite of my attempt to keep my feelings neutral, the fact is that I was repulsed. As much as I tried to make sense of it, it seemed clear that it represented a much more reprehensible, perhaps unforgivable, level of behavior, even in comparison to what Murray had told me before. But now, at this moment, sitting beside an old man who was willingly recounting the most sordid details of his life, I was overcome by a sense of understanding, even empathy, for the circumstances that might drive a man to such depths of immorality.

"You don't have to explain yourself to me. I'm not judging you. It seems to me that back then you were just in a certain mode . . . where life itself didn't have the same significance. Like in the peaceful life we're living here and now, somebody pisses you off and maybe you think to yourself, 'He can go fuck himself,' or maybe you even tell the guy to fuck off. Back then, in the circumstance you were in, you were just killing everybody anyway. And you didn't know where the next mortar would land or whether the next bullet would have your name on it. So, some guy rubs you the wrong way and instead of cursing him out, you shoot him. You're in a position where you're doing things, and they're things you wouldn't normally do. But it's all just happening."

Murray took a deep breath and was almost in tears. His face had the look of a man who had just relieved himself of an unbearable burden. His voice cracked as he spoke: "That was Iwo Jima. It was a tough world. Very tough." He took another deep breath and looked sorrowfully at his wife's picture.

"I wish you hadn't heard this." A tear rolled down his cheek. The clock kept ticking, and we sat together silently for several minutes.

After Murray seemed to regain his composure, I resumed the interview with a less intimidating line of questioning: "How long were you on Iwo Jima?"

"I don't know. I didn't keep track of days all the while I was in the military. But it was from Iwo Jima that I was discharged. I went back to Hawaii on a Liberty Ship."

"Did your whole group go back to Honolulu?"

"No. Just me and a bunch of other guys that they were sending back. Honestly that whole trip back is kind of foggy to me. I don't remember why I was sent back, and I have no recollection of boarding that ship. The next clear memory I have is being in the hospital in Hawaii. And my sinuses were just killing me. I remember the doctor there went up through my right nostril with a needle about four inches long and the size of the lead in a pencil. He went through some kind of a membrane—I could hear it crunching—and he injected some water in there, and my head felt like it was going to bust from all the pressure. All of a sudden . . . boom! It let loose, and all the crap that was in my sinuses got washed out. Now he wanted me to stay in the hospital a couple of days. Then they moved me to another area in the hospital. I stayed there for about a week, then the doctor called me into his office and told me, 'I don't know what you've got, but you're not fit for duty. We're going to send you back to the States.' And that was it. I boarded a hospital ship, it was an eight-day voyage to San Francisco, and I was in the hospital there for about three months.

"I remember seeing the Golden Gate Bridge and being happy as hell. They had me in the psychiatric ward, and I really didn't see a lot of doctors. I never gave that any thought. I remember one time I was standing in a chow line and I saw a guy that I worked with at the copper mine. His name was Matt. I asked him what he was doing there, and he said, 'Well I'm just waiting for the end of this damned war.' There was a medic standing next to him, and whenever Matt moved he'd move right along with him. The guy followed Matt everyplace, even into the head. I asked Matt, 'What's with this guy following you around?' Matt says, 'Well, they were going to send me overseas, but now they think I'm crazy, so they're watching me.' After I got back home, maybe a few months later, I went to one of the local beer joints, and there was Matt with a gun and a badge. He was a deputy sheriff! Turns out he was faking being crazy the whole time. I said to him, 'Matt you son-of-a-bitch! Last time I seen you, you was in the nut house, and now look at you!' And he says, 'Be quiet . . . you're the only one who knows.' Matt wasn't too responsible, and he wasn't much of a deputy either. I wouldn't have wanted him to be watching my back during the war."

"What else can you tell me about your time in the hospital?"

"Not very much. The military, for the most part, sends men back, and they spend a little time teaching them how to become a person again, instead of a killer. They didn't do that with me. They taught me how to kill, and that was it. All that time overseas, and I only had one thing on my mind: 'kill, kill, kill.' That's what they had instilled in us. And after I got out that's what came right with me. When I was discharged, I went home. They never deprogrammed me. And I had trouble adjusting to civilian life. A lot of trouble."

Murray shook his head, stopped for a minute, and took a long drink of water. "You know, when I went in the service I didn't have a single cavity. By the time I got through I had seventeen. Most of them were repaired while I was overseas. The drill they had over there worked by the dentist cranking his foot, like an old sewing machine. That made the cables run and the drill turn. I can remember every one of those seventeen cavities. It hurt like hell. And after I got home I still had trouble with my teeth, and I had to have them worked on some more."

"You know, during the war, my grandfather was a dental technician in the Navy. He served in the Pacific. Maybe he worked on your teeth."

"He might've. But we had our own dentist for our battalion. He was a young fellow, and I didn't pay much attention to him. Except when he was drilling into my teeth, of course."

"When you were finally discharged, do you remember how you felt? Were you happy about it?"

"Yeah, I was happy. But I was pissed off, too. To think of all the time that I wasted. A short while after I got out of the hospital, my wife and I were walking down the street in San Francisco. A car backfired near us, and I threw myself face down onto the sidewalk. Does that help you understand how I felt after I was discharged? When I finally made it home I got off the train and my mother and father and my two kids were waiting for me at the Salt Lake City station. I remember one of my little girls ran toward me and I picked her up. And we all hugged and kissed one another, but I really didn't feel much. I sure didn't feel like celebrating. I was just a different person entirely than when I left. Before I went in the service I was kind of on the timid side. I wasn't boisterous. I wasn't quarrelsome. I wasn't really hard to get along with. When I would go to dances and have a few drinks—which I always did—a lot of the guys would want to start a fight somewhere. I was just the opposite. I was a lover, I wasn't a fighter! After the military, if somebody crossed my path, I wanted to kill them. That's the first thing that entered my mind. I'd get angry with some guy, and I wanted to kill him. That was my first thought."

"Did you get into a lot of brawls?"

"No. I had the presence of mind to tell myself I had to change my ways. It was against the law, and I couldn't do it. What the government should have helped me figure out I had to figure out on my own."

"You never killed anybody outside the service, did you?"

"No. I didn't. And it's good that I didn't."

"Can you think of any specific instance when you thought, 'Well, I'm going to kill this guy right now'?"

"Yes. I was on a job up in northern California, shortly after I came home. It must've been the late 1940s and we were putting in a natural gas pipeline. There was a guy there by the name of Chuck, and I thought we were real good friends. Well, the superintendent of the job didn't know shit from Shinola. And he was a drunk. So, he got fired, and my so-called friend took over as foreman. I was running the dragline, and we were working in twelve-hour shifts. So, the guy that was on the shift before me didn't know what he was doing, and two nights in a row, he left it to where the cables were almost broken. I had to change those cables twice. The second day I go to see Chuck, since he was in charge of all the equipment, and I said to him, 'We gotta change that cable again, it's busted.' He lit into me: 'You don't know what you're doing . . . you can't be busting things like that . . . we've only got a limited supply.' Blah, blah, blah. I could see him getting madder and madder. Finally, he says, 'Let's go outside and settle this once and for all!' And I said, 'Settle what?' So, he says, 'We'll settle this between you and me!' I said, 'Chuck, I just got back from fighting the Japs, and I didn't come all the way home to fight you. But now I see why you were back here with the 4-Fs while I was in the Pacific. You didn't belong out there.' And with that, I turned my back on him, and I went back to work.

"A couple of hours later, Chuck comes out to where I was working and says, 'You're fired.' So I said, 'Good.' I shut the machine off, got my lunch bucket, and headed for my car. The next thing I know, the boss of the whole job comes up to me and says, 'Where are you going?' So I told him, 'I'm going home, Chuck just fired me.' And he tells me, 'Well get back on that machine and get back to what you were doing.' And he goes and fires Chuck.

"That night Chuck came up to the room where I was staying. He called me a dirty SOB and says he was gonna beat the shit right out of me. That it was on account of me that he got fired from that job. Well, he took a swing at me, and I hit him right between the eyes. He went down like I'd shot him. As he was bent over, I came up with my knee and caught him right flush in the face. That knocked him on his back, and I jumped on top of him and grabbed him by the throat. I was screaming at him, 'If I get any more trouble from you, I'm gonna kill you!' I wanted to kill him real bad. He's the only guy I can remember that I felt that way about."

"What stopped you from killing him right then?"

"I didn't want to go to jail."

"That's it?"

"I had a family. And I didn't want to go to jail. If I could have gotten away with it I probably would have killed him. I was very tempted. As it was, he had both his eyes black and a broken nose. Nothing more was ever said about it, and I never did see Chuck again."

"Did you ever spend any time in jail? Or in the brig while you were in the Navy?"

"No."

"Let me ask you a hard question: Back in the war—I know it was horrible, it was chaos—but did you like killing people?"

"I liked killing Japs. Yeah."

"And when you came home, did you miss it? I would think that would be difficult, after being in combat. I can only imagine . . . like I don't like to take any shit from anybody, you know what I mean? I would think that if I had been in combat, trained that way, living that way, where any minute I could get killed myself . . . I would think it would be hard to control yourself given those circumstances."

Murray took a long pause and pondered my inquiry carefully. He repeated the question to himself, quietly: "Did I miss killing people?" He grabbed a handful of chocolate-covered almonds from a jar next to his chair and slowly savored them one by one while he looked up at the clock. Finally, he answered.

"Overall, no. Usually everybody got along real well. I did my job the best I could. It was difficult because it was hard work and long hours. It was tiring and it could make you very irritable. At least it did me. And I was irritable to start with after I got home. I don't think anybody could have been any more out of this world than I was, for about ten years. I shake my head when I think about it. What a jackass I was. I don't know why I did the things that I did. I guess I'll never know.

"I should've had someplace to have went before I was sent home. But by the same token I realize they didn't know anything about PTSD; they didn't know what to do for it. By the time they found out, it was too late for me. It took me a long time. I bounced around for ten years. And I suffered tremendously. Consequently, my family suffered also. I couldn't settle down. I had to be on the move. If I didn't like the way things were going on a job, I would quit. When I got home, I had thirty days to go back to the copper mine to keep the job that I had before. Well, the thirty days came and went. Then my old supervisor went to a lot of trouble to get me my job back because I had exceeded that thirty-day period by quite a bit. I went back to work at the mine, but only for two weeks. The schedule came out, and they had put me back on the night shift. I walked straight to the office and quit.

"I did nothing for quite a while. Then I worked at a used car lot up in Ogden. I was doing a lot of drinking. And I behaved just like a playboy. I don't know why my wife stuck with me. I was very irresponsible. She stayed at our house in Sandy with the girls, and I'd go up to Ogden and not come home for days at a time. I'd disappear and I wouldn't even let her know where I was. One time my uncle came up looking for me and I told him some bullshit story about how busy I was. Well . . . I was busy horsing around. I don't understand why my wife let me come back. More than once. I'm sure she knew that I was cheating on her, but she never did mention it. I was very fortunate that she stayed with me."

"When you look back on it now, do you know why you were behaving that way?"

"I have no idea. I took no responsibility. I wasn't faithful to my wife before I went in the service, but I didn't cheat on her the way I did afterwards."

"Do you think there was a part of you that wanted to be back on the islands?"

"Yes. I have thought a lot of times, even recently, how come I didn't fall on one of those islands? Why did I come back home? What was my purpose in life? I still wonder why I'm living this long."

Murray stopped and took a sip of water. He became palpably morose. It seemed to me that he was dredging up the memories of every regrettable decision he had ever made, all the deplorable acts he had ever committed. When he continued, his voice trembled.

"There are times even now when I feel like I deserved to be one of them that stayed there. Don't ask me why . . . I've already told you why." And with that, he began to weep.

I couldn't help but feel sympathy for an old man who had just confided that he was ashamed of his longevity, chagrined by his own existence.

"You have a beautiful family that would disagree with you. Your daughters and your grandchildren. Your whole family of people who not only love you, but who are out in the world and doing a lot of good."

"But they're not in my shoes. And everybody hasn't heard what you've heard. I still have nightmares. It's the same dreams over and over. And crazy thoughts go through my mind. You know, I wish I had never enlisted. It's the biggest regret in my life. I often wonder what my life would have been like, what sort of man I might have been, if I had never chosen to go into the military."

It's not every day that one hears such a compelling statement from a veteran of World War II, and now I had heard it from Murray twice in one afternoon. I was flustered and not sure how to proceed. We sat together, but alone in our respective thoughts, for quite some time. Murray shared a few of his almonds with me. Eventually I thought of a line of questioning that wouldn't seem trivial following such a profound revelation.

"So, when you left the military, the war was still going on. Do you remember how you felt when we dropped the atom bomb on Japan? Looking back on it now, do you think it was the right thing to do?"

"Well . . . I didn't feel sorry for them. It took a lot of their lives, but it saved a lot of our lives, and it helped us reach our objective. Do I think it was the right thing to do? In one way, yes, but in another way, no. It really did a lot of damage to thousands and thousands of people. But I wasn't unhappy about it. The question in my mind was how did they do it in the first place. It amazed me that we had such a weapon of destruction. During that time, you know, there were still Japs that had been put into internment camps here in the United States, and some of them right here in Utah. I think there were a lot of them that they treated poorly that they shouldn't have. Like grabbing somebody who was in college, somebody who'd spent his whole life in the United States, just because his father and mother were born in Japan. They did a person like that a great disservice. And some of them fought over in Europe, and they did real well. I don't think it's right to hold somebody account-able for something their parents did, or didn't do. That's one of the things that went on that the government didn't want you to know."

"It seems like now, today, you're a much more thoughtful person than you were back then."

"That's true. Back then, I was not very thoughtful of my fellow man. I really don't know why. But things bother the hell out of me now. Like these people that have no place to sleep and nothing to eat. That bothers me—that I can't do anything about it."

"If I asked your three daughters what kind of a father you were, what sort of answers do you think I'd get?"

Murray became a little defensive.

"I was a good father to my older daughters. I was a good father to both of them. I put food on the table. There wasn't anything they wanted that I didn't get for them."

"But all the time you spent womanizing and drinking and doing those other things, that was time you could have been spending with them. I'm not trying to give you a hard time, I'm just asking the question."

"Yes, that's true. It's very true. And I have a hard time right now forgiving myself for not doing like I should have done. And I gave them a few spankings, which I'm sorry for. I wish I hadn't. My thinking now is different. There are other forms of punish-ment that are just as effective; I don't believe in spanking at all."

"And when Catherine was born, were you a different father to her?"

"Oh yes . . . I was a different father. It was 1955, and we had moved to California a year or two earlier. My wife and I were having marital problems, and I thought it would help if we had another child. Of course, I was hoping for a boy, but I couldn't have gotten a better child than I did. Catherine . . . she was the apple of my eye. She never knew what the word 'no' meant; I took every opportunity to spoil her. But she never did get spoiled. It just wasn't her nature. I paid a lot more attention to Catherine than I had to my older girls. Before I went to work every morning, I'd lie in bed while my wife was fixing my break-fast, and I'd have little Cathy right on my chest. I just loved her to pieces. And Catherine and I stayed very close. Until she got to be about sixteen and figured out there was a difference between boys and girls. Then everything fell apart."

"After Catherine was born did you cut back on your drinking and the cheating on your wife?"

"Yeah, to a certain degree."

"But you didn't stop."

"Not entirely, no. I was very lucky . . . my wife must have seen something in me that I didn't see in myself. I could have searched the world over and I wouldn't have found a better woman."

Murray stared at the photo of his wife. It almost seemed as if he were having an intimate, private conversation with her.

"Yes, I was a much better father to Catherine. But I never slacked off on doing things for any of my girls. I did everything I could for them. Both my older daughters would tell you they weren't slighted, that I didn't show any favoritism to any of them. Neither one has any gripe about what kind of a father I was."

"And yet you're living here, with Catherine."

"Yes. Well, my middle daughter—Sylvia—she's married to a guy, and he changed her entirely. She was the sweetest girl. She was very soft-spoken. And the older one—Rae—she was very soft-spoken, also . . . and . . ."

Murray's voice tapered off, mid-thought. He took a long drink of water. He looked to me like a man who was remembering that perhaps he wasn't quite the father to his older girls that he was portraying himself to be—that his relationship with them wasn't what he might have hoped for. The look in his eyes betrayed the feelings of regret that he would have preferred to keep hidden. I thought it a bit odd that after all the terrible things he had confessed to me, he was obviously hesitant to admit to his failings as a father. But then again, maybe it wasn't odd at all. I decided to stop grilling him on the subject and to move on.

"How many grandchildren do you have?"

"Well, Catherine has four kids, Sylvia has five, and Rae has six."

"So you've got fifteen grandchildren. And do you enjoy being a grandfather?"

"Well, yes. To some of my grandchildren."

"What do you mean by that?"

"Just what I said. I enjoy being a grandfather to some of them. Others of them, it's 'Glad to see you, so long.' Catherine's kids are the ones that I feel happy to be their grandfather. And you know, I have almost fifty great-grandchildren. And I have two great-great-grandchildren! Of course I wouldn't know either one of them if I seen them."

"You know, one of the things in my life that makes me sad is that my great-grandmother, my mother's mother's mother, didn't come to my medical school graduation. I thought I'd be one of the only people whose great-grandmother was around to see him graduate medical school. She was in pretty good health at the time and everybody offered to pick her up and take her, but she just didn't want to come. Nothing I can do about that now, though."

"Hmm . . . that is too bad. Where was that?"

"My medical school was in Brooklyn, New York. But my graduation was at Lincoln Center in Manhattan. And my great-grandmother Ida was living at her house in Brooklyn at the time."

"You know, I do believe in God. And I believe in a hereafter. I believe that I will see my family again. What it will be like, of course, I don't know. My wife was such an angel. She was such a good person. I can look back now and see what a wonderful, wonderful woman she was. Marrying her was the smartest move I ever made."

"We haven't really talked too much about the past fifty years of your life. What were you doing in the 1960s?"

"I had PTSD bad back then . . . so some of the time I was just running around like a chicken with his head cut off. But I did several things. I went to night school to get a real-estate license. While I was in the real-estate business I came upon a wood fence dealership that a guy wanted to sell. That was in River-side, California. So, I bought that fence company, along with another guy, by the name of Sam, who was the Stake President of the local LDS church. When he and I took that company over it was down to one crew. We expanded down to Orange County, which is about thirty miles south of Riverside. Eventually we went all the way down to San Diego, and we had five crews working for us.

"I was doing all the outside work: soliciting business and making sure the jobs were going all right. My partner was an accountant, and he took care of the office and all the paperwork. We had that company for several years. There was a lot of development going on in that part of California at that time. We signed a contract for a new development where they had plans to put in five thousand houses on I don't know how many acres. Right after that, somebody came along and offered to buy our company, and it seemed like a good time to sell. So that's what we did. And I haven't had to do a day's work since. Of course, my money didn't all come from that business. I did a lot of investing too.

"By 1972, I moved back to Utah, to a house on 4500 South in Midvale. My folks were still alive and all the rest of our family was here. We stayed in that house for twenty-seven years. I was still having a hell of a time sleeping . . . waking up every night, screaming, sweating. I can remember I was driving along one day in the car, and a cloud came in front of the sun and made the sky dark. It scared the hell out of me. Why? Don't ask me, I don't know. But I pulled over and jumped out of the car. My heart was racing. I realized then I couldn't keep going like I was, and I had to try and get some help. Finally, I got a hold of this old psychiatrist here at the VA hospital. A wonderful doctor he was. Schmidt. He was in the military himself. Overseas. He knew what I went through. And he knew how to handle me. I saw him for several years, and he helped me quite a bit. Until he died.

"After we came back to Utah, I did do a little construction work for my nephew. He had a partner that he had met in South America on his church mission. They were buying properties here in Salt Lake and all the way up north to Ogden, and they planned to develop and build houses on the land. I owned a backhoe at the time, and they paid me two thousand dollars for each foundation I would dig. Most foundations I could dig in a day or two, so I could dig about three foundations in a week . . . and that was a lot of money back then. Eventually I quit doing that, and I haven't worked since then."

"So, what have you been doing for the past thirty years?"

"Playing golf."

"I didn't know you played golf!"

"Five days a week! I loved golf. If my legs hadn't failed me I'd still be out there playing. When I was a young man, golf wasn't even in my vocabulary. I started to get interested in the game while I was in California in the 1960s. After I retired for good and sold my backhoe I took a series of lessons, and that's when it got into my blood. I really went after it with a vengeance! How crazy can you get? There were three of us who used to work up at the copper mine, all retired, and we'd meet every morning at eight o'clock. One guy was the personnel manager and the other was an equipment operator like me. We had all worked together before the war. We'd go all over, wherever . . . Salt Lake, Provo, Bountiful. I got to where I had about a ten handicap, and once in a while I'd get in the high seventies."

"You were a damned good golfer! Did you ever have a hole-in-one?"

Murray held his thumb and index finger two inches apart.

"I was that far! It was at the Meadow Brook Golf Course. With a seven iron on a par three. I was exactly pin-high and off by just two inches." Murray grunted and shook his head.

Having been confounded by the game of golf for almost forty years myself, I knew exactly how he felt.

It was getting late, and I needed to wrap up our session, so I started asking some random questions.

"Do you remember what you were doing when JFK was assassinated?"

"I was in California, in my house, watching TV. And a news bulletin came on and it shocked the hell out of us. And one of the reporters I remember seeing that day was Mike Wallace, and you know he just died yesterday. I liked Mike Wallace. He reminded me of another guy I really liked . . . Edward R. Murrow. I used to watch his program on TV all the time. You know, somebody once said that the four most frightening words in the English language are, 'Mike Wallace is here.'"

"That is pretty funny. You know, one of the principles I live my life by is to always conduct myself so that if at any minute Mike Wallace comes around the corner with a camera crew, I won't have anything to worry about. Did you like JFK?"

"Well, everybody liked him. He was a real likable guy. Was he a good president? I don't know. He wasn't in there long enough. But I was very upset when he was shot."

"What did you think of the war in Vietnam?"

"Now you're rubbing me the wrong way."

"Well, I just want to get your opinion."

Murray pointed his finger at me while he spoke quite vociferously, "My opinion is that it was unnecessary! What the hell! The French had been in there for years and couldn't do anything, so they got out. And we rushed right in and started over again until we finally figured out the same thing ten years later and got the hell out of there. And we're in the same situation today, in Afghanistan. We have no business being there. In 1943, we fought in a war that was necessary. We did it for a reason. We had to do what we did. I think that it should have stopped right there. That was enough."

"How do you feel about your grandson Louis being in the Marines?"

"I think it's great. I'm proud of him."

"Did you give him any advice when he enlisted?"

"Yeah . . . don't volunteer for anything! He's up to sergeant now, and he's in drill instructor school. He's just about to graduate. I wonder what he's going to think of me after he reads about everything I've told you."

"Did you ever tell your wife anything about your experiences over in the Pacific?"

Murray answered emphatically: "No! No, you're the only one. You've heard more than anybody else. I never wanted my family to know what a cold-hearted son-of-a-bitch I was. I couldn't have found a better woman than my wife if I'd have looked the world over. To put up with what she put up with . . . and she didn't even know all of it. But she probably does now. And I'm hoping that if she does, that she forgives me."

"Is that important to you, for people to forgive you?"

"Yes, it is. Very important. I care now about what people think about me. I didn't give a damn before. But I know that the number one thing is that you have to forgive yourself. There's a little poem I recite every morning:

> When you get what you want in the struggle of life
> And the world makes you King for a day,
> Just go to the mirror and look at yourself,
> And see what that man has to say.
>
> For it isn't your mother or father or wife
> Whose judgment upon you must pass.
> The person whose verdict counts most in your life
> Is the man looking back from the glass.

You may be like Jack Horner and chisel a plum
And think you're a wonderful guy.
But the man in the glass knows you're only a bum
If you can't look him straight in the eye.

He's the man you must please, never mind all the rest,
For he's with you clear to the end.
And you will have passed your most difficult test
If the man in the glass is your friend.

"You know," Murray continued, "there's another verse to that, but I can't think of it right now. I'll have to give it some thought."

[Author's note: Remarkably, Murray had just recited, nearly word-for-word, the poem "The Guy in The Glass," by Dale Wimbrow, first published in 1934 in *The American Magazine.* Murray never did recall the final verse, but here it is:

· You may fool the whole world down the pathway of years
And get pats on the back as you pass,
But your final reward will be heartache and tears
If you've cheated the guy in the glass.]

"Would it matter to you at all whether I forgave you or not?"

"Yes. I'm ashamed. I'm ashamed of the things that I've done and the way I conducted myself when I was younger. I should have taken more responsibility. I could've been a lot better husband than I was. I could've been a lot better father than I was. And I'm ashamed that in my life I didn't do more to help mankind."

"Was your father a good husband?"

"As far as I know, yes, he was. But he was very distant to me, as I've told you. We weren't close at all."

"Maybe that's why you didn't learn the proper way to behave until later in life . . . because he didn't take the time to teach you properly."

"There's a possibility of that. But my father was a very hard worker. And my father was a good provider for us. No, I have only myself to blame for the pattern my life followed."

"Well, I've given a lot of thought to the things that you've told me. I think you are who you are, and you probably did the best you could with what you were given. All of us can only play the hand that we're dealt. And I think your redemption comes from the fact that you were able to correct yourself, that you became a more thoughtful person, that you were a better father to your third daughter. It seems that in the course of your life you were able to learn some valuable lessons. And for what it's worth, I forgive you."

"Thank you. But there are others that I hurt by doing the things I did. And I feel like I've betrayed myself by telling you the things I've told you."

"But you must know, at least on some level, that no matter what you tell me I'm not judging you negatively for it . . . that I don't think of you any differently. Maybe you won't admit it, maybe you're not even aware of it, but I think you know that I understand the things that you're telling me, probably better than anyone else would. Doesn't that feel good to you? Doesn't it feel good to finally share the whole entire story of your life with someone who is just accepting you at face value? Don't you believe in the old saying, 'The truth shall set you free'?"

"Yes, that's right. You're probably right. Otherwise I wouldn't be talking to you. You are a straight shooter, I'll give you that. But right now, I'm feeling a little worn out."

"Well, we've probably talked enough for today. And anyway, I have to go home now and make dinner for my wife."

"You cook dinner for your wife? How come?"

"Well, because my wife works very hard, and because I'm the good cook in the family."

"What does your wife do?"

"She's a doctor. She takes care of people with cancer—leukemia and lymphoma, actually."

"Oh boy."

"So her job is harder than mine, and she works very long hours, so I cook her a nice dinner every night."

"Well, good for you. You get an 'A-plus' in my book."

CHAPTER 7

MY MIND IS IN SUCH A TURMOIL

Bruce Quinn has been coming to Utah for a ski vacation every year since that trip we took in 1994. In fact, counting our first few trips to Vermont and Colorado, 2012 is the twenty-second consecutive year that he and I have been skiing together. This year his trip was later in the season than usual, and he showed up the day after my most recent interview with Murray. My mind was preoccupied by everything we had covered in that session, and I decided it wouldn't be a violation of my agreement with Murray to disclose the details of our discussions to Bruce, who would have no way of identifying him and no chance of ever meeting him. Bruce is a special friend to me and a unique individual. He is generally quiet and soft-spoken, but a very pensive man who has strong opinions on a wide variety of subjects. In the long course of our friendship, he and I have had animated debates over such diverse topics as the proper way to ski moguls, the proper way to manage kids in the pediatric ER, and the proper way to manage our beloved and infuriating New York Jets (a topic on which the people actually managing the Jets could clearly use a few pointers).

That first night I prepared a nice pasta dinner for Julie, Bruce, and Bruce's wife, Antonella. After dinner, as we were finishing our wine, I told them all the pertinent details of Murray's combat experience. As I finally wrapped up with the gruesome events that transpired on Iwo Jima, Bruce, who had been characteristically quiet throughout my discourse, gave me a very familiar look—one that I can only describe as quizzical while at the same time deeply perceptive. He half-asked, and half-stated, in his deliberate, baritone voice, "So basically, you're interviewing a murderer."

I was rendered momentarily speechless. I stared at Bruce, and while Antonella countered his statement with some sort of an opposing argument that I can't really recall, I came to the recognition that perhaps, in a certain sense, Bruce was right. You can call it what you want—fragging, friendly fire—or you can try to explain it away as an irrational act during a time of war. But at its core, what Murray had done was kill a comrade in the midst of battle, and most likely intentionally. In the civilized world, we call that murder. While outwardly I challenged Bruce's assertion—going back to my previous assumption that combat is such a perverse circumstance that the normal societal rules just don't apply—I inwardly knew that there was much more than a grain of truth to what he had just said. I found myself defending Murray, and rather vigorously at that. But why was I defending him when I knew in my heart that what he had done was wrong? And what should I do about it? How would the family of M. S. Blair feel knowing that their father, or their grandfather, who all these years they thought of as a fallen hero, was gunned down by one of his own men? And ultimately, should they know? Is it their right? Or would it be cruel to reveal such ghastly details—particularly after the man who committed the act was no longer around to be punished for it? Conversations with Bruce are always thought-provoking but never easy. That's probably one of the reasons why I love him.

After a few days of skiing, it was time for me to get back to work. About a week later I found myself back at Catherine's house, but this time in my role as her medical acupuncturist. After finishing the session, as I was about to leave, she said, in a rather matter-of-fact tone of voice: "By the way, the other day Jason was cleaning out the garage and he found something you might be interested in." And with that, she handed me a scrapbook—yellowed with age, pages crumbling from decades in the arid Utah air, and barely held together with a single brown shoelace. Inside the front cover was a handwritten title: *Murray's correspondence from the U.S. Navy. Left: May 6, 1943 at 7 PM on Union Pacific Railroad.* Affixed to each page, Murray's letters to his wife, still in the original envelopes that carried them home. Dozens of letters. I got goose bumps. "Something I might be interested in?" This was gold! A potential treasure-trove of information, right from the original source, right from the time that the history was actually happening. Facts that wouldn't be tarnished by years gone by. Details that wouldn't be muddled by the hazy memory of a ninety-five-year-old man. I tried my best to conceal my enthusiasm and respectfully asked Catherine if I could take the scrapbook home with me for further investigation. She agreed without hesitation, and off I went, barely able to restrain myself from peeking at the letters every time I stopped at a red light.

The instant I got home I opened the book. My hand trembled as I carefully opened the first letter, dated May 7, 1943—the very first day after Murray's departure—and postmarked Cheyenne, Wyoming. As soon as I started reading it, I got an uneasy feeling that I was being more than a little voyeuristic, intruding on a private conversation between a husband and wife, a dialogue that was never meant for public consumption. But my intense curiosity trumped any momentary hesitation, and I kept right on reading.

Dearest Sweetheart:

Well here we are sitting on a side track. I just had my breakfast, of scrambled eggs, link sausage & fried spuds, plenty of coffee, and a roll. We have a tourist pullman, with a sleeping birth each. I spent the first night tossing and turning & waiting for daylight which finally came, & imagine my surprise to see the ground all covered with snow.

Well we are moving now so I guess I better stop writing. Kiss my babies & tell 'em daddy loves them with all my heart. No matter what dear always remember I have always loved you & always will. Tell the folks hello.

Love,
Murray

Later that same night, there was a quick postcard from Omaha, Nebraska, and the next day a beautiful little postcard from Chicago (See images on next page).

Murray's next correspondence was from Camp Peary, Virginia, dated May 10.

Dearest Sweetheart:

Well here I is, we arrived last night, made up our beds & went to sleep. Got up at 5:30 this morning & went to chow. We are now waiting for a medical examination, and from there on I don't know what will happen.

107—Navy Pier, Chicago

NAVY PIER, CHICAGO
The Navy Pier is the Largest Commercial and Pleasure Pier in the World, built and controlled by the City of Chicago and is located at the mouth of the Chicago River. It is three quarter of a mile in length and is devoted to commercial and recreational purposes, all the features of which are under Municipal control, open night and day free to the Public. The Pier was built at the cost of five million dollars and was constructed under the supervision of America's most able engineers.

Well honey here I am in the windy city of Chicago. It's pretty cold here, but we are pulling out in 1 hr. so I guess I can stand it.
Love

Mrs.

Sandy Utah

POST CARD

We are in a pretty nice camp & the boys all seem to be pretty good guys, they are nearly all married. Our camp is situated about 55 miles from Norfolk, and the scenery down here is beautiful. It's the only place I saw on the whole trip, that I would like to live in.

Tell the folks hello & kiss the babies for me, tell them daddy loves them. I love you honey with all my heart, & will look forward to the day I can hold you in my arms again.

Love,
Murray

The next day, another letter.

Dear Wife:

Well honey here it is another day. We didn't get through till almost 10:30 last night, and we got up at 5:30 again today. They gave us a physical exam, and issued us our clothes. I now have approximatley [sic] $115 dollars worth of clothes, & I have still to receive a few more!

They gave us all a haircut yesterday, & boy are they some haircuts! They done everything but scalp us, but you'll never know the difference fifty years from now. They are pretty good about fitting our clothes to us, & they are very careful about giving us the right size shoes.

Take good care of my babies, because when daddy gets back home he's not going to do nothing but love them, and you honey.

Write soon because I'm very lonesome, dear. Tell the folks hello & tell the babies not to forget their daddy & to be good girls.

Love & Kisses,
Murray

Murray kept writing every day, the mood of the letters be-coming gradually more despondent. By May 16, only his tenth day in the service, it seemed as though he already regretted his decision to enlist.

Dearest Sweetheart:

Well honey here it is Sunday, just a week ago since I came into this camp, it seems like a year. I guess there is no use kidding myself, I'm sorry, but being it's all water over the bridge I'll have to make the best of it.

Yesterday they gave us all two shots in the right arm, & a vaccination on the left arm, & my right arm is so sore I can hardly move it. Some of the boys passed out, and others were sick to there [sic] stomach, but I guess I'm too mean to get sick. On top of that we had to drill until 5:30 last nite.

We can go to a picture show nearly every night if we want to, but I am so tired by the time we get through that I could drop. Last nite it was Cary Grant & Ginger Rogers in Once

Upon a Honeymoon. It was pretty good but I was too tired to enjoy it.

Write me often honey, because if I don't have your courage to keep me going I don't know whether I can make it or not. Once you enter into the services of Uncle Sam, it's tough. They break you down & make you like it. They break you down, then reconstruct your life according to their liking. They asked us a few days ago what we wanted to do, & I told them I wanted to operate a shovel. So last nite they picked 14 men out of this barracks to go to a technical school, and I was one of the 14. But when I got over there, they was going to make a dinamite [sic] expert out of me, & I told them to go to hell. The instructor said, do you know you're in the Navy, & you do as you're told, not what you want to do? I said "yes sir", (that's essential) but I talked him out of it finally. But I don't know what they will spring on me next.

Kiss my babies & tell them not to forget there [sic] daddy. He loves them dearly.

Love,
Murray

The next correspondence is dated May 23.

My Dearest Sweetheart

I received your letter & it was really what the doctor ordered. Write as often as you can, because for the next 5 weeks while I'm in boot camp, that's all I've got to look forward to. I'd give most anything to see you & to hold you in my arms for a minute. I've been busier than hell all week. There isn't much I can write you about honey, they gave us orders not to tell our wives anything about what we are doing that would help the enemy. So, about all I can tell you we're doing is working like hell, & I don't mean maybe.

The weather here is hot and humid, and it rains almost every day. I imagine it is about 100°, and my face is burnt black. The boys in my barracks are mostly from Texas, Mississippi, and Missouri, they are singing them Southern songs now but they sure don't pep me up any.

They gave us a typhoid shot yesterday, and there was some mighty sick boys. I felt a little green myself, I had quite a fever last nite, but I feel a lot better today.

They tell us the toughest part of boot training is over, I hope so, it has sure been tough. We asked one of the officers why it was so tough, & he said "Boys there is two Navies, the one they told you about at the recruiting station, & the one your [sic] in." I haven't suffered any hardships other than tired feet & sore muscles. My muscles have been stiffer than hell, especially that muscle that hangs between my legs. I may have to cut it off, to get my pants buttoned, in a couple of more days.

Kiss my babies and tell them daddy loves them dearly. I love you, dear, more than could be told on paper.

Goodnite dear,

Murray

In his next letter, dated 5/27/43, Murray seems to be adjusting to life in the military. He also briefly mentions an inspection by Secretary of the Navy Frank Knox.

Dearest Sweetheart.

Well honey I received your letters & boxes of cookies & candies, I really enjoyed them but they didn't last very long. I gave nearly all the boys in the barracks a piece of candy & a couple of cookies, & they said to thank you. The cookies were pretty well squashed. If you send any more, and I hope you do, put a little more packing around them.

I'm getting a little more used to taking orders & liking it, I'm not having any trouble getting along. Things are getting a little easier, at least they seem easier to me. We are getting a little more towards advanced training & that is more interesting. They are not teaching us how to take prisoners, but how to kill. Everything they teach us is to kill, they preach it to us day & nite.

Did Sylvia have a nice birthday? I shore [sic] wish I could have been there. I have dreamed about you nearly every nite the past week, & this morning when I woke up it seemed so real I felt like crying when I realized where I was at.

Sec. Knox of the Navy was here at the camp yesterday and we had to clean everything up & make it shine. Today after chow we're going to practice throwing hand grenades.

I'm glad ma is able to go to California with you. I won't write you another letter until you reach your mother's house and you write me with her address.

Honey I love you ever so much. Kiss my babies & tell them to think of their daddy.
Love,
Murray

Frank Knox was born in Boston, Massachusetts in 1874. He left college to enlist in the Army, and fought in Theodore Roosevelt's Rough Riders during the Spanish-American War. When the United States entered WWI, he rejoined the Army and served as an artillery officer in France. Although he had been a faithful disciple of Teddy Roosevelt, he was vehemently opposed to Franklin Roosevelt's domestic and economic policies, including the New Deal. In 1936, he was the Republican Party candidate for vice president, the running mate of Kansas Governor Alfred Landon, who was defeated by FDR in one of the biggest landslides ever in a presidential election.

As hostilities in Europe escalated, Knox became an outspoken supporter of Franklin Roosevelt's foreign policy, calling for an end to American isolationism. In 1940, Roosevelt appointed Knox to the position of secretary of the Navy, and under his guidance, the US Navy became the most powerful in the world, its personnel increasing from 190,000 men in 1940, to over three million by 1944. He traveled the world to inspect naval units and observe battlefront activities, believing that cabinet members should "get out in the field and see actual conditions" in order to make more intelligent decisions and to improve the morale of the troops. He is estimated to have flown over 140,000 miles during his time as secretary of the Navy, but his extensive travels took a toll on his health. He died of a heart attack in April 1944.[12] The United States would be a better place today if even a few of our politicians followed the example set by Frank Knox.

Murray's next few letters were sent during the first week of June, and they were addressed to his wife at her mother's home in Riverside, California. In those letters, he mostly complains about the weather ("hot, sultry, & almost unbearable"), his commanding officers ("I think 'CBs' stands for confused bastards"), and mess detail ("it was a mess, alright, washing all those dishes"). He also mentions "the fellow that sleeps in the bunk above me is a good guy, from Texas. He's a real good egg, & I believe I will go to Washington with him next week when we get our leave."

Then, on June 11:

Dearest Sweetheart.

Well I have a little news to tell you this time, they had a Bob Hope program here night before last, & we were only allowed nine tickets for the sixty men in our barracks. So we all drew a slip of paper out of a hat, & I was lucky enough to draw one with a T on it so I went to the show. We had to march about three miles to where they were holding it & we didn't get back until 1:00 in the morning. It was a pretty good show, Bob pulled off some pretty raw jokes about Frances Langford & everybody rather enjoyed it. They weren't broadcasting over the air so they weren't too fussy about what Bob said.

[Author's note: Frances Langford was a screen actress and Bob Hope's long-time vocalist, most well-known for the songs "I'm in the Mood for Love" and "Hooray for Hollywood."]

I have been bothered with sinus trouble the past week, & yesterday I went to the hospital & they drained it & made me stay in the hospital overnight. Then they released me for light duty. The air is so damp down here I don't think they will be able to clear it up. I wrote to Marell & told her to send me some nose drops, & I will put a few of them in my nose every day.

Yes dear I remember the 5th of June six years ago, & I remember a lot of days in that six years that I caused you a great deal of sorrow & tears. Would that I had those days to live over, but being as that is impossible, I ask only that I have a chance to make you forget any sorrow I ever caused you. Because when we are once again together dear I'm going to make everyday a honeymoon, and you & I are never going to be separated again, until death do us part.

But enough of that, I can't afford to let my mind dwell on the past too much, because it makes me too homesick, & that is one thing I must not do. I have exhausted my supply of news, dear. I love you dearly, & I am counting the days till I can hold you in my arms.

Love
Murray

Murray's next letter was dated June 20, 1943, after he returned from his leave.

Dearest Sweetheart

Well here it is Sunday and am I tired. We left here Wed. nite at 6:30 on the train and decided to stay in Richmond the 1st nite, but there wasn't a damn thing to do. So we got up first thing the next morning & caught the train for Washington. On the way there the train jumped the track, & we were going to be held up there for 5 or 6 hours. So 16 of us went over to a farm house & convinced the farmer to haul us 18 miles to a town where we caught a bus, & we didn't get to Washington until 1:30 P.M. Thursday. Then my bunk mate & I went to the New Ebbitt hotel & got us a room, $6.50 per nite. Cheap, huh?

Then we went all over town & saw all the historical spots, the Capitol Building, the White House, & then we got good and drunk. I drank Tom Collins & pink ladys [sic] then that nite we went to a stage show & had dinner at the Roosevelt hotel. The next morning we had to come back, that's the fastest I ever saw 62 hrs. go in my life, they really flew by.

Well I've got to go take a shower & get ready for dinner, then I've got to try to get my clothes clean, that I got dirty on my leave. I love you dear & miss you more than you'll ever know. I hope & pray you never stop loving me for even a minute.

oxoxoxox
Murray

Murray included a postcard from the Ebbitt Hotel along with his letter. (See image on page 110.) The hotel was built in 1925, and eventually demolished in 1986. The Grand Hyatt Washington currently stands at that location.

Over the next month, Murray wrote to Phyllis about every two or three days. In all of his letters he mostly complained about the mundane activities of military life, the amount of time spent just sitting around and waiting, and the frustration of not knowing when his next orders would come or what they would entail. There seemed to be quite a bit of misinformation being spread around, as typically one letter might report a bit of scuttlebutt concerning the plans for his unit, and the next letter would offer a different scenario entirely. Another common theme within Murray's correspondence was his concern about his family's financial situation and the difficulty involved in

getting the money from his paychecks back to his wife in Utah. In a letter dated July 15, 1943, Murray writes:

> *My Darling.*
>
> *Well I finally got time to write you a letter. Nite before last they brought us in at 5:30 & instead of going to the barracks like we generally do they put a 60 lb. pack on our back, & it was raining like hell to make it more enjoyable, & they marched us in the mud through the woods until 11:00. To top it off they double timed us all the way back, we was damn near dead, there was quite a few boys that fell out & had to be picked up by ambulance. It was really rough but I guess we'll all live.*
>
> *They took us out this morning & loaded us in those landing boats & took us accross [sic] the bay & stopped about 100*

*yards from shore, let the end of the boat down & all of us had
to jump out & swim to shore. It was a lot of fun, even if we did
have to jump in the water.*

    *I just now came from the rifle range, we have been
shooting carbines they say were built special for the C.B.s. I
scored 132 out of a possible 200, I don't think that's very good,
but the instructor said that was better than average, & out of
the fellows in my barracks there is only about 4 or 5 that shot
better.*

    *I have been trying to get to the post office to mail this
money to you, but it's closed by the time we get in at nite.
So if you need some money before I get it sent, ask dad for
some & you can pay him back. It worries me when I get to
thinking about you, & how you will get along while I am gone.
You said in your last letter you had bought a yellow dress &
you thought you were too extravagant but honey as long as
you have any money & god knows it won't be much, you buy
whatever you want to. I know I wasn't the best provider in the
world, & you had to do without a lot of things, but honey when
we are together once again I'll make it all up to you.*

    *Well the mail man just came in. I received a letter from you
today, & you tell them soldiers I'll cut their god damn throats.
Be careful honey, they will stop at nothing, although I can't
blame them for following you, I'd follow you myself. But you
stay in at night. I'm still a virgin dear, I'm saving it all for you. I
love you sweetheart.*

    Murray.

In the beginning of August, it seems that the bulk of the
men in the battalion were given a furlough, but the men from
the West Coast had to wait until the end of the month to get
home to their families. Murray describes this in an undated
letter that was postmarked August 3, 1943.

    My Darling.

    *Well the boys all got off this morning, there is only about
165 of us left out of the whole battalion, 1200 men. It's hard to
see them go & have to stay behind, I sure wish I was coming
home too. I guess I'll enjoy it just as much the last of this
month, but right now I'm just so homesick & lonesome. Just
think honey if everything goes alright I can hold you in my
arms in about 3 weeks, gosh I can hardly wait.*

Yesterday they had stuffed peppers for dinner, that was a nice change of pace & they tasted awfully good. I decided to go to a show last night, it was Cab Calloway in Stormy Weather, it was pretty good. Some of the boys have got a hot crap game going on right in my barracks. There are some really shooting some hot dice, but one fellow lost $100, the simple ass.

I sure had an enjoyable day yesterday, I went out on a road job & worked for about an hour on a drag line, & the rest of the day I was running a bulldozer. I also got to drive a jeep, they sure are funny little things. I sure had a lot of fun. If I can get a few more days like that it won't be so bad. But the next 3 days I'm on guard duty, on 4 hrs. & off 4 hrs. & so on for 3 days.

I haven't had a letter from you or from ma & pa for five days now. Are you all mad at me or what? Also I was just wondering if you have forgot how to bake cookies. I'd sure like some. I love you sweetheart & miss you so much.

Love,

Murray

P.S. I only had one envelope left, so give this other letter to Marell.

By mid-August, after three months in Virginia, the group was ready to relocate. Murray sent Phyllis another undated letter, postmarked August 14, 1943.

My Darling,

I received your letter last nite, & as I have a few minutes I'll drop you a few lines. I hope this is the last letter I ever write in Camp Peary. We are supposed to be leaving tomorrow for someplace, they won't tell us where but the scuttlebutt now is that we are going to Gulf Port Mississippi.

It's awfully hot here & for the past 2 days I haven't done anything, & it sure makes the time drag. I just came back from supper & I sure did enjoy it. For a change they had ham, pickles, cheese, potatoe [sic] salad, iced tea, & two kinds of cake. It sure did taste good.

The boys have all come in off their leaves, and listening to them tell about the good times they had home it makes me more anxious than ever. My stomach is all jumpy & I can't hardly sit still. I'm telling you honey I can almost feel you in my arms. I had the nicest dream about you last nite. I dreamed

I came home & gosh I was just showering you with kisses & honey they was sure nice & I was so happy. I love you dear be sure & have your pretty yellow dress on when I come home, & have your hair pretty like I like it. Tell Pa to have the fatted calf ready for the prodical [sic] son.

I love you dear.

Love, Murray

P.S. Did you get the letter with the two dimes in it for the kids?

Hello Rae & Sylvia daddy will be home to see you pretty quick.

A letter postmarked August 18, 1943:

My Darling.

Well sweetheart, we finally made it, we got in at 4:00 this morning, boy we sure was tired but they let us sleep all day so I don't feel so bad now. We came thru N. Carolina, Georgia, & Alabama. The cotton is all in bloom & it sure is pretty, but you ought to see how the negroes live, boy anything that has got a couple of walls & a piece of roof on it they are living in.

I sure like this place a lot better than the other camp. We are situated about 3 miles from the gulf of Mexico. We have big double decked barracks with big fans in them, & we each have a nice big closet with shelves to put our clothes in. We got different officers when we moved over here. I don't think very much of them, but I haven't had a chance to talk to them so I really shouldn't pass judgement until they prove themselves no good. But I don't like them from the 1st look at them.

I think I will get my leave between the 20th & 25th. What do you want me to wear when I first get off the train, my white suit or my blues? I want to look just like you have been imagining me. I love you, love you, & love you, & I hope you don't mind when I get home if I kiss you wherever we are because I don't care if we're in the busiest part of Salt Lake if I feel like kissing you I'm going to. I had a nice dream about you last night, I was holding you in my arms & we were dancing. Honey you will never know how much I miss you, & when we can be together again I'm going to be like a regular little puppy dog following you around. I'll make love to you so much you will be sick of it. I don't care what you ever do you won't be

able to make me mad at you. I'm really going to throw a lot
of love in your direction. By the way dear are you still having
those bleeding periods, cause if you are when I get home I'm
going to put a stop to them. Tell me what date would be the
best to arrive in order to miss them things.

I love you dear, I've got to go to bed so I'll close now.
Love, Murray

The next several pages of the scrapbook consisted of a hand-written diary that Phyllis kept while Murray was home on leave. She provides quite a bit of detail regarding their activities, and a lot of information about the friends and family with whom she and Murray visited. What follows here is a series of excerpts from her narrative:

Aug. 22, 1943

Murray arrived this morning at 9 A.M. to spend five days home. Five short days. It all seems like a wonderful dream now his being here.

Sat. afternoon we drove over to see Dave & Mervine, Dave was awfully tickled to see Murray. We decided to go out that nite, so the four of us went over to a dance. It was wonderful to be held in his arms just as I had dreamed so often. After the dance we went back to Dave's for coffee, bacon, & eggs. Murray really enjoyed it, he ate six eggs.

Sun. morning we laid in bed & read the funnies, got up & had breakfast & went to Salt Lake. We came back around 4 o'clock & had a family dinner of fried chicken & corn on the cob & watermelon, with all the trimmings. That evening we just sat around & talked.

Mon. we went out with Dominic & Evelyn, we drove over to the carnival in Murray & went to the penny arcade, & played a few concessions, then just walked around for awhile & had a dish of ice cream.

Tues. morning Murray went fishing with Dominic & they caught three, he came home & went to sleep & then we spent the rest of the afternoon together. In the evening we were invited over to Dave's, & Mervine had a lovely rabbitt [sic] dinner, it sure was good. After dinner we all went to the show in Midvale. It was Heaven Can Wait with Don Ameche, & we all enjoyed it.

Wed. we went up to Bingham so Murray could see all the fellows he used to work with. They all told him how good he

Within the pages of the scrapbook, a single souvenir
was firmly affixed: a menu from the Coon Chicken Inn.

looked and wished him good luck. The two of us went to the
Coon Chicken Inn for the evening, we had a wonderful time
just enjoying being together. After they closed we went back up
to Bingham & Murray saw all the fellows he worked nites with.

Thurs. we just spent the day together, we washed Murray's clothes & even enjoyed that. Mother had us all down to
dinner & after we went to the Apache for awhile.

Fri. morning at 11 A.M. Murray left to go back to camp. It
was the hardest thing I've ever had to do, telling him goodbye.
I tried not to show it but inside I was breaking. The time simply
flew by on wings. We were hardly separated for a moment,
cramming all the memories we could into those five days, not
knowing how long they would have to last us.

I first learned about the existence of the Coon Chicken Inn
while watching the outstanding 2005 film *C.S.A.: Confederate
States of America* by brilliant filmmaker Kevin Willmott. The
film is a faux-documentary that creates an alternative history
of our nation based on the scenario of the South having won

the Civil War. The Coon Chicken Inn was a successful restaurant chain in Salt Lake City, Seattle, and Portland from 1925 until 1957. The entrance to each restaurant was through the mouth of a smiling black porter, the character whose image is depicted on the menu. From the xenophobic epithet that was the restaurant's name, to the unashamedly stereotypical depiction of a man of color that was used as its trademark, the very existence of this establishment is a testimony to the normalcy of racism that was so prevalent in this country prior to the Civil Rights Movement. As Willmott himself suggested, the owners and patrons of the Coon Chicken Inn were not necessarily overt racists, but this was the manner in which many white Americans viewed black people at that time. Quite hypocritical, considering that in Europe our nation was strenuously fighting against a Nazi regime that was founded on the principles of anti-Semitism and racial hygiene. Not surprising though, in light of the shameful manner in which we in the United States have historically treated those deemed 'different,' be they American Indian, black, Jewish, Muslim, or gay.

I do not believe that Murray, or his wife Phyllis, were racists . . . at least they were no more racist than the typical Utahn of their generation. But the fact that they thought nothing of patronizing the Coon Chicken Inn, and that Phyllis herself was smitten enough by her evening there to save the menu—which to our modern eyes is so obviously offensive that it might well be considered obscene—right alongside her husband's precious letters, gives us insight into the gratuitous, smoldering bigotry that was apparently ubiquitous in 1943.

On a somewhat less somber note, the menu itself gives us a glimpse into the economy of America circa 1943. Sandwiches for forty-five cents, a full dinner for ninety-five cents, or the 'De Luxe' for $1.75 . . . and maybe wash it all down with a twenty-cent milk shake or a ten-cent cup of coffee.

One thing surprised me as I read the notes that Phyllis so meticulously kept throughout Murray's furlough: There was not one single word about any interaction between Murray and his daughters. I have no idea what to make of that omission, particularly in light of Murray having closed so many of his letters with a greeting for his girls. Were children so marginalized in 1943 that their presence wasn't even worth mentioning? Were Sylvia and Rae staying with their grandparents to allow

Coon Chicken Inn menu, 1943.

Murray and Phyllis some romantic time? And it also seems a bit odd—especially considering the lascivious tone of some of Murray's letters—that Phyllis didn't comment about any amorous interludes between her and her husband; although one could assume that such matters were not commonly written about by women of that generation. In any event, the absence of any acknowledgment of the girls during Murray's time at home is puzzling, but its significance will remain a mystery.

On August 29, Murray sent Phyllis a postcard from St. Louis, and on September 1, he sent her the following brief letter from his base in Gulfport:

My Darling:

Well I finally got here after a helluva trip. I arrived in camp 13 hrs. late, and they have me listed as A.O.L. (absent over leave) and have restricted me to the base for a few days and they took my identification card away from me. It's as if they have made me a prisoner at large. I don't know what the matter was, because all the trains were on time, but I think the agent in Salt Lake must have made a mistake in the schedules.

I go up before the Captain in the morning. I hope the old boy is in a good mood. Everyone seems to think he will let me off with just a warning.

*I started school today, it's supposed to be a mechanics
school but all I did all day long was change two tires. Pretty
soft, huh?*

I love you sweetheart. Kiss my babies.

Love, Murray

Murray's next correspondence was postmarked September
8, and while he doesn't mention what sort of punishment he
was given by his commanding officer, he does seem pretty anxious to return to civilian life.

My Darling,

*I've sure been lonesome since I got back here. I just don't
seem to be able to fall into the swing of things. I guess I
haven't woke up from the beautiful week I spent with you. I've
been fixing the brakes on a truck this morning, & I cut a couple
of my fingers & it didn't help my feelings out a bit. Gosh honey
when I get back home for good I'll just devote the rest of my life
making love to you & making you happy.*

*I didn't get to finish this letter last nite, so I'll add a few
lines to it today. I was so homesick last night, I went over to
Gulfport & really got drunk, but I got back in camp & to bed by
10:00 so I don't feel so bad today. I recieved [sic] another letter
from you honey, & please don't think of me as going out with
another woman. I don't care what everybody says or thinks,
my mind body & soul is existing for nothing except the day
we can once again be together. Without the memory of you,
& the satisfaction in knowing I'll have you to come home to
when it's all over, I just wouldn't give a damn about anything.
So sweetheart when anyone tells you I'm stepping out you
should know different, because after holding you in my arms,
& having your love, I couldn't ever have anything to do with
another woman.*

*So please don't ask me things like that darling, it makes
me think you don't believe in me, & it almost makes me cry to
think of you sitting home alone. If I ever thought you went out
with another man, I would go completely out of my mind. So
darling as long as I have complete confidence in you please do
the same with me.*

*We have an inspection this afternoon, and I've got to
straighten my locker up it looks like a bunch of gypsies lived*

*in it. I don't know what is the matter with me, I just can't seem
to get goin'. I went & asked them if I could get out to go back
to my job, & they told me that men here don't get releases to
go back to work. Maybe you can ask pa to go up to the copper
mine & see if they could pull some strings so I could come
back to work there. They could tell the draft board that they
are awfully short of shovel men, & maybe they would release
me. If pa can do something have him do it fast, because there
is nothing I can do here on my end. I'm going to try & figure
out another angle to get out, & I don't think I will be here much
longer.*

*I've sure got the blues today, and it's been raining all
morning, which doesn't make it any more cheerful. I know
I may have seemed changed when I was home, I suppose I
have in some ways, but darling there is one thing that will
never change & that's my love for you. I love you dear with
the deepest & biggest affection I will ever feel for anyone or
anything.*

Love,
Your husband & sweetheart.

It is very interesting to me how urgently Murray wanted to
get out of the military after only the first four months of his
training. It would appear that he deeply regretted his decision to
join the Navy long before he ever experienced the rigors of being
overseas or the horrors of combat.

These two most recent letters also struck a very visceral
chord in me. There are some familiar themes that provide insight
not only to Murray's personality but also to the essence of my
relationship with him. As I have mentioned previously, Murray's
behavior, particularly toward Catherine, is eerily suggestive of
my own father's vitriolic manner. I have come to recognize that
my father is the prototypical narcissist—that realization having
come through years of painful interactions and countless sessions with helpful therapists. I have long suspected a similar
diagnosis for Murray, and as Catherine's physician, it has been
very clear to me that she exhibits many signs of being the child
of a narcissist. Now, having the opportunity to eavesdrop on
what would have otherwise been a private correspondence between Murray and Phyllis, getting a candid glimpse at Murray
circa 1943, I can see definite evidence of Murray's narcissistic

personality. In fact, the content of these letters is so strikingly reminiscent of the letters I received from my father while he was incarcerated for embezzlement at a federal penitentiary that while I was reading them, I felt like someone had just punched me in the gut.

When Murray blames the station agent for getting the schedule wrong, it is the narcissist shifting blame to anyone but himself. When Murray concocts a scheme to get out of the Navy, it is the narcissist refusing to honor his commitments; instead expecting others to shoulder the burden alone. When Murray tells Phyllis he would go out of his mind thinking of her with another man, it is the narcissist projecting his own guilt onto everyone around him. After all, having interviewed Murray seventy years after these letters were written, we know that despite his overtures to the contrary, he never in his life stopped cheating on his wife; although I do believe that the regret he expressed to me was indeed genuine. But in 1943, he cloaked his own guilt in the carefully constructed smokescreen of denial and projection. And when Murray tells his wife that he wouldn't give a damn about anything if he didn't have her to come home to, it is the narcissist holding somebody else responsible for his own personal happiness.

We can look back on Murray's own cold, distant relationship with his father and recognize the very origins of his narcissism. The poor self-esteem that is the harbinger of the narcissistic personality has its roots in a childhood that is devoid of love and lacking in parental acceptance. By his own admission, Murray wasn't close to his father, who never even took the time to listen to his son play the violin, and their relationship remained strained until the day the old man died.

So, the rapport I've forged with Murray may be at least partly explained by my familiarity with narcissists and my ability to navigate through their miscellaneous bullshit. And the very deep bond I have formed with Catherine may similarly be understood as one wounded child of a narcissist empathizing with another. In any event, these letters have given me a heightened awareness of the dynamics of the Jacobs family, and a deeper knowledge of Murray Jacobs the man.

Murray's next letter was postmarked September 9, 1943, and it included big news from Europe.

My Darling Sweetheart.

I just heard over the radio where Italy surrendered, boy that sure sounds good to me. That means it will be just that much sooner I can be back home with you. The boys here are so excited & are sure making a lot of noise about Italy's surrender. I don't think we will be here too much longer, because the officers had a meeting last night & they announced that we are going to California when we leave here. They won't tell us when, but I don't think we will be here over 2 or 3 weeks more.

I went to a show last night. It was Coney Island with Betty Grable. Boy she was nice. But not half as nice as a sight of you would have been. I go to the show nearly every nite, because when nite falls, & this beautiful moon comes up I get the blues so bad I would go out of my mind if I had to just sit around & wish for you. I miss you so much I'm about ready to go nuts. I want you to come to visit me so bad, but I know we haven't the money. I'm going over to supper darling, will be back in a few minutes.

The boys caught a four foot alligator while they were down swimming today, it sure is an ugly thing. They've been dragging it all over the barracks. The next couple of days I'll be doing guard duty, I go on for two 4 hour stretches & then off for 12. I don't have to do anything else so it's not bad.

I love you sweetheart with all the means god gave me to love a woman with. Kiss my babies & tell them daddy loves them.

Yours forever & ever
Murray

Murray continued to send letters to Phyllis about twice a week, always telling her how much he missed her and usually sharing whatever rumors were circulating about the battalion's relocation to California. In a letter postmarked October 1, he discusses his detailed plan to get out of the Navy.

My Darling Sweetheart.

I recieved [sic] a letter from the Copper Company today, to give to the Battalion Commander. It states how long I worked for them & what type of work I did, & that they are in need of my services. I'm going to take it over tomorrow & see if they will do anything about it. If they won't I'll write & let you know, & you can go to the Red Cross & ask them if they would try to get me released on the grounds that you can't make a go of it on the wages I am earning, because I know they are releasing men on those grounds. You could take a list of all the debts we owe, & scrape up a few we don't, & also tell them that the kids both need their tonsils out, & tell them that we haven't the money for it, which we really haven't. Also state that Pa has been down sick, & that we can't get any help from them, & you'll have to make it sound real bad. I'm ready to get out of this outfit anytime they will hand me an honorable Discharge.

I've been laying here on my bunk today just about half asleep thinking back from the time I first met you. I wish I had it to do all over again. I would sure make you a lot happier than I have in the past. I'm never going to do anything again to make you sorry you married me. Well hon it's time to go to bed so will close with this thought. May god keep you safe & keep you loving me always. Good night darling. I love you with all my heart.

Love

Murray

P.S. Don't say anything about me trying to get out, until I find out all about it.

In a letter postmarked October 3, Murray, obviously distraught, tries to reassure his wife. The situation brings to light the difficulties in communication that were probably typical in 1943, but seem implausible in today's world of ubiquitous cellular phones, e-mail, and instant messaging.

My Darling:

I received your letter this afternoon, & I hope I don't ever receive another one like it from you. My mind is in such a turmoil, I don't hardly know what to say. I'm sorry dear that you haven't anymore confidence in me than you have. I know I haven't made your life very happy, but dear I know if you will just wait until I get back home, if god grants that I do, that you will not be sorry that you have stuck by me.

I can't understand why you haven't received any letters. I was out of camp for 8 days, out in the swamps with a gang of men working on a drainage ditch. While I was out there I wrote you a couple of letters & sent them back into the camp. I have been almost nuts since I got that letter from you. Honey, you must remember, I'm in the armed services, & we may go out on manouvers [sic] or out on the ocean for a couple of weeks or we may go out on a little island & of course the post office doesn't follow us. So please don't be so impatient & get mad at me, cause I'll write as often as I can.

I went over last nite & saw the old man (skipper) about getting out to go back to my job. He talked to me & explained that the only ones they gave a discharge like that was men with undesirable characters. He said that I wasn't an undesirable & that where we are going he would need every man he could get, but if I insisted he would give me an honorable discharge. Well honey I thought it over, & as bad as I want to come home to you I had to turn it down. If I had done something like that, I wouldn't be able to hold my head up again. I'll explain it all more thoroughly when I get to see you.

We are leaving tonite, & they told us we are going to California & it will take us 5 or 6 days to get there. We will only be in the U.S. for a month or two longer, & from there on I don't know. I would like to look into your beautiful face once more, & kiss your sweet lips, & hold you ever so tight, before I leave for god knows what. If I get out of here I want to walk down the street with you, & have you really be proud of me because you & everybody else will know I done my part.

I love you darling with all my heart
oxoxoxox
Murray

Of course, we can never know exactly what the battalion commander said to Murray to cause him to have such an abrupt and dramatic change of heart. But it must have been one hell of an impassioned plea.

So after about six weeks in Mississippi, Murray boarded a train bound for California.

On October 7, 1943, the battalion arrived at their new camp, Port Hueneme. That day, Murray wrote Phyllis a letter.

My Darling,

Well honey here we are in Hueneme that's pronounced why-knee-me, isn't that a helluva name? But I sure love it because I'm not so far away from you now. First we went through Louisiana, then Texas, & boy what a state it's just as flat as a dollar. We passed through a big oil field by the name of Gladewater, there must've been hundreds & hundreds of oil wells. We passed by big stockyards full of cattle and a lot of farms that looked like they were mostly growing cotton and corn. There were some quite nice looking ranches about 4 or 5 miles apart. Then we went through Arizona, & I was sure glad to get a look at some mountains. But talk about your dry country, that really takes the cake.

Honey your mother lives only 100 miles from here, so if you want you can come down to her place & we can find you a place close by after you get there. I don't know for sure how far we are from the different towns but we are 13 miles from Ventura. You will have to get a map & figure it out from there. I hope you can come to me in a hurry, because I don't think we will be in the U.S. very much longer. It's quite cool here so bring some warm clothes with you. I had to buy me a new blanket, they are sure good blankets. I'd like to bring about 6 of them home with me when I get out. They are all wool, & we get them for $7.50 apiece.

I love you sweetheart with all my heart.
Love,
Murray

The next day, Murray wrote again.

Hello Darling,

We finally got settled in huts, 10 men to a hut & an oil stove & we sleep on army cots. I just came back from chow. We had roast pork, mashed potatoes, sour kraut [sic], string beans, pumpkin pie, coffee, bread & butter. Not bad huh?

I sure hope you can come to me in a hurry, because from the way they are talking I guess we will only be here long enough to outfit the battalion with equipment which takes from 3 to 6 weeks. They already have our boats down at the dock & are loading our heavy equipment on them. We have been changed from a construction battalion to a combat battalion, which means that we will go out with the Marines & take bases held by the enemy. I don't know which direction we will go in, but you can rest assured honey that I will do everything in my power to come back the same way I go (standing on both feet.)

I guess I shouldn't be writing stuff like that, but I am so blue and lonesome tonite. The train with all our pay records on it was wrecked on the way here, & how long it will be before that gets straightened out, nobody knows. We were supposed to have got paid today, but now they say we will just have to wait. I'm so worried about getting you down here, because I know we don't have enough money.

I had the nicest dream about you last night. You had that nice new nightgown on, and I thought I was holding you in my arms & just kissing & kissing you, I could feel your lips so sweet & soft. Gosh it was nice, until that time I woke up. Honey if you can try & get Marell, Evelyn, & Pa to each lend you a few bucks so you can come to me, before I go completely nuts & do something I'll be ashamed of for the rest of my life. Please honey.

I love you sweetheart & miss you so much.

Hello Rae & Sylvia Daddy loves you.

Love

Murray

Then, suddenly, inexplicably . . . the letters stop. The next entry in the scrapbook is a note in an official "War Department V-Mail Service" envelope postmarked December 17, 1943. In reviewing the itinerary of the 100th NCB, it appears that the battalion left for their embarkation point on November 20, 1943, and sailed from the United States on November 21. They arrived in Oahu on December 1, and remained there for seven weeks, until departing for the Marshall Islands on January 20, 1944. So why, after diligently writing to Phyllis at least twice a week for five months, was there no correspondence from Murray in the six weeks between October 8 and November 20? It is of course possible that Phyllis did manage to scrape up the funds to go to California, where Murray could see her frequently, rendering the writing of letters unnecessary. It is also possible that, for one reason or another, she didn't save the letters from that period, although given the thorough and meticulous manner in which she maintained the scrapbook that seems unlikely. Unless Murray could remember the details, this question would remain unanswered.

The envelope postmarked December 17 contained a brief note that was dated December 6, 1943, and marked with an official stamp: "PASSED BY NAVAL CENSOR."

> *My Darling.*
>
> *Just a few lines to let you know I am alright. Yesterday was Sunday, & I went around the base, it surely is a large place. I went over to the dock & they were unloading some jap prisoners. They sure was awfully young, most of them looked to be about 17 or 18 years old & all of them seemed to be quite happy over the fact that they were prisoners. I guess they know they will get treated better here, & get more to eat, than in their own country.*
>
> *How are the babies? Are you going to have Sylvia's tonsils out? I love you darling.*
>
> *Love*
> *Murray*

The scrapbook contained a few more official envelopes, but none contained any personal notes from Murray. Rather, each carried a generic holiday greeting that was sent while the battalion was located at Majuro. Apparently personal correspondence was frowned upon while deployed in enemy territory.

The names on the notes (next page) were not redacted by the Naval Censor, but for the purpose of this publication.

Notice that Murray managed to sneak a tiny "I LOVE YOU" past the censors, hidden in one of the Easter flowers.

That was the last letter within the pages of the scrapbook. For the next nine months, there wasn't a single piece of evidence that Murray corresponded with Phyllis. But at the back of the book, there was a single envelope . . . the only one that wasn't glued in place. It was postmarked March 3, 1945, from San Leandro, California. Inside the envelope, was a letter, which was also dated March 3.

> *My Darling:*
>
> *I'm sorry I didn't get to talk to you yesterday when I called. But I was anxious to let you know I was back in the states.*
>
> *I am in a hospital located a few miles from Oakland. From what the doctor says I'll be here for at least a month. So if you will get your stuff all ready you can head this way as quick as*

you can and find a place to stay. I want you to bring my blues
& pea jacket with you.
   I love you darling with all my heart and soul.
   Love
   Murray

When it's all said and done, the letters, while providing considerable insight into Murray's frame of mind—especially pertaining to his relationship with his wife—and giving us a snapshot of military life circa 1943, nonetheless fall somewhat short of revelatory. The absence of substantial correspondence during the entire fifteen months that Murray was deployed overseas leaves a void that still fails to confirm, clarify, or refute the pertinent details that were revealed during my interviews with him. And unless Catherine stumbles upon another scrapbook hidden away somewhere, we have no choice but to accept Murray's account of the events of his time in the Pacific, as he recalled them seventy years later.

But there was something bothering me about the date of that last letter. Murray was discharged on April 13, 1945—about six weeks after that letter was sent. That made sense, given that the doctor had predicted he'd be in the hospital for about a month. But it occurred to me that March 3, 1945, was right around the time when the battle of Iwo Jima was happening. In fact, the first amphibious assault on the island took place on February 19, 1945; the flag was raised on Mount Suribachi on February 23; and hostilities continued until March 26.[3] This discovery created quite a discrepancy in Murray's story, since even if he was taken off the island on that first day of combat, it would have been impossible for him to be back on United States soil by March 3. Back then, the routine transport of military personnel was accomplished by sea, not by air, and if one considers that the journey from Iwo Jima to Pearl Harbor would require at a very minimum eight days, then another eight days to get back to California, the absolute earliest date that Murray could have been in that hospital would be March 7, 1945. Since the postmark on the envelope must be considered accurate beyond a shadow of a doubt, there was no way Murray could have participated in the landing on Iwo Jima, and certainly no way he saw that flag being raised four days later.

Well, that was one fucking detail that was refuted by the letters. Now it was my mind that was in a turmoil.

CHAPTER 8

SAY WHAT'S ON YOUR MIND

Several months had passed since I mailed the request for Murray's military records to the National Personnel Records Center in St. Louis. I was thrilled when seven weeks later I received a notice that his file was successfully located. According to the National Archives website, a catastrophic fire at the facility in St. Louis in 1973 resulted in the destruction of over sixteen million official military files, mostly involving personnel who had served in the Army and Air Force. Thankfully, Murray's records were not amongst those that were ruined by the fire, nor the subsequent damage caused by the water that was used to extinguish the blaze. Otherwise the documentation of his military service would have been lost forever. As soon as I got the good news I mailed away a check for sixty dollars to cover the cost of having the file reproduced and the photocopies mailed to me. But that was almost a month ago, and I was still eagerly awaiting my documents. And now, more than ever, I needed the information that those documents would contain.

I really wasn't sure how to proceed. I had chosen not to reveal to Murray the fact that I found no evidence of combat on Majuro to avoid challenging the authenticity of his memories. He builds an airstrip in the Marshall Islands, is involved in a fierce battle in the Palau Islands, and then gets the two jumbled up in his ninety-five-year-old mind. So what? What would be the purpose of confronting him with those details? But Iwo Jima? One of the most iconic wartime images ever recorded, and he thinks he was there to see it, but he really wasn't? Seems almost impossible. And just for the record, there wasn't one neuron in my brain that thought he was making that story up. Being from Brooklyn, and therefore genetically skeptical, then having my distrust intensified by years as a doctor—particularly working in the emergency department—I have one of the most sensitive internal bullshit detectors you'll ever come across. Some people are "glass-half-full" people, and others are "glass-half-empty" people. I look at a glass and assume it has poison in it. And my expert observation, as a profoundly cynical individual, was that Murray believed with every ounce of his heart and soul that he fought on Iwo Jima and that he personally witnessed that flag being raised.

My next visit to the house was once again in my capacity as Catherine's doctor. As I arrived, Murray was just finishing a session with his psychologist from the VA hospital; apparently I'm not the last doctor in the United States to make house calls, after all. Gita Rakhsha, PhD, has been treating Murray for his PTSD for several years, and in recent months, as Murray's mobility has deteriorated, she has consented to conducting their sessions at his home. What a fortunate coincidence, and a great opportunity for me. I introduced myself and quickly thought about how I could unofficially consult with her about this situation without violating my agreement with Murray and without inadvertently coercing her to violate the confidentiality of her own doctor-patient relationship. She seemed very excited about my project and happy that I was taking the time to talk to Murray. Given that Murray had not actually given me the letters (he didn't even know I was in possession of them), I felt comfortable telling Dr. Rakhsha about the discrepancy I had discovered regarding the dates, and also about the fact that my research suggested he had not seen combat on the island where he thought he had.

Dr. Rakhsha shared with me that in her considerable experience working with veterans, it is not at all unusual for this sort of confusion to occur. Particularly amongst combat veterans with PTSD, their memories often get cloudy immediately following their traumatic experience. Then they try to fill in the gaps with data they acquire subsequently. For example, in Murray's case, if he had been hospitalized for so-called battle fatigue after seeing combat on Peleliu, he might have filled in the holes in his memory with images of Iwo Jima that he saw in the newspaper. In such cases, she explained, the memories that are created are absolutely real to the individual, and with the passage of time, they become increasingly detailed.

It was a fascinating, nuanced conversation between two very motivated and dedicated professionals. Each of us wanted to extract information from the other, but neither was the least bit willing to breach the trust that had been established with

Murray. I asked Gita pointedly whether she felt that I should address the inconsistencies I had uncovered with Murray, and she responded quite definitively that I should not. There was no question in her mind that Murray had experienced the things he had told me about. (Although I did not disclose any of the specific details of Murray's combat experience, Gita did confirm that one of the events Murray frequently referred to was being immersed in water that had been turned red by the blood of his comrades.) She was convinced that confronting him with errors in the when and where of his experiences could only cause him harm, potentially resulting in a state of mental chaos and depression from which he might not be able to emerge.

Although I appreciated the opportunity to meet with Dr. Rakhsha, I was not sure that I agreed with her. I spent the next few days thinking about what to do, and I found myself more and more convinced that telling Murray the truth was the most ethical approach. What right do I have to withhold somebody's own truth from them? That has always been my approach as a physician: full disclosure of the facts as best as I can explain them. Some doctors routinely present the patient with an intentionally bleak scenario, hoping the patient will be pleasantly surprised when things work out OK. Others purposely portray a situation through rose-colored glasses, often giving the patient false hopes that are likely to be shattered. In spite of my intrinsic pessimism, I take a more balanced approach. I believe that my responsibility to the patient is to provide them with accurate information in language they can understand so that they can make sound decisions for themselves. In this case, however, I was dealing with a condition—PTSD—that was way outside my area of expertise, and a type of patient—an elderly combat veteran—with whom I had no experience at all. On the other hand, Murray was not technically my patient. And in fact, as a journalist, his reaction to the results of my research could become an important part of the story. I certainly did not want to cause Murray any distress or harm, but ultimately, I came to the conclusion that telling him the facts, at least about him not being on Iwo Jima, was the right course of action.

I went back to see him about a week later. I was palpably nervous as I entered the house, knowing that this meeting was likely to be very different than our previous encounters. For the first time, my intention was not just to examine the morality of

Murray's actions, but to question the veracity of his memories. I started by asking Murray to review the events that had ultimately led to his discharge: "I know you don't know why you were sent home, but I'd like you to take me through the steps of the process. How did you get from an island in the middle of the Pacific Ocean to being on your way back home?"

"The last place I was at was Iwo Jima. I saw that flag being raised . . . you know that whole thing was staged. The battle wasn't even over yet, and they put that flag up to show the people back in the States that we were winning the war—to boost their morale, if you can believe that. I can't remember exactly what happened, but the next thing I knew I was on a Liberty Ship headed back to Honolulu. It was in the hospital there that I had that big problem with my sinuses, then the doctor told me they were sending me home; that I wasn't fit for duty. I have no idea what he saw that made him say that. I don't think he ever told me. But then I boarded a hospital ship, and it took us eight days to get back to the United States. I remember that was a beautiful ride . . . the ocean was smooth as glass. Once I got to the hospital in San Francisco, my wife came and stayed with some people we knew in Oakland. During the week, I had to stay in the hospital, then on weekends I'd get liberty and could go stay with my wife."

I became very uncomfortable. I was about to straddle the fence between being an aggressive investigative reporter and a compassionate friend to an old veteran who was caught in a tangled web of confusion.

"So now let me ask you a different question. I wasn't there, so I don't know. You know I wasn't there, obviously. You land on an island—and on the surface this is going to sound like a stupid question, but bear with me—you land on an island, and how do you know what island it is?"

Murray gave me that piecing look that I hadn't seen in a while, and he barked, "I didn't! For a long time, I didn't know what island it was. And as a matter of fact, I didn't care. All we were told was . . ." Murray shook his head and grunted rather than finishing his sentence. He was already getting frustrated, and I had hardly even said anything yet.

"We didn't give a damn! We knew there was an island there, and there was Japs on it, and we had to take it! It was confusing, but we made it!"

"OK, I understand what you're saying. And maybe you might understand why it's not such a silly question after all. It seems to me, if you just plopped me down some place, if there wasn't a sign—I mean if you dumped me off an airplane and put me somewhere, how the hell would I know where I was? Unless I saw the Empire State Building, then I'd know it was New York. Now you've told me a couple of times that the last place you were at before you were sent home was Iwo Jima. So how do you know that?"

"How do I know it?"

"Yes . . . how do you know that you were on Iwo Jima?"

"Well hell, after we was there we found out. It was later that they told us where we were at."

Now I'm really nervous about proceeding, thinking back to the ominous warning I was given by Dr. Rakhsha. I start the next question four different ways before I finally stammer out something that resembles an actual sentence: "What would you say to me if I told you that it is not correct that you were on Iwo Jima?"

Murray looked right at me and responded in a stern and deliberate voice. "I'd say I don't care . . . believe what you want to. I'd say, well go ahead; go back to your books. And I'd say to you that I don't care whether you believe me or not."

I could tell by the sadness in his eyes that Murray was hurt by what I had just said. I was really hesitant to continue, speaking slowly, and stumbling over every word: "Well, what if I said it's not a matter of believing . . . that I have proof you weren't on Iwo Jima?" I was so ambivalent about accosting Murray with my evidence, I was babbling almost incoherently.

Murray grew impatient.

"Say what's on your mind!"

Murray's abrupt outburst jolted me back to a more lucid state.

"I have, in my possession, a letter from you to your wife, that was sent from that hospital in California."

"You do? How did you get it?"

"Catherine gave it to me. Jason found it in the garage."

"Well, I never did see it."

"You wrote it. So you saw it once." I was much more comfortable now that the cat was out of the bag, and feeling more assertive. "And the postmark on that letter is March 3, 1945."

"OK."

"The landing on Iwo Jima took place on February 19, 1945."

"OK."

"Now, unless you were going back and forth by airplane, which I don't think you were, there ain't no way you're getting from Iwo Jima to California in twelve days."

Murray remained obstinate: "The hell I didn't!"

I was just as unyielding: "Well, you go ahead and tell me how you did that."

"You figure it out!"

"I did figure it out, just going based on what you've already told me. You're on Iwo Jima, even if you were there for the initial invasion—which you told me you weren't—that's February 19. Remember February's a short month; only nine days to February 28 then three more days until March 3. Now, you've got to get back to Pearl Harbor, right, on that Liberty Ship. That's the first step, and Iwo Jima is several thousand miles west of Hawaii. You told me you were in that hospital in Honolulu for about a week. That's the second step. Then you've told me it was an eight-day voyage on that hospital ship back to California. So, I'm looking at that timeline and I'm saying how is it possible you could have gotten back to San Francisco to mail that letter on March 3?"

Suddenly, Murray's demeanor became much less belligerent, and almost sheepish.

"I don't know. Too many years ago for me to worry about it."

"I understand. And I'm not asking you to worry about it. Remember you once told me I'm a very precise person?"

"Yes, you are."

"Well, I'm just trying my best to get the facts straight. Personally, my theory—and I'm going to be honest with you—is that you hit those islands, one landing after another, and what you just told me is the damned truth: that you didn't know where the hell you were. Each one was just another piece of beach with Japs shooting at you. I think you did that enough times, then something happened—whatever battle fatigue is, whatever it was that made that doctor say you weren't fit for duty—and the whole experience became one giant hell in your mind. And once you came out of whatever funk you were in, once you were back in the States, Iwo Jima was in the news, and in your mind, that's where you put yourself. But I don't think there's any way you were there. And I really don't care whether you were there or not. I'm just trying to write an accurate story. Because we know for sure the date of the landing on Iwo Jima, and we know that the postmark on the envelope must be correct. That's my theory. And I'm wondering what you think about what I've just said."

"I don't know. I don't know what to tell you. We never asked what island we were on. We never knew. And I don't think they wanted us to know. Every time we were briefed before a landing, they never referred to it by name. Then later on, we would say, 'Where the hell are we?' And we'd find out. But I'll tell you what . . . I don't know about the dates, or the letter, or whatever. But those guys raising that flag . . . I watched them do that. How did I see those guys raise that flag?"

"I don't think you did. I believe that you are absolutely certain that what you're telling me is the truth. But I think that whatever happened to you that made them pull you out of combat . . . well, quite honestly, I think that it fucked up your memory. I think you probably saw a different flag going up, on a different island, and that it's your mind playing tricks on you. Let me give you an example: Just recently I went to visit an old college buddy of mine, a guy by the name of Mark Heiberger. We started reminiscing, and he's telling my wife a story about something that happened when we were taking a class in children's literature together. Except I never took any class in children's literature. But Mark insisted that I was in that class with him, sitting right next to him, and I couldn't convince him otherwise. Now Mark is a real bright guy; in fact, he might be the best dentist I've ever come across. And he's never been anywhere close to combat, not to mention the fact that he's half your age. But in his mind, he was one hundred percent sure that I was in that class with him, even though I know for a fact that I wasn't. Now if his memory can deceive him like that, isn't it possible that your memory, after everything you've been through, could be deceiving you as well?"

Murray slumped down into his chair. His voice became weak and barely audible.

"No, I don't think that. I don't think that at all."

He sat for a long while in solemn silence, audibly breathing in his oxygen and staring out the window. The tension in the room expanded until I couldn't take it anymore.

"So, what do you think about me asking you about those dates?"

"I don't know." Murray kept looking out the window.

"Well you must think something. Are you pissed off at me?"

Now Murray abruptly turned and looked me straight in the eye.

"No! No, I'm not pissed off at you. I just don't understand. You know, that hospital where I was at . . . there was one area in that hospital where the guys couldn't get out at all. Those guys were really screwed up—but good. One guy wouldn't go to bed unless they'd give him his rifle so he could sleep with it. Of course, they didn't let him near any bullets. But I knew him from before; not real well, but I did know him. And he wasn't all screwed up before he went overseas. I never did find out what ever happened to that guy. But as far as those dates, I don't know what to tell you. If those dates are correct . . . well, I couldn't be in two places at once. I don't know what happened. Why would I think I was on Iwo Jima if I wasn't?"

"If it's OK with you, I'd like to tell you what I think happened."

"What do you think happened?"

"Keep in mind that I'm trying to be a detective, figuring out something that happened seventy years ago. But I wasn't there, so maybe I'm right and maybe I'm wrong. But I think the last place you were at was not Iwo Jima, but it was Peleliu. And I don't think when you landed there you knew where the fuck you were. After all, if you blindfolded me, and dropped me in the middle of the desert in Utah, how in God's name would I know where I was? The same thing holds true for you guys. There wasn't any sign on that island that said, 'Welcome to Iwo Jima,' was there?"

"There was no signs anywhere."

"So, the ramp comes down, bullets are flying, shit's happening, people are dying, there's blood everywhere. At that moment, how would you know where you're at, and why would you care?"

"You don't give a shit. Except you wished you were someplace else."

"Right. It's just one bloody mess that you were involved in. But remember I told you those pictures in your drawer that you gave me were from Peleliu? Those photographs were taken on Peleliu. And I think it was so bad there that you, and a helluva lot of other guys, wound up with this battle fatigue, or what we call now PTSD. And you got shipped back to Hawaii, and you were in that hospital for who knows how long, and when you finally came out of the daze you were in, you tried to piece together, 'Where was I and what the hell happened?' And right around that time is when Iwo Jima was happening, and you incorporated that image of what took place on Iwo Jima into your own memory, as if you were actually there. And that's what has been in your memory your whole life. You had experienced so much stress and trauma that your mind created a different circumstance of where you were in order to fill in the gaps in your memory. And that's what I think happened."

"Well, that's possible. It's possible. I don't know, Dr. Z. I may have been on some other island. But . . . if I'm wrong about this, if I wasn't there on Iwo Jima, then you can throw the whole damned thing out. How can you believe anything else I've told you?"

"That thought crossed my mind. I've thought about that. But I think that's incorrect. Just because you didn't know where you were, it doesn't mean you didn't experience the things you remember. That happens all the time. Like if I say to my wife, 'Remember that time we went parasailing in Bermuda and what a great time we had?' And she says to me, 'That wasn't Bermuda, it was St. Martin.' That doesn't mean we didn't go parasailing. It just means that one of us doesn't remember where we were when it happened. People misremember details of their lives all the time. So, no, I don't think you throw everything else out. It doesn't really matter where you were. Does that make sense to you?"

"Yeah. It does. But I've been trying to put all this out of my mind for so many years so I don't get into that same rut again. Waking up every night . . . the same dreams over and over again. It was hard to take. I don't want to go back to that! That was no good! I'm going to have to quit talking now, 'cause I'm getting worked up. OK?"

"Of course it's OK. You want me to leave?"

"No, I want you to stay. But I want to talk about something else. Why don't we talk about golf?"

"OK, let me ask you a question. For me the hardest shot is when you're in the thick rough right close to the green. You know how sometimes just beyond the fringe they keep that rough real thick? Whatever I try, it's not working."

"That is a hard shot. You have to open your clubface. Because when the club hits that thick grass, it's going to turn, so you have to compensate for that. You'll have to practice that one, I can't just tell you."

"What do you think is the most difficult shot, the one that you'd practice the most?"

"I think a real challenging shot is when you're about six feet from the hole. A putt that you should hit, but that you don't always hit. But there are several shots that are hard; it depends a lot on the golf course that you're on. If you play the same course frequently, you get to know all the things you need to know when you go out and play. Knowing the course is very, very helpful. Which course do you like the best?"

"I like Mountain Dell."

"Very good. I like it too. As long as I don't have to walk—it's too hilly.

"You know I'm trying to give you a satisfactory answer. About those dates. And I don't know what's wrong. There's something wrong—somewhere. I don't know what to tell you. In my mind . . . well, I just can't tell you."

"Does it bother you to think that maybe your memory is wrong?"

"Yes. It's bothering me now."

"Well, I hope you're not angry at me."

"I'm not angry; I'm just confused."

"Do you like your psychologist from the VA, that lady I met here at the house last week?"

"Oh yeah, she's all right."

"When I told her I had found this discrepancy in the dates, and I told her I was going to talk to you about it, she said, 'Oh I don't know if I would do that.' She told me that I probably shouldn't tell you about it."

"She did? I wonder why she said that?"

"Well, I figure that you and I are honest with each other. I feel like there's nothing I can't tell you and there's nothing you can't tell me. No sense in bullshitting you—I don't have time for that and neither do you. Honesty is the best policy as far as I'm concerned."

"The best. If somebody tells me something I want to know whether I can believe it or not. I don't like bullshit. I've ran into quite a few guys in my lifetime that has told me things and no doubt they've been lying. I've got no use for those people. But this thing about the dates . . . I just don't know what to make of it."

"I'm sorry to have caused you this confusion. As a doctor, and as your friend, I would suggest that you ask your psychologist about it. She might be able to help you with it. Ask her. That's if you really want the answer. Maybe you should spend some time thinking about that."

"No, I don't want to think about it. Because I spent too many years thinking about it and so many more years trying to forget it. For now, I've had enough. Maybe we should call it a day. It's about time for my supper."

Murray made his way into the kitchen, and I started packing up my gear. As I was putting on my coat, Murray sat down at the counter and unwrapped a sandwich. He motioned for me to come over and asked, "Have you ever seen a real pastrami sandwich?" I walked beside him and said, "Of course I have . . . I'm a Jew from Brooklyn. My people invented the pastrami sandwich." As I put my arm around his shoulder, he proudly proclaimed, "Well, take a look at this." It was a sandwich from a local chain restaurant, some pale meat masquerading as pastrami between two slices of bread pretending to be rye. I didn't have the heart to tell him that an impostor like that would be illegal in New York City—I felt I had burst his bubble enough for one day.

"Looks great," I said, violating the commitment to honesty that I had made only moments before. "You enjoy your dinner."

As I was leaving, Murray had one more thing to say: "Now, if you find any more discrepancies in this thing, I want to know about it."

Those words echoed in my mind during my drive home. I took them as an affirmation that I had indeed done the right thing by telling Murray the facts; that his psychologist had underestimated his fortitude. As I arrived at my house I was deep in thought, recapitulating my conversation with Murray, wondering if when I was convincing him of the credibility of his story, I was really trying to convince myself. Then, when I reached into my mailbox, I was jarred back to reality by a large manila envelope. From St. Louis.

CHAPTER 9

TENSE, RESTLESS, AND IRRITABLE

I brought the thick envelope into the house and set it on the dining room table. It was from the National Personnel Records Center and contained the copies of Murray's records that I had been anxiously awaiting. I was very apprehensive about what those documents would reveal. Despite my overtures to the contrary, I had not been entirely truthful with Murray, as I had an altogether different theory about the events that led to his discharge. I was, indeed, convinced that he most likely saw action on Peleliu. After all, in addition to the photos that he had in his possession, there was videographic evidence of an individual on Angaur to whom he bears a striking resemblance. But I believed there was a distinct possibility that the wound he suffered was actually a self-inflicted gunshot wound, a desperate effort to get himself discharged in the face of harrowing combat. Furthermore, if Blair, his commanding officer, had suspected as much, and threatened to initiate a court-martial, that certainly might explain Murray's decision to kill him.

I also thought it was possible that Murray's file would be sketchy and only marginally helpful. Who knows how thoroughly records were kept back then? The contents of that envelope represented my best hope for uncovering the truth, and if they were a dead-end, then I might have no choice but to settle for conjecture and supposition. I wanted to open that envelope, but there was a part of me that was afraid to find out what it contained. I left it sitting there—untouched—for several hours. I had a really bad feeling about what I was going to find inside, and I thought that maybe if I didn't bother it, it wouldn't bother me. Until Julie came home from work. As usual, she served as the voice of reason. She saw it lying there, and said incredulously, "Are you nuts? Open that envelope right now!"

I sat down in a comfortable chair, my hand trembling as I tore into the envelope, revealing over a hundred pages that had been copied from Murray's official military file. Julie settled into the sofa just a few feet away as I started examining the documents one by one. I had a familiar sensation, reminiscent of childhood days when I was about to receive the results of a test or be dealt some harsh criticism by my father. The documents were in a haphazard order, certainly not arranged chronologically; in fact, there was no evidence of even the most rudimentary attempt at organization.

First was his "Notice of Separation from the U.S. Naval Service," in duplicate, each embossed with an official seal. It confirmed that he received an honorable discharge on April 13, 1945, at a rank of machinist's mate first class.

Next, a memo from the chief of naval personnel authorizing reimbursement for "first class rail transportation of dependents (wife and daughters) from Salt Lake City, UT to Riverside, CA on 10 Oct. 1943." That would confirm that Phyllis and the girls were, indeed, able to visit Murray while he was at Port Hueneme.

Next was Murray's application for enlistment, dated April 10, 1943. It included his employment record, which indicated that he worked as a shovel operator at the Utah Copper Company from March 1935 through April 1943, at a salary of nine dollars per day. It also included a full set of fingerprints and a "Beneficiary Slip," in triplicate, directing the payment of six months' pay to Phyllis in the event of Murray's death. Murray also signed an affidavit, in triplicate, stating that he was not receiving a pension nor disability payments from the government of the United States.

The next document was a letter typed and signed by Murray, addressed to the chief of naval personnel, dated December 12, 1944. It was his formal request for discharge from the Navy. The letter is excerpted here:

> I enlisted in the U.S. Naval Reserve on May 5, 1943, at which time my father and I owned and operated a shoe repair business in Sandy, Utah. At the time of my enlistment it was thought that my father would be able to operate this business satisfactorily. Recently my father has been advised by his doctor that it is absolutely necessary that he refrain from

hard work or long hours. He is suffering from stomach ulcer, arthritis, and anemia.

My father is now faced with the alternative of preserving his business and losing his health completely, or saving his health and losing his business, which is his only means of supporting himself and my mother. Additionally, this is the only shoe repair business located in this community, and as such is considered an essential industry, as his customers include a large number of workers from the Utah Copper Company.

I am thoroughly familiar with the operation of this business, and could handle it capably if I were released from the service. Every other effort to secure help in the shop has met with no success.

It is my earnest desire to aid my country, however I also feel I have a definite obligation to my family in that I should do everything possible to protect my parents means of support and help preserve my fathers failing health. I have been overseas for a period of thirteen months, and served in the task force in the Marshall Island Campaign, serving a period of six months on Majuro Atoll.

Your prompt consideration of this request will be appreciated.

Along with the letter was a notarized, handwritten letter from Murray's father, addressed to the chaplain of the 100th US NCB dated November 17, 1944. Again, I have excerpted that letter:

Dear Sir—

I have written my son Murray Jacobs several times asking him if he could get released from the service to help me in my shoe repair business. He has consented to do so if it is possible for him to get an Honorable Discharge and he wrote me that it would take a letter from four prominent citizens and in contacting them they were willing to do so and I am enclosing those letters for your consideration.

Whatever you can do will be greatly appreciated. I have been working 16 or 18 hours a day since Murray left me. I have tried in every way to get help but it seems impossible, so my last effort is to get my son to take over the business. I have been advised by my doctor to take it a little easy but that is almost impossible as I have a large community which depends upon me to keep their shoes in good repair.

Now I don't want to ask for anything out of reason but it seems to me that my work is very essential to the War Effort and I trust you will see my point of view. Please don't think me un-patriotic for I want to do anything I can to bring this hectic war to a close, which I hope will be soon.

I thank you from the bottom of my heart for anything you can do. May God bless you all.

Guy Jacobs

Accompanying that letter were notarized letters from William L. Hewlett, the local barber; E. C. Elkington, of the Jordan Drug Co.; Horace Burkinshaw, owner of the Burk Theatre in Sandy; and Isaac Sorensen, bishop of the Sandy ward of the LDS Church. Each letter requested that Murray be released from the military in order to assist his father. All specifically mentioned that the shoe repair business was essential to the community and that Guy's health was failing. There was also a letter from Guy's personal physician, Robert T. Jellison, MD, in which he documented a chronic history of bleeding peptic ulcer that necessitated "confinement in the hospital" on multiple occasions.

These letters were accompanied by a document from the Salt Lake County Chapter of the American Red Cross, outlining their official recommendation for what was referred to as a "Dependency Discharge." The following is an excerpt from the report of Intake Supervisor Wanda F. Johnson:

At present the seaman's wife receives each month $100.00 family allowance for herself and two children, and a $30.00 allotment. This is her only income but is adequate for her support.

At present the parents owe $1,000.00 mortgage on their home, which is valued at $3,700.00. They own a 1937 Chevrolet sedan, and at present they have $400.00 in savings.

According to Dr. Jellison, Guy Jacobs cannot continue his strenuous work without seriously impairing his health, yet it is obvious that continuance in this work is necessary for financial security. If his health fails as indicated under the present strain, their savings are not adequate to provide maintenance for him and his wife, and they would lose their property and have to be taken care of by the State, since no other member of the family has sufficient resources to support them.

According to the community and family and past record of the seaman, Murray Jacobs is capable and willing to continue in his father's business and could adequately support both his family and his parents if he were discharged from service.

Miss Johnson's report was forwarded to the Naval District Headquarters of the American Red Cross, where it was received by Assistant Field Director Abraham L. Kaminstein. Unbeknownst to anyone at the time, Kaminstein was destined to become one of the most important and influential figures in the history of American and international copyright law.

Abraham Lewis Kaminstein was born in New York City on May 13, 1912. After graduating from the College of the City of New York, he received a law degree from Harvard. In 1944—at the time of his involvement in Murray's case— Kaminstein was stationed in Hawaii with the American Red Cross. In 1947, he began his career at the United States Copyright Office of the Library of Congress, and in 1960, he was appointed register of copyrights, only the seventh individual to hold that position since it had been established in 1897.

Kaminstein was a leading force in altering the copyright system to favor the interests of authors, songwriters, and other creative persons. The Copyright Act of 1976, the first major revision of copyright law since 1909, was prepared under his direction, and it remains the basis of copyright law in the United States today. Kaminstein also played a prominent role in revising international copyright law, helping to make the United States a leader in the global copyright community. He retired as register of copyrights in 1971. After his death in 1977, a tribute to him was made on the floor of the House of Representatives, and published in the Congressional Record.

Every writer, poet, artist, musician, playwright, and filmmaker in the world today owes a debt of gratitude to the visionary efforts of Abraham L. Kaminstein. Sadly, few even know his name. I located his son, Dana Kaminstein, PhD, who generously furnished me with this biographical information. According to Dr. Kaminstein, his father was a tireless worker who was respected and beloved by those who worked with him, and he viewed himself as a champion of the common man. And on December 6, 1944, his role was that of an advocate for one common man, a Navy Seabee from Utah whose family appeared to be in dire financial straits. In a memorandum to the officer in charge of the 100th Naval Construction Battalion, Abraham L. Kaminstein provided the official recommendation of the American Red Cross to approve the Dependency Discharge of Murray Jacobs, and he forwarded the necessary enclosures. As any good lawyer would, he reminded the recipient of his memo that the report of the American Red Cross was to be considered confidential, and he asked to be advised of the disposition of the case. Thus ended our protagonist's fleeting involvement with a man who later went on to become a distinguished figure in US legislative history.

What follows is a series of endorsements, first from the officer in charge (OinC) of the 100th Naval Construction Battalion, Commander H. D. Cavin; then from the OinC of the 33rd Naval Construction Regiment; a third endorsement from the OinC of the 7th Naval Construction Brigade; and finally a fourth endorsement from the OinC of the Hawaiian Area Brigades. All these documents recommended unequivocally that Murray's request for discharge be approved. A memorandum from the Bureau of Naval Personnel, dated March 3, 1945, responded as follows:

> Regarding request for Discharge for Own Convenience-
>
> By direction of Chief of Naval Personnel, subject man's request for discharge is not approved. Retention of subject man in the Service is authorized. He should be advised to register for increased allotment in favor of his dependents.

This whole sequence of events was very interesting and elicited mixed feelings. Having read Murray's letters to his wife, knowing how badly he wanted to get out of the Navy even prior to going overseas and remembering the schemes he was concocting during his training, it was easy to imagine that this was just one more shameful attempt to beat the system and avoid fulfilling his obligations. It seemed particularly unscrupulous, considering that by 1945 our military had been depleted by so many casualties that we were desperate for able-bodied men to join and bring the war to an end. On the other hand, one might consider that there was at least some veracity to Murray's request. It certainly seemed that his father was ill and had limited financial means, although describing a rural shoe-repair business as essential to the war effort required a stretch of the imagination. Given that his application had the endorsement of four levels of officers within the chain of command, it was a blatant example of military bureaucracy that his request was arbitrarily and summarily dismissed.

The next document in the file was Murray's "Quarterly Marks Card," in triplicate, indicating his ratings for proficiency, which were average throughout his enlistment, and conduct, which were consistently above average.

The following document was dated March 2, 1945, and originated from the US Naval Hospital in San Leandro, California. On it, Murray verified that he had returned an overcoat that he apparently wore on the journey from Hawaii back to the mainland. Needless to say, this document appeared in triplicate. While perhaps superfluous, it did offer further proof of the date of Murray's return to the United States.

Next, there was a form documenting Murray's change in rating, effective March 1, 1944, from machinist's mate second class to machinist's mate first class. It was accompanied by a page that certified Murray was serving outside the Continental United States, and he was thereby entitled to wear the Asiatic-Pacific Campaign Ribbon.

The next several pages were Murray's initial physical examination at the time of his induction, dated May 1, 1943. The exam revealed no specific abnormalities. His serologic test for syphilis was negative. This was followed by a "Clothing Issue Statement," which documented every article of clothing that Murray received upon entry into the service. There was also an "Application for National Service Life Insurance," dated May 11, 1943. At a cost of six dollars and ninety cents per month, deducted from Murray's pay, Phyllis would have received $10,000 in the event of his death.

The next page chronicled Murray's transfer to US Naval Hospital #10 in Aiea Heights, Hawaii, on February 2, 1945, and it was followed by the documentation of his transfer to a transport ship headed to the United States on February 21, 1945. The following page indicated that he arrived at the US Naval Hospital in California on March 2, 1945. These records offered absolute evidence of what I already knew: Murray could not possibly have been on Iwo Jima. There were then several forms that confirmed that Murray received an "Honorable Discharge, By Approved Medical Survey" on April 13, 1945—ironically only a month after his discharge was denied by the Bureau of Naval Personnel.

The next page, "Summary of Service," could have been very revealing, but it was not.

National Recruitment Station, Salt Lake City, Utah	5/5/43-5/8/43
US Naval Training Center, Virginia	5/8/43-8/14/43
100th Naval Construction Battalion	8/14/43-2/2/45
US Naval Hospital #10, San Francisco, California	2/2/45-3/2/45
US Naval Hospital, San Leandro, California	3/2/45-4/13/45

Unfortunately, there was not a single reference to Murray's exact whereabouts for the entire time he was with the 100th NCB—precisely the type of perfunctory documentation I was afraid I might find. Of interest was that the location of Naval Hospital #10 was listed incorrectly as being in California rather than in Hawaii.

The last twenty pages of Murray's file consisted of his medical record in its entirety. There was another copy of his initial physical examination report, some cursory documentation of a few other physical exams, his complete dental record, and his immunization record. There were a few more detailed notes regarding the treatment of his sinusitis. Then there was his admission note to the US Naval Hospital in Aiea Heights, dated February 2, 1945:

Chief Complaint: Severe headaches.

Present Illness: Patient complains of a recurrence of headaches, with eye pain and extreme malaise. He has had attacks of increasing severity and frequency for the past year and lately has been almost incapacitated. He has lost 15 lbs. in weight in the last 4 months, and complains of a multiplicity of symptoms.

Physical Exam: Moderately developed and nourished adult male acutely ill. T-100.2; P-88

Tenderness over frontal sinuses. Chest clear to percussion and auscultation. Abdomen, no masses or tenderness.

Diagnosis: SINUSITIS, Acute maxillary.

On February 7, 1945, there was a note documenting a consultation by the neuro-psychiatric department:

This man has personal and domestic problems that are of concern to him. He is worried over the poor health of one of his children, who needs to have a tonsillectomy, and his father who has peptic ulcer but is compelled to work never the less.

He displays many anxiety manifestations. History of bed wetting to age 12, walked in his sleep a few times. Fairly good prior adjustment. Overseas since Nov. 1943. For 3 months increasingly nervous, sleeps poorly, develops gas and knots in stomach. No appetite.

He appears mildly apprehensive, markedly restless. He constantly wrings his hands.

Impression: In my opinion his anxiety is responsible for his symptoms, and in his present condition he is not suited for duty in a combat area. It is more practical for this man to be evacuated to the mainland for further treatment and disposition.

Diagnosis changed to PSYCHONEUROSIS, ANXIETY NEUROSIS #1517. ORIGIN WAS NOT DUE TO OWN MISCONDUCT. DNEPTE. Suggest transfer to OPEN WARD, MENTAL.

[Author's note: The military abbreviation 'DNEPTE' signifies 'Did Not Exist Prior To Enlistment']

The next form was the admission note at the US Naval Hospital in San Leandro, California, which was dated March 2, 1945:

Chief Complaint: Difficulty in sleeping, apprehension, and worry about family.

Present Illness: Tense, restless, and irritable. Worried about father. 15 months sea duty with CB's. Not psychotic. Not suicidal. No acute physical illness.

To service- May 5, 1943. To foreign duty Nov. 21, 1943. Saw no combat.

Those three words hit me like a baseball bat in the chest. I could feel my heart start racing and a lump in my throat. I looked up at Julie; she looked back at me and asked what I had found. I ignored her and kept reading.

Patient was admitted to Aiea Heights with a diagnosis of Sinusitis, Acute Maxillary because of complaints of severe headaches. He received treatment for his sinuses and was noted to have many anxiety symptoms. On 2-7 his diagnosis was changed to Psychoneurosis, Anxiety neurosis. He remains tense, apprehensive, fatigued, restless, and anorexic. He does feel that he has improved and is sleeping somewhat better.

Family History: Father age 55 years has peptic ulcer. Mother age 50 is nervous. Patient is 2nd of 3 siblings. Oldest sister has frequently been treated by a physician for nervousness. Father and mother frequently in conflict because of father's infidelity.

Past History: Normal birth. Enuretic until age 12 years. Walked in sleep until 12 years. Afraid of the dark until 13 years. Still afraid of water.

Afraid of the water? Then why the fuck did he join the Navy?

Had nightmares until age 13 years. Failed in 6th grade. Has 11th grade education. Steadily employed from 1936 until entering the service in 1943. Smokes and drinks moderately. First heterosexual experience age 16 years. No conflicts. Married age 20, has two children ages 7 years old and 5 years old. Has made a good marital adjustment in spite of difficulty at the start of married life. Prefers to be to himself. Good civilian and Naval record.

Physical Examination: General appearance good. Neurological examination essentially negative. Patient is a tense, anxious, and restless individual who is sincere and conscientious. During interview he builds up tension, develops facial tremors, and his palms perspire. He is very unhappy in the service and is markedly concerned about his need to be home to help his family. He feels he is of no value to the Navy in his present state, and the longer he stays in the service the worse he gets. He shows good intelligence and has good insight and judgement.

Impression: This is an anxious, tense individual who can not tolerate service life. He is preoccupied with his belief that he is needed at home and that he is contributing very little in the service. Because of his neurotic background and anxiety precipitated under no significant stress, he will be recommended for a discharge. He is too serious a potential liability to warrant retention in the service.

I could barely breathe. My hands felt jittery. I couldn't possibly begin to process the information I had just obtained. But I kept on reading. The last few pages were the report of the Board of Medical Survey, dated April 2, 1945.

Facts are as Follows: This man is a 28 year old MM1c, U.S. Navy, with 19 months active duty prior to admission to the sick list. He had 15 months duty outside the continental United States but never experienced combat action.

He was admitted to the Sick Bay on January 26, 1945 at the 100th Naval Construction Battalion at Oahu, Territory of Hawaii (T.H.) with diagnosis Sinusitis, Acute Maxillary. He was transferred on February 2, 1945 to U.S. Naval Hospital, Aiea Heights, T.H., at which time many manifestations of anxiety were noted. Diagnosis was changed to Psychoneurosis, Anxiety neurosis #1517, and on March 2, 1945, he was admitted here.

On admission he was tense, insomniac, restless, and fatigued. Psychiatric evaluation reveals a long standing and well fixed anxiety reaction in a man who could not adjust to service life. He is markedly concerned about real domestic problems at home. He was enuretic and somnambulistic until 12 years of age, was afraid of the dark throughout childhood, and has always had a fear of the water.

During his stay in this hospital, he has shown only slight improvement. The admission diagnosis has been retained. Maximum benefit of hospitalization has been obtained. It is the opinion of the Board that this man is unfit for retention in the Service. His disability is not the result of his own misconduct, and was not incurred in the line of duty. His condition existed prior to enlistment, and was not aggravated by service. Probable future duration—permanent.

If discharged, he is not likely to become a menace to himself or others, and is not likely to become a public charge. He
is fully competent to be discharged into his own custody. He
has been informed of the Board's findings and does not desire
to submit a statement in rebuttal.

I slumped down into the chair and looked back at Julie. I
slowly repeated the devastating words I had just read—"never
experienced combat action"—and tears welled up in my eyes.
My worst, unimaginable nightmare was unfolding right before
her eyes.

"I have nothing," I said to her, my voice trembling. "I'm writing a book about nothing."

CHAPTER 10

WHAT COULD BE SO HORRIBLE?

In the weeks that followed I mourned the loss of my project much as one might lament the death of an old friend. I had spent the better part of a year with Murray, not just interviewing him, but also developing a friendship. I was not only invested in the story, but I had become emotionally attached to the man. I found myself progressing through the five stages of grief, as first described by Elizabeth Kübler-Ross in her 1969 book, *On Death and Dying.*

At first, I experienced denial. How could Murray have provided me with such vivid, detailed accounts of combat that he had never actually experienced? How is it possible that he is still, to this day, being treated for Post-Traumatic Stress Disorder at the VA hospital if he never endured any trauma in the first place? If someone were to fabricate events in his life, why on earth would he create a scenario in which he committed war crimes, torturing prisoners and killing his own officers? As I replayed our conversations over and over in my mind and listened to the recordings of our interviews, I couldn't wrap my brain around the likelihood that all the things that Murray had so solemnly—and reluctantly—confessed to me had never really happened.

Then I became angry. Not so much at Murray; mostly at myself. Sure, I felt betrayed. I had spent all those hours listening intently to stories that turned out to be bullshit. But I knew—definitely and beyond a shadow of a doubt—Murray wasn't lying to me. He believed every word he told me; in his mind, he had experienced every horror he described. I couldn't in good conscience be angry with him. After all, he wasn't the one who coerced me to listen to his stories. I was the one who coaxed him into telling me. No, I was pissed off at myself for choosing to ignore the signs that were there all along—signs that seemed so obvious now. When Murray told me about violent combat on Majuro, and I discovered that the island had been taken with hardly a shot fired, I concocted a scenario in which he was just confused about where he was. Same thing when I uncovered proof that he couldn't possibly have been on Iwo Jima. As it turns out, when Murray said, "If I'm wrong about this, then you can throw the whole damned thing out," I should have. And when he asked me, "How can you believe anything else I've told you?" I should've taken him at his word. For a grizzled old ER doctor from Brooklyn, who prides himself on his cynicism, I sure let myself get duped this time.

And then I started bargaining . . . maybe not in the way Kübler-Ross described it, but bargaining nonetheless. Maybe I wasn't really an idiot for believing Murray. His psychologist at the VA was still treating him for PTSD, wasn't she? And maybe—just maybe—it was possible that Murray was telling the truth and his medical record was wrong. I went back and read those notes again, but I couldn't convince myself that they were anything but accurate. The documentation was quite thorough, even by today's standards, and two independent doctors statements very clearly and unambiguously declared that Murray had not been in combat. Moreover, when I went back and looked at Murray's letter to the chief of naval personnel, his desperate plea to be released from the military, I noticed that he never once mentioned that he had encountered the enemy. He talked about being overseas, that he served on Majuro, but at no time does he describe himself as having fought for his country. It seemed to me that if I were the one writing that particular letter, that's the first argument I would have made—assuming, of course, that I had actually experienced any fighting.

No matter how I tried to spin it, the bottom line was that the credibility of everything Murray had told me was now in question. As my anger gradually transitioned to an overwhelming feeling of sadness, Julie remained incredibly supportive. I think during those few weeks the most common words she uttered to me were, "I'm sorry, honey." She wasn't used to seeing me so defeated; I can usually apply my problem-solving skills to overcome whatever obstacles life puts in my way. She even went so far as to suggest I use the story I had gathered as the basis for a novel. But in my own morose way I had already surrendered to the idea that my book was dead . . . *morto*. My intention to simply document the wartime events that shaped a veteran's life had morphed into a journey into the confused mind of an old man who was apparently pretty damned fucked up even before he joined the military. I hadn't necessarily hoped to tell the tale of the next Audie Murphy, but I wasn't really interested in regaling readers with the story of a bed wetter, who was afraid of the water, who wanted out of the Navy after only a couple of weeks of boot camp, who cheated on his wife relentlessly (if even that was true), and who never actually came face-to-face with the enemy.

As I became increasingly despondent, I sought out the wisdom of my own psychologist, Dr. Dawn Fleming Jackson. I shared my experience and feelings with her, and as usual she provided me with valuable insight. She observed that while the combat exploits of a Navy Seabee during WWII would indeed be interesting and of historic value, the psychological pathology that Murray was displaying was perhaps a far more unique story. How did he manage to convince himself that he had experienced the things that he had described so vividly? When exactly did those events start taking shape within his mind, eventually becoming entrenched in his memory? And why did he envision himself as having perpetrated some of the terrible crimes to which he had confessed?

In the course of our conversation, I mentioned that Murray was being treated for PTSD, and we came to realize that his psychologist, Gita Rakhsha, is one of Dawn's closest friends. Now what's the chance of that: I'm a fifty-two-year-old doctor trying to write a book about a ninety-five-year-old veteran, and his shrink and my shrink are good buddies. I'm not a particularly religious man, but I do believe that coincidences like that are something more than random happenstance. I took that synchronicity as a sort of sign that, conceivably, the path of my life was brought across the path of Murray Jacobs' life for some greater purpose—that my project might have some merits that I hadn't yet recognized. Furthermore, Dawn expressed to me that she was very intrigued by the story of my relationship with Murray. Why did I become so interested in him in the first place, and why had my emotional involvement become so deep? Her enthusiasm helped convince me that the project shouldn't be abandoned, but rather redirected. If the book had a whisper of life left in it, perhaps it was my voyage with Murray that should provide the foundation—something along the lines of the best-selling book by Mitch Albom, *Tuesdays With Morrie*. And so it was that Dawn Fleming Jackson, PhD, encouraged me to reanimate this project from the dead. She helped me attain the final stage in the grieving process: acceptance. After that session, I realized that I didn't have nothing after all. I didn't quite know what it was that I had, but I felt pretty confident that it wasn't nothing.

In his 1994 book, *Finding My Way*, John Schneider, PhD, described an entirely different concept of managing loss, a model he referred to as transformative grief. His approach involves three fundamental questions: What has been lost? What remains? And what may still be possible? In contemplating my own situation, I found myself seeking answers to each of those questions. What I had lost was clear enough: I had lost all faith in Murray's credibility. Therefore, I no longer had the opportunity to write about a previously untold morsel of World War II history. What I was left with also seemed relatively straightforward. I had the story of an apparently troubled child who grew to become a troubled young man. He had a hard time adjusting to married life and an equally hard time adapting to life in the Navy. During the course of nearly two years in the service, he became increasingly anxious and dysfunctional, and he made fervent efforts to get himself discharged, demonstrated as early as his letter to Phyllis on September 8, 1943, and as late as his letter to the chief of naval personnel on December 12, 1944. I don't know what transpired in the fifteen months between, but it would appear that while he was definitely overseas in Hawaii and the Marshall Islands, he was never in direct conflict with the enemy.

As he became progressively more stressed about issues both real and imagined, his deteriorating mental status landed him in the psychiatric unit of a naval hospital in California, and ultimately led to his honorable discharge as recommended by the Board of Medical Survey. Evidently, he did not have any greater success adjusting to life as a civilian, as his marital troubles continued, and his relationship with at least his two older daughters did not flourish. Somewhere along the way, he began to concoct memories of wartime incidents that were so intense, so realistic, that they became assimilated into the essence of his being. In fact, these so-called memories were so convincing that even a seasoned psychologist at the VA hospital believed their authenticity, and he continued to be treated for PTSD seventy years later.

So, if that's what I'd lost and that's what I was left with, Schneider's final question remained: What might still be possible? I knew that Murray was sincere in his belief in the reality of everything he told me, and I was equally certain that he was experiencing real anguish from his fabricated memories. If somehow I were able to convince him that none of those horrible events had actually happened, maybe I could relieve him of his mental suffering. Maybe he would be able to live the remainder of his life without having such terrifying nightmares. Maybe he could go to his grave peacefully, without the burden of thinking he had done such hideous things. Maybe the ultimate purpose of my work would be to absolve a tormented old man of sins that he had never really committed.

On the other hand, perhaps the primary function of this book would be to describe a very unique form of mental illness. The vast majority of WWII vets never discussed their wartime experiences. Many others may have embellished their experiences and exaggerated their contributions; cases of so-called "stolen valor" are unfortunately common. But this, a man who never discussed the combat he never experienced, all the while believing—really believing—he had been immersed in the blood of his fallen comrades, he had shot and killed one of his own officers, he had cut off the heads of dead Japanese soldiers, and he had sliced off the genitals of a living prisoner and forced him to eat his own penis?

I personally have never heard of such a story, and I believe that alone makes it a story that might be worth telling.

This would be a very daunting challenge. I would need to present Murray with much more proof than a couple of typed doctors' notes in order to dislodge decades-old misconceptions from the recesses of his mind. And with regard to his psychopathology, several questions would need to be answered. When did Murray first begin to imagine these events that he had never actually experienced? How did he construct such elaborate, detailed thoughts? Why did he envision himself as a war criminal? One might postulate that while hospitalized, he could have encountered some combat veterans who shared their own experiences, and in the fragile emotional state he was in, he incorporated their reality into his own. And in creating this alternate universe for himself, perhaps it was his underlying poor self-esteem, fueled by some real guilt and shame about having not given his best effort in serving his country, that led him to perceive himself as having tortured prisoners and having killed his commanding officer. Of course, this sequence of events is conjecture on my part. I have no idea what actually happened, as I wasn't there with Murray in 1945.

I devised a three-part plan of action in order to gather more evidence and get these questions answered. The first part was the easiest: Since I had convinced myself that Murray had most likely experienced combat on Angaur and/or Peleliu, I needed to go through his records a second time, carefully looking for any proof of his whereabouts during the invasion of those islands. The battle of Angaur took place from September 17–October 22, 1944, and the fighting on Peleliu lasted from September 15–November 27, 1944. As I scoured Murray's file, I found one single entry: a dental procedure performed on September 16, 1944, by the same dentist who had worked on him several times previously. Since the 100th NCB was back in Hawaii at that time, and since it would be highly improbable that anyone would take the time to fill a cavity in the midst of violent combat, I believe that this small piece of documentation effectively rules out the possibility that Murray was one of the seventeen men who detached from the battalion and participated in the invasion of the Palau Islands.

My next step was to try to find out what ever became of the only two men that Murray mentioned by both first and last name. His good buddy Doyle "Yardbird" Smith, who Murray had so intensely described as being blown to bits by a mortar, and Lieutenant M. S. Blair, who Murray claimed to have killed "accidentally" on Iwo Jima. The deaths of these two men haunted Murray, and if I had any hope at all of exonerating him it would be absolutely necessary that I ascertain what happened to them during the war. One possibility was that each was KIA (Killed in Action), and Murray felt some sense of responsibility for their deaths, by virtue of the fact that he had in a sense abandoned his unit prior to fulfilling his enlistment. That certainly could explain his overwhelming feeling of guilt and his recurrent nightmares. The other side of that coin is that one or both of them survived the war, and in fact might even be alive to this day. Either way, I needed to uncover their fates, and the obvious starting point was to try to retrieve their records from the National Archives in St. Louis. I was able to get a little more information about each of them from the duty roster of the 100th NCB—namely their home addresses at the time of their enlistment. Doyle K. Smith from Goose Creek, Texas, and Lt. Mahlon S. Blair from Terre Haute, Indiana. Unfortunately, without their service numbers, the National Personnel Records Center didn't have enough identifying information to provide me with their files.

Right around that time, Julie and I took a trip to Portland, Oregon to visit our nephew Peter Asch, Julie's middle brother's oldest son. Pete and I have had a special relationship ever since the first day I met him when he was about eight years old. He was always a great kid, and now he's a fine young man with a wonderful family of his own: his wife, Aggie, and their daughter, Sidney. Pete graduated from Rutgers University with a bachelor's degree in history and then earned his master's degree in history at NYU, with an advanced certificate in the field of archival management and historical editing. He spent a lot of time during his undergraduate and graduate education taking oral histories from veterans, so naturally, during the course of our visit the conversation turned to this book that I was trying to write. This book that had me on a rollercoaster of emotion and I was just barely climbing from the nadir of despondency to a point where I was starting to feel some excitement about it again.

So, the five of us were sitting outside at a local café, having a coffee. Aggie was discreetly breastfeeding Sidney, and I was telling the whole story of Murray Jacobs, everything he told me, and how I only recently found out from his records that he hadn't experienced combat. And Aggie, an adorable redhead who is about as sweet as anybody could possibly be, said in a quiet and calm manner, and without ever diverting her gaze from Sidney, "Oh, so you're writing a book about a guy who didn't do anything." Like Carlo getting strangled by Clemenza, I never saw it coming. Especially from her. She was so innocent, so matter-of-fact when she said it, like a skilled assassin delicately slipping a knitting needle through my eye socket and scrambling my brain. Until the moment she reads this, she probably won't have any idea how painful that comment was to me. But the real source of my pain was the truth within the statement. And the fact that I know that many people who read this book will feel exactly the same way. In fact, I'd probably feel the same way if I were reading it.

But I remained steadfast in my pursuit of the truth. I asked Peter if he knew of any way to uncover more information about what might have happened to either Smith or Blair. Sure enough, two days later, my beloved and resourceful nephew came through for me: He had located each man's obituary.

From the Terre Haute (Indiana) *Tribune*, dated Tuesday August 8, 1978:

> Word has been received of the death of former Terre Haute resident Mahlon S. Blair, who died Sunday at Winter Park, Florida. He was born in Clinton, Indiana and moved to Florida nine years ago. He was a Navy veteran of World War II and a retired electrical engineer. Surviving are his wife Lucille and his son Robert of Charleston, South Carolina, and two granddaughters.

And from Jasper County, Texas, dated September 16, 1981:

> Funeral for Doyle Smith, 63, of Kirbyville, Texas, will be at 10:30 a.m. today at E.E. Stringer Funeral Home with burial in Magnolia Springs Cemetery. He died at 4:05 a.m. Wednesday in Albuquerque, New Mexico after an illness. A native of Magnolia Springs, he lived in Kirbyville most of his life. He was a World War II veteran and a retired pipefitter with Local 195. Survivors include his wife Beatrice and one son, Milton Smith of Pasadena.

Of course, without their military records I can't be one hundred percent certain that these are the same two men who served with Murray in the 100th NCB. I am quite confident about Blair, considering how unusual the name "Mahlon" is, and I'm pretty sure about Smith—a pipefitter, who is the right age, and who lived in Kirbyville, just a short drive from Yardbird's listed home in Goose Creek. I suppose if I wanted to be even more thorough I could try to locate Beatrice, and if she's still alive inquire as to just how well-endowed her deceased husband was, but discretion being the better part of valor, I think I'll just let that sleeping dog lie.

So now I have fairly compelling evidence that Murray's good buddy Yardbird wasn't blown up by a mortar somewhere in the Pacific and that his commanding officer Blair wasn't fragged. In fact, it seems as though both of those men went on to lead peaceful, productive lives in their hometowns, raising their families and practicing the same trades that likely brought them to the Seabees in the first place. The final component of my plan was to try to discover the origins of Murray's fictitious memories. I decided that my best course of action would be to interview three people: his sister Evelyn, his psychologist, and his daughter Catherine. I considered interviewing his two older daughters as well, but in light of their contentious relationship with their father, I opted against it.

Evelyn was my obvious starting point. First of all, she is the last person alive today who knew Murray before and after he served in the Navy. If she could remember what Murray was like when he returned home, or better yet, if she could recall exactly what he had said back then about his time in the service, then I would have some real clues as to the genesis of his pathology. Secondly, it should be a relatively easy interview—after all, what elderly woman wouldn't appreciate the chance to reminisce about the old days and tell a few stories about her brother? I asked Murray's permission to talk to her, and he agreed without hesitation. He even offered to give her a call and let her know that it was OK with him for her to answer any questions I might ask. I did feel a little duplicitous about the whole thing, since I hadn't told Murray anything about what I had found in his records. But I overcame my guilt and called her.

"Hello, Evelyn. This is Dr. Scott Zuckerman. I'm writing a book about your brother, Murray, and he told me it would be OK to give you a call and talk to you."

"Well, I don't want to talk to you."

"I'd just like to ask you a few questions about your brother."

"Well if you want to know anything about Murray you can just ask him."

Click.

If we still lived in an era of dial tones, I would have been hearing one. Apparently, the cantankerous gene was dominant in the Jacobs family. So much for an easy interview. I decided to start with Catherine instead.

I knew that interviewing Catherine would be tricky at the very least. I would need to ask her incisive questions without revealing any of the information that I had already gathered. I started by establishing some ground rules for our discussion.

"Generally, you and I have a doctor-patient relationship, and everything you tell me is kept in the utmost confidence. I take my responsibility to guard your privacy very seriously. However, the work we're doing today stands apart from that relationship, and I intend to make use of anything you tell me. On the other hand, our conversation will be informational only for me; I've promised your father that I will maintain a strict level of secrecy about everything he has disclosed to me, and I intend to fulfill that commitment. With that understanding, I'd like to start by simply asking you, what is your impression of your dad?"

"I would describe my father as a person who is well-seasoned. He has lived a really big life. He has done much traveling; he has gone places and seen things that most people only read about. He has stories that are often unbelievable, but I know for a fact they are true."

"Can you give me an example?"

"Well, he was on an airplane headed to South America with the CIA agents who were sent to assassinate Che Guevara."

"That's interesting. That's a story he never told me. How did that come to pass, and how do you know for a fact that it's true?"

"He was traveling with my cousin, Jerry, his sister Marell's son. He and Jerry were in business with each other. They were entrepreneurs before it was in vogue. They were in South America together most of my early adolescent years. They bought gemstones, artwork, fabrics . . . all kinds of things. At one point, they were trying to buy a silver mine. According to my dad, and verified by Jerry, it was 1967, and in the course of conversation these men, in a roundabout way, revealed that they were headed to Bolivia to assist in capturing Che Guevara."

"Tell me more about your impression of your father. Not of his life, but of him."

"He's a very kind and generous man, but the way he goes about things . . . it always seems to play out wrong. He tries to do nice things, but the manner in which he goes about it sometimes doesn't seem nice. And he's always been like that. When I was a child, we would go for car rides—that was a very popular thing to do when I was growing up in California. We had a white Cadillac with those big fins and a red interior. My dad was so proud to own that car. So, he'd take us out for a ride and it'd be like, 'Look there's Disneyland! Doesn't that look like fun?' But we wouldn't stop. Or, 'Look there's Knott's Berry Farm! Doesn't that ride look cool?' But we wouldn't stop. Or SeaWorld. Or the San Diego Zoo. We would drive past all these fun places and then we would just go home. And you can imagine how that felt as a kid . . . you know. But I don't think he was doing it in a mean-spirited way; I think he was just misguided.

"I'd also describe my father as controlling and manipulative. He might try to help people, but his help always comes with strings attached. It always has to be on his terms. And he's always been that way, too. It might seem like he was giving you a gift, like he would give you a couple thousand dollars, but it came with contingencies, rules, guidelines. And my dad has always been very impulsive—he thinks he knows what he wants, he gets it, and he's immediately unhappy with it. I think he's an unhappy person in general."

"Well, it would seem reasonable that he's unhappy now. Just from my observation, not based on anything he's said to me, at his stage in his life there's things that he would like to be doing, things that he has a memory of being able to do, and he's no longer able to do it. So being unhappy under his present circumstances is different than being an unhappy person. When you were fifteen was he unhappy?"

"That's complicated. I know things now that I didn't really understand then. He was unfaithful to my mother. He had a long affair with his high school sweetheart, who lived in Idaho, and while my mother was dying he would take trips up there and stay with her. He thought my mom didn't know, but she did know. And it really hurt her. And my sisters were really hurt, too. I just took the stance that I don't think it's right for us to judge, that we don't know what he's going through. I certainly don't condone what he did, but now he has to live with himself, and I know that he is not a happy person about those things.

"He and my mom were expecting my oldest sister before they got married. They kept that a secret from everybody. And after they got married, my father would still drink and hang out with women; he was clearly not ready to be a responsible husband

and father. However, they were married for almost sixty years by the time my mother died. My mom endured a lot. She would tell me what it was like to have people come in and repossess the furniture, to have to pawn her wedding ring to pay off my father's debts. My sisters won't talk to me about him. I don't know if he was a good dad to them. They had different parents than I did."

"Was he a good dad to you?"

Catherine paused for a moment before answering: "Yes. When I came along I was 'Daddy's girl'; truly the apple of his eye. I was born in 1955, and my mother was older. She was thirty-six, which was considered old, and I was breech, so it was a very difficult labor. And my father adored me, at the cost of ignoring my mother, and that continued for a very long time. I didn't know it then, but my mother was very jealous of our relationship. When I was twelve she wrote a letter that she probably meant for only my father to see, but I read it. She said she was leaving, that she was sick of him, and that she couldn't stand me anymore. In the letter, she relinquished custody of me and said she didn't want anything to do with me ever again. She drove through Arizona, got as far as the Mexican border, then called from a pay phone and came home."

"How did you rectify that with her?"

"I cried a lot."

"But then how did it get rectified?"

"It did not. She said it was a mistake. But in my house, growing up, there was not open communication. My family practiced shunning. My mother and father could each go weeks without uttering a word to me if they were angry. Weeks. They would either ignore me entirely or just stare at me with an icy glare."

Oh yeah . . . I'm very well-acquainted with that particular look.

"Give me an example of something you might have done to bring about that sort of treatment."

"Well, I got pregnant. That's a good example. I was sixteen. Dad didn't respond too well to that. Mom was at the doctor with me, so she had a heads-up. My father left . . . he departed . . . he went back to South America. My mom had the support of her friends, but when her friends would come over I was asked by my mother to go close myself into a bedroom. So that I didn't embarrass her."

"In light of that story, your description of your father as a 'good dad' is interesting. You're more forgiving, perhaps, than I would be."

"Probably so. Of course, I can't comment on how forgiving you would be."

"But that notwithstanding, you're quite forgiving of your father."

Generally, Catherine speaks rather loudly, at a brisk pace with an abrupt cadence. But in this instance her voice became soft and she spoke very deliberately: "Yeah. I am. And maybe that comes from the early relationship we had. My sisters actually were resentful of my relationship with my father. Dad would get up very early for work when I was a baby, and he would lie in bed with me sitting on his chest. That apparently made my sisters very angry. Of course, I can understand how my sisters would resent the attention my father gave me, and I can also understand how they would be angry about his behavior toward our mother. But I can't change who he is, or how he chose to behave. He beats himself up every day . . . 'Why did I do this? I hope your mother forgives me.' He didn't realize what he had until it was gone. He remarried twice after my mother died, and—"

That statement took me by surprise, and I interrupted Catherine: "Interesting that he never mentioned that to me either. When did your mother die?"

"My mom died in August 1996. Andrea was six months old. Two weeks later it was my father's eightieth birthday, and he wanted a party, so I had a big open house. By that time the woman in Idaho had become very ill, and unbeknownst to me, her son and daughter-in-law came to my house—I mean I didn't invite them—and they brought a plaque that she had made for my father. My sisters, of course, were quite taken aback. I remember that it was so odd, so awkward, so really strange, that I didn't even know what to say. So I decided to just say nothing, because whatever would have come out of my mouth wouldn't have been the least bit productive. My dad was fine; he thought nothing of it. He asked that woman to marry him, but she said no. So, three months later he married a Mexican woman, Isabelle de la Cruz, and that marriage was annulled after a few months because of what my father chalked up to 'cultural differences.' But she still comes and visits. She's an absolutely wonderful woman, about twenty years younger than my dad. It was another example of my father doing something impulsively, but then growing tired of it almost immediately.

"After that he got married again, to a woman named Pearl Labrum. She is deceased; she died last year. They were married in 1998 and stayed together a couple of years. And since then he's had a few different girlfriends, one of whom still calls him . . . constantly."

"Do you like your dad?"

Catherine thought for quite a while before answering: "I like him because he's my dad."

"You know, I want to add the disclaimer that while your answers to these questions will probably make their way into the book I'm writing, I have no intention of discussing them with Murray. I'm not trying to create World War Three in your house."

"Yes. I know that. Let me tell you that I do like my dad, but I don't always like the things he chooses to do or the way he behaves. I can still find that little girl in me, whose daddy would come home from work and put her on his shoulders . . . and I can remember that and hang on to that. Like he says to me, 'What ever happened to that sweet little girl I used to know, who was so loving?' And I'm thinking, 'This isn't loving? You're here, in my home, and I'm caring for you. This is loving. Just because we yell at each other doesn't mean it's not loving.'"

"If I were you, I might not like him that much. I like your dad. Of course, I know him only in his current state, and I have a very specific relationship with him. But according to the things you've told me, I wouldn't blame you for not liking him. He didn't cheat on my mother. He didn't shun me when I needed him. He hasn't said to me some of the things that he's said to you."

"To my knowledge, he was a philanderer before I came along, and then he had this relationship that I knew about, after my mom was diagnosed with her terminal illness. She was dying. In between there, I don't know of any untoward extramarital activities." As she continued, Catherine's voice became palpably louder and she spoke pointedly.

"My father was a hard worker. I would see him get up early. He would come home exhausted. You know? In addition to the business he had with Jerry, he was operating heavy equipment." She paused for just a moment, and lowered her voice. "My father derived great pleasure from certain things. But talk about being controlling—my father has a very narrow view of how things should be. For instance, golf. My father was a scratch golfer; he was really, really good. He quit playing golf, probably ten or fifteen years before he physically had to, because he wasn't playing to the standard he had in his mind. So it was like, 'If I can't play the way I think I should still be able to, then I'm not going to do it at all.' It's all or nothing with him."

Catherine was abruptly vacillating between an emotional defense of Murray and a clinical description of the many exasperating aspects of his personality. I decided to bluntly cut to the chase: "I know you've been through enough therapy, I would think you would have had this discussion . . . do you think your father is a narcissist?"

Catherine replied without hesitation: "Yes. Most definitely yes, I do. My dad is absolutely a narcissist. My father—and my mother—were psychologically and emotionally abusive. Emotional blackmail. To me and to each other. I mean, I was raised on guilt. Whatever it was, it was my fault, even if it wasn't, and until I begged forgiveness there would be no making amends. Now, believe me, I was not an easy child. And as I grew up, I was not who he imagined I would be."

"But we're not talking about you . . . we're talking about your dad. You don't have to apologize to me. What I don't want is for this to transform into a therapy session for you, but I will just state, it's not possible for the child of a narcissist to be who their parent thinks they should be. It's just not possible. Because . . . well, that's part of what defines the experience of the child of a narcissist." I wasn't sure if I was trying to convince her of what I was saying or trying to remind myself. "Anyway, I want to ask you a couple more very specific questions. Through the course of your life, what has been your knowledge and understanding of your father's military experience?"

"This is my impression: My father enlisted in the Seabees, in part because of a sense of duty, partially because of finances and benefits, and possibly because he thought he could get away from the day-to-day responsibilities of having a family. But I don't know, that's just my impression. I believe he did what he was told, he was good at what he did, but he suffered shell shock, or battle fatigue—whatever they called it during World War II—and he has had extreme anxiety as a result of that. I was always told he had a medical discharge—honorable, but medical. I have gone my whole life without my father ever really talking about it . . . ever . . . and never really understanding what it was that he experienced."

"When I was a little boy I knew my grandfather was in the Navy. It was told to me. He told me. When you were growing up, a lot of kids your age had parents who had been in the military. So, when you were a little girl, did your father tell you he was in the Navy or the Seabees?"

"Before I was in kindergarten, I knew that he had been in the Navy. At that time, my mother had a job at Rohr industries in San Diego. They make parts for jet aircraft. And I remember very clearly associating that my father had been in the Navy and my mother worked in a factory helping to build jet engines. And I had a sailor hat that was one of my dad's from his time in the service. But he never talked about it. When I was much older, after my daughter Amy was born, which was in June of 1972, my parents, without any discussion, sold everything and moved our family to Utah. They wanted to avoid any potential interaction with Amy's father—who was actually a very nice person and about to start medical school—so they took me to another state. Right in the middle of my senior year of high school. That was very traumatic for me. So, we move into this house in Holladay, and I come home from school one day, and my dad is literally unconscious on the couch. He cannot move. And he stayed that way for a really long time. I later found out that he was having some kind of an 'episode'—now we call it PTSD—and that he was really not OK. During that same period of time, my aunt Evelyn was having some sort of mental breakdown. I thought the whole thing was kind of strange. I remember thinking, 'I hope none of this gets passed down genetically.'

"Anyway, after that I remember we started going to the VA hospital pretty regularly. By 1974, my dad was getting treatment that I knew about. Maybe he had treatment before and I just didn't know it. He was on some drug, probably Librium, for a very long time. I was told that he was having flashbacks and depression and anxiety caused by his war experience. They weren't calling it PTSD back then."

"Did you ever talk to your grandparents about what he was like before or after the war?"

"No. They died the year we moved here. And as I said before, my family really wasn't very communicative, so I never had that kind of discussion with them. It would be awesome if we could go back in time and ask all the questions we didn't think to ask when we were younger. They died within a couple months of each other, right after we moved to Utah."

"Do you remember when you were growing up your father's distaste for the Japanese?"

"Yes. Even as a small child I remember him referring to them as 'slanty-eyed devils.' When I was growing up, my father had friends who were African-American, he had friends who were Hispanic, guys that he worked with, but he called everybody a derogatory name. By the late 1960s, I realized that my father was a bigot. But his distaste for the Japanese was profound. And he did not get over that. As far as he was concerned, the Japanese were not OK."

"So, I'd like to wrap it up with one final question. You obviously know that I've spent a lot of time with your dad, and you probably know that there's things your dad has told me that he's never told anybody else. Things he's never discussed even with his psychologist. Knowing you as I do, I can't imagine that you haven't thought about what it is that he's revealed to me. So, I would ask you a two-part question: What do you think he may have told me, and what is your worst fear—when this project comes to an end, and you open up this book—that you might discover he has told me?"

"I don't understand the question . . . you want to know what I hope he has been telling you?"

"No. What do you think he has been telling me?"

"Well, what I think he's been telling you is what I hope he's been telling you; they're the same thing. I think he has been delineating his wartime experiences in detail, from his point of view. What he was personally experiencing, what he was going through, what he was doing on a day-to-day basis. Not just what he saw, what was going on around him . . . but what it was like for him. What *happened* to him. What was so traumatic that it sent him over the edge? And I have given it a lot of thought, way before you started this, which is why I'm so grateful that he would talk to you. I think that he saw people forced into situations where they did heinous things to human beings because of the situation that they were in. And then they were required to live with that . . . to just get on with their lives. And my expectation is that not only did he see those things, but he participated. And I think he feels that if he were to say these things to me, that it would change my perception of him, that I would not look at him the same way, that I would no longer see any good in him."

"And can you envision something being revealed that would indeed change the way you perceive him?"

"No." Catherine answered instantly, almost before I had finished asking the question, and without the slightest hint of uncertainty. "No. And I think that's because within my mind, whether it's fantasy or not, I have created a place where I'm OK with my dad. I'm OK with the things that I know about, I'm OK with the things I might not know about, and I'm OK with him."

"So, is there nothing that you could imagine that you would dread hearing?"

Again, Catherine answered without equivocation: "No. I even imagined that my father just couldn't take it and he actually shot himself, so that he could go home. I have imagined that he has looked someone in the eye and killed them, that he cut someone's head off, that he disemboweled someone. I have thought that he might have accidentally killed one of his own men. I have run through all of this in my head over the years. What could be so horrible that he will not speak of it? What could be so horrible that he thinks I wouldn't understand and I could not handle it? What are the most awful things I could think of? And the things I just mentioned are the worst things I could dredge up in my imagination. And in any of those scenarios, I am still OK with my father."

"Of course, there could be worse case scenarios than that."

"I suppose that's true. I've thought he could have been a defector."

"A defector? If he was a defector you would have been brought up in Tokyo."

"Well, he could have gone AWOL [Absent Without Leave]."

"That would be a deserter."

"Yeah . . . a deserter. That would really disappoint me. But then I've thought if he was a deserter it was probably due to some precipitating traumatic event. So, I've gone through all of this in my head, long before I ever met you, trying to understand my dad. As best I can. When I think about my dad, yeah, he's done a lot of things that are not nice. But when you are narcissist—you know—he is how he is. He's not going to change.

Someone with a personality disorder isn't going to change. He's almost ninety-six years old. He can't see beyond whatever his needs are. And it was always about him. I wish I had taken the opportunity before my mom died to have some kind of resolute conversation. A conversation where I got to find out about something other than the awful things. There had to be things that weren't awful. I would think. Sixty years is a long time to stay with someone. I wish I could have asked her what her perspective was about what happened to him during the war. That would have been compelling. But now she's gone, and I have no choice but to accept my father at face value. And that's why I'm so thankful that you're taking the time to talk to my dad, and that he's so willing to talk to you. Maybe I'll finally get some of the answers that I've been searching for. Maybe I'll finally get to know the truth about what the heck happened to my father."

CHAPTER 11

WAR IS UGLY

While my conversation with Catherine was certainly interesting, and provided me with some additional information about Murray's life and his relationships, it failed to yield any clues about the origins of his delusional thoughts. As I suspected, an interview with his sister was far more likely to be enlightening, so I tried calling her again.

"Hello, Evelyn, this is Dr. Scott Zuckerman calling. If you remember, we spoke on the phone last week, and I'd just like to ask you a few questions about your brother, Murray."

"Well, we got along just swell all our lives."

Excellent. At least this time she actually said something. I figured I'd better get right to the point before she changed her mind.

"Do you remember what Murray was like when he came home from the Navy after the war?"

"He was a nervous wreck when he came home, and he didn't want to talk about it. And I don't want to talk about it either. You can talk to Murray . . . I've had enough."

Click.

She hung up on me again. This appeared to be one tough old broad. Maybe the Navy should have signed her up back in 1943, instead of her brother. I decided to interview Murray's psychologist instead. I told Murray that I wanted to have a conversation with Dr. Rakhsha, and he consented, with the stipulation that I would not tell her any of the details he described in our discussions. I agreed, although I was a little bit disingenuous in the sense that I had every intention of disclosing to her the facts contained within his military records—facts that I had not yet even discussed with Murray himself. Murray signed the necessary documents allowing Dr. Rakhsha to talk to me, and

I set up an appointment to meet with her at her office in the VA hospital in Salt Lake City.

Gita Rakhsha, PhD, is an attractive woman of Iranian descent, and she has been practicing psychology since 1999. She has a youthful appearance that belies her many years of experience working with veterans suffering from PTSD. She is soft-spoken, chooses her words carefully, and speaks with just a hint of a Persian accent. She was fifteen minutes late for our appointment, and as soon as I sat down, she informed me that we'd only have about a half-hour before her next patient was expected to arrive. She began our conversation by asking me a rather pointed question: "I know you're writing a book about Murray, but I'm not really sure what you intend my role to be. I would like to ask you: What is your purpose in talking to me?"

"My purpose is two-fold. First, I'd like to get your impression of Murray. Obviously you cannot give me a thorough analysis, in just a few minutes, of a man who has had an issue for which he's been treated for many, many years. But I'd like to hear your general impression of him and his clinical circumstance. Secondly, I'd like to share with you some information that I have discovered. You and I are in a unique situation, because although you are Murray's psychologist, and therefore maintain strict confidentiality with him, he has given you permission to release information to me. He has not given me a similar consent; in other words, there are things that he has told me that he has requested that I do not reveal to anyone until after he is deceased. That being said, I am in possession of information that I obtained independently that I would like to share with you, and I would like to get your response to that information."

"That sounds great. And I want to let you know that my primary priority is for Murray's care. The bottom line is that my role is that of his psychologist. So, to that end I can absolutely share with you what my perspective is.

"In terms of his clinical issues . . . I don't know how much you know about PTSD, so forgive me if I'm telling you things you are already familiar with. PTSD is one of the possible reactions to having experienced a traumatic event, or events. There are many theories as to how and why it develops. Basically, there is an absolute physiologic impact. So it's not just psychological or emotional, although those are huge components of the condition. Neuroimaging evidence shows us that there are changes in the central nervous system, specifically in the cerebral cortex and the hippocampus.

"Our fundamental responsibility as human beings is survival, so we are wired to react to trauma in order to survive. There is a physiological response to traumatic events that is part of our natural survival reaction. That being said, we are equally wired with a natural process that allows us to recover from trauma. So, for example, if I'm hit by a red car, the next time I see a red car, I'm going to be anxious, and I may have many of the same physiological reactions that I experienced at the moment of the trauma. But in time my system resets itself; there is a cognitive and behavioral learning process that takes place. In PTSD that natural recovery process is somehow disrupted. So, in patients with PTSD, the fear or panic network of responses becomes established and it never resets.

"So, for example, with our Vietnam vets, it could be something as subtle as the air being balmy. This is not conscious; they are not aware of why they are experiencing the physiological moment of their trauma. But then the memory of the trauma can appear to them to be as equally life-threatening as the trauma itself. Their ability to discern between the event and their memory of the event has been erased."

At that moment, her phone rang and she took the call. As the clock kept ticking, I grew increasingly impatient, as I had a specific agenda to address in the already limited time that was made available to me—and it didn't necessarily include a dissertation about PTSD. As soon as Gita hung up the phone I abruptly tried to get the conversation back on track: "So how does all that apply to Murray?"

"There are very specific criteria for the diagnosis of PTSD. Criterion A is the experience of a traumatic event. It has to be a really significant stressor, one that changes your paradigm about life. It can be a something like having your own life threatened or witnessing the death of another person. Like if you saw your buddy get killed in front of you. So, in terms of Murray, he has that, right? He has seen life and death up close. He definitely experienced that."

"Can you tell me what he has shared with you about those experiences?"

"Well, the water running red because of the blood. Having seen throats slit. I mean, he has told me a whole bunch of things. What he's told me about his experiences is that first the bombers would go in, then the Marines, and then the Seabees would arrive, unload supplies, and then construct the landing strips. And that not all the Japanese were killed by the air strikes and there would be firefights, mostly during the night. He talks a lot about being wet and cold. And extremely hungry. So, he has numerous criterion A—he absolutely has had those. Criterion B are intrusive symptoms, in which the traumatic event is re-experienced. These can be recurrent, involuntary memories of the criterion A events. Nightmares. Flashbacks. Dissociative moments. For example, one of my Iraq veterans, when he sees a little heap of garbage on the road, for a split second he is back in Iraq when an IED [Improvised Explosive Device] exploded. Murray definitely has intrusive memories of the things he experienced—memories that he does not want to have. So, he absolutely has criterion B; he has nightmares, he's told me about hallucinations.

"Criterion C are avoidance symptoms. He doesn't want to think about it, he doesn't want to talk about it. If something comes on the TV he walks out of the room. He drank for a long time; he's told me about his drinking. A lot of our vets do that— it's the only way they can stay away from their memories. Murray is emotionally distant and he has intimacy issues. Some vets abandon their families entirely because emotional connection is so difficult. So, in terms of his diagnosis, he's told me plenty of avoidance symptoms, and his life story—from what I can gather—demonstrates them.

"Criterion D are negative changes in cognition or mood. So, persistent feelings of horror or helplessness. Feelings of guilt or shame—"

"Do you get a sense that he feels guilt about things that he did?"

"Oh, *absolutely.* Survivor's guilt is a huge part of PTSD."

"That's not the sort of guilt I'm talking about, although I believe that's true, too."

"Survivor's guilt, as you understand it—I think—is because 'my buddies died and I didn't.' But I refer to it as also being because of what you needed to do in order to survive. You kill civilians. You kill children. You do all kinds of things that your moral being is against. Murray has not told me specific things. But I have heard it from vets so many times that I don't have to hear it from him. I *know* he has done things because he needed to survive. Things that as a moral human being he cannot accept. That's part of the guilt. I just saw a Vietnam vet; that's his issue. He didn't have any other trauma, but he killed an officer—what's called fragging. So yeah, Murray hasn't told me those things specifically, but he doesn't need to. When he talks about guilt I can read it. I don't know the details, but you can fill in the blanks. War is ugly.

"The last cluster of symptoms, criterion E, is called hyperarousal. That's a chronically revved-up system: trouble sleeping, an exaggerated startle response. Murray is hypervigilant; he's always scanning for threats. He's told me about that. Like he sleeps with his gun. Under his pillow! From what he has told me—and his daughter has corroborated—he has exhibited these symptoms."

I noticed Gita glancing at the clock, and I realized our time was dwindling.

"When I met you at Murray's home, I had just found out that he was not on the particular island that he thought he was, specifically Iwo Jima. This is not supposition on my part; I have very substantial evidence—and gathering evidence dating back to WWII is a very difficult task. I'm sure I don't have to tell you that. You and I had a discussion about whether I should tell him about that discrepancy and how he might react to it. You advised against it, but I went ahead and told him anyway. And he had a very interesting reaction to it. First he became angry with me; then he became confused. Catherine told me he had a pretty tough night; that he didn't sleep well and that he was a little angry at her for giving me the letters that led to my discovery in the first place. But his words to me were, 'If you find any other holes in this whole thing I want to know about it.' I thought that was a really positive sign, that he really wanted to know the truth."

"Good."

"Anyway, I would like to share some information with you, and while you don't owe me any degree of confidentiality, I would not want you to discuss this with either Murray or his daughter, at least not at this point in time. It took me several months, but I have finally come into possession of Murray's original military records."

"Wow."

"What would you say if I told you that he never saw combat?"

"That's interesting." There was a lengthy pause as Gita stared at me, her face entirely devoid of any emotion whatsoever. "He never saw combat? Really? I would be surprised."

She didn't seem surprised. At least outwardly she appeared entirely calm and cool. I dropped what I thought was a bombshell right in her lap, and her voice didn't change; not one bit. If she was surprised then she was doing a damned good job of hiding it. I have to admit I was annoyed by her lack of reaction.

"I've done quite a bit of research to finally come to that conclusion. When Murray told me about his first combat experience, he talked about being on the island of Majuro, about men that he had killed, about the water being red with the blood of his comrades. But when I looked into it, I found out that there was no combat on Majuro—the Japanese had abandoned the island before the invasion took place. I didn't really think too much of that; I thought he was just confused. I thought it had just become one big battle in his mind; that it didn't really matter what island he was on. What's really the difference, anyway? People are shooting at you . . . it doesn't matter the name of the island where you were being shot at."

"That's absolutely right."

"That being said, every military source I have found states that there was no combat on Majuro. Based on the documentation I have in my possession, when the fighting on Iwo Jima was happening, he was in California. And there is nothing in his record to suggest he was ever in combat. In fact, there are documents that specifically state that he never saw combat. And in December 1944, just four months before he was discharged, he wrote a letter asking to be released from the Navy."

"Really? On what grounds?"

"Ostensibly to help his father run his business, because of his family's economic hardships. Interestingly, in that letter he specifically says that he had been overseas, but he does not mention having been in combat. I would think that if I were trying desperately to get out of the military, that I would mention that I had been in harm's way, that I had been fired upon by the enemy."

"Yeah. That is interesting."

"And then I have all the medical reports from his military file. In February 1945, he was given a diagnosis of 'Psychoneurosis,

Anxiety neurosis #1517.' The language they used then seems to be quite different than our terminology today. And in March 1945, there is an entry which includes some particularly interesting details of his past medical history: had nightmares until age thirteen, enuretic until age twelve, walked in sleep until age twelve, afraid of the dark until age thirteen, afraid of the water. And that report clearly states, 'Saw no combat.' When I read those words I was stunned."

"How did you react?"

"Well, quite frankly, I was stunned. You seem to be a much more calm individual than I am—your response to this information is far less effusive than mine was." I was becoming increasingly irritated by her stoic reaction. "And then I have the report of the Board of Medical Survey, which states, 'fifteen months duty outside the continental United States but never experienced combat action.' That report directly resulted in his discharge, because of this so-called psychoneurosis or anxiety neurosis disorder: 'this man is unfit for retention in the service.'"

"Oh. Interesting."

"To me it's beyond interesting. Because I believe that he really believes that he was in combat. This is not a guy who I believe is bullshitting me. The things he has told me . . . he is certainly not portraying himself as being heroic. Not in any way. As I said, I promised him that I wouldn't share specifics with you. But he admitted to me that he committed war crimes. And he described them in very explicit detail."

"Do you think those things actually happened?"

"Well, they all supposedly took place on the field of battle, so if it's true that he never saw combat, how could those incidents have possibly happened? Have you ever seen such a thing? Does this information change his diagnosis?"

"Well, that's very interesting. Because he exhibits all the symptoms. When I think about his diagnosis, and how he presents, he's so classical. There's no 'ifs' and 'buts' about it; in his case it's just so classical for PTSD. So, when you ask me if this changes his diagnosis, I want to say, 'as reported by him and his family, no.'" Suddenly Gita appeared much more intrigued, as if the information I had unloaded on her had finally sunk in. And she stopped looking at the clock.

"But by the criteria you just told me, the diagnosis of PTSD requires substantial trauma."

"That's what I'm the most curious about. What was it? Because I see him as a sincere person. You asked me if I have seen this before. We have vets who come in and they have learned how to report PTSD so they can get service-connected disability payments. So, there's that secondary gain there, and we have to be aware of that. But in Murray's case I believe there is no secondary gain. I've worked with him pretty intimately, and I think he's very sincere."

"I agree with you. I believe that every ounce of his soul is convinced he was on Iwo Jima. This is not a man who was trying to convince me that he saw that flag-raising so I'd write some great book about him. By the way he acts, and by the things he's told me, that's not what this guy is about at all. So, have you seen a case like this? Where a veteran really believes he was in a circumstance that he never actually experienced?"

"Have I seen fabrication of facts? In order to explain one's experience? Yes. Most definitely yes. And it's not unique to PTSD. Fabricating data, not because of secondary gain, but because you need to understand what you have experienced. I've seen that before. But I'm wondering, if he really didn't experience any of those things, but he has these vivid memories and images . . . that's what I'm curious about. How did he get the details of his criterion A events? I don't know how he did that. Thinking about how people do that, it may be that he heard it from other veterans—maybe when he was in the hospital. And when did he start experiencing these symptoms? It sounds like maybe since childhood. And let's talk about childhood stuff. Because he has predisposing factors that I didn't know about until just now. Like if he had nightmares all his life, if he was an anxious child—those are important details to think about.

"But I'm just so curious about how he developed his criterion A. As a psychologist, that's the real interesting thing for me. That's a key issue. You can develop PTSD through vicarious experience of traumatic events. Vicarious traumatization is something that psychologists need to address. Maybe that's what happened. He heard horror stories at a time when he was not processing information in a coherent way. Maybe. Who knows?"

"I've been trying to interview his sister, because I would like to find out from her what he was like before the war and what he was like after. And she is probably the only person alive today who might remember what he said about his experiences when he first came home. But even though Murray called her, and he tried to convince her to talk to me, she's hung up on me twice. She doesn't want to talk to me."

"Because why?"

"Well, I think because she's a very grumpy ninety-year-old woman. I'm not going to give up trying, but I may have to accept the fact that she just won't talk to me. She may already know what you and I have only recently discovered. But I don't have any way of confirming that unless she opens up to me. That being said, so far, I have not shared this information with either Murray or Catherine. But I would like to tell him about it, for two very distinct reasons. Number one, I think his reaction to this information becomes a part of his story . . . and his story has taken a very bizarre turn."

"It has."

"And I still think this is a fascinating story, because I've never heard of any WWII vet have this story. And I don't know if a story like this has ever been published."

"'A story like this' . . . meaning what?"

"Look, I started this project just to document an old guy's war record. A history that he never shared with anybody. Like a lot of the WWII vets didn't tell anybody. And that's all I wanted to do: get his story and eventually share it with his family. And then he starts telling me about these war crimes and atrocities that he committed, and it became a very different story. Quite frankly, it became a story about the horrors of war, and how we should be careful judging the guys in the military today, who are on video all the time. Because the guys back then did the same things; maybe worse."

"Well, who knows?"

"Well definitely the things Murray told me were worse than anything you might have read in a newspaper in 1944. But in any event, now it's become the story of this psychological tragedy that has taken place within this man's mind. And he seems to have lived his whole life believing that he did these terrible things. But in fact, he didn't do them.

"And that brings me to the second reason that I would like to tell him about this at some point. I believe that he bears a great burden for the things that he thinks he has done. One of the things he told me, at the end of a particularly tough interview—one in which he confessed something that really took me by surprise—he looked me in the eye and he said, 'I never wanted my family to know what a cold-hearted bastard I was.' And I believe that he really feels that way. And I think— and maybe you can tell me if I'm wrong—that maybe it would help him to not have that burden, and to not have to carry that heavy weight with him to the end of his life. You said earlier that he absolutely feels guilt about the things that he did. I might be able to relieve him of that guilt. For example, he told me about a close friend of his, whom he said was blown to bits right next to him. I don't know if he ever talked to you about that."

"Not specifically, no."

"Well that obviously didn't happen."

"Not if he wasn't in combat."

"It took quite a bit of research, but I discovered that his friend wasn't killed in combat; that he was discharged from the Navy, went home and had a family, and died in 1981 in his home town in Texas. And I'd like to share that information with Murray, to alleviate some of his guilt. What are your thoughts about that? What do you think about me revealing these facts to him?"

"I have mixed reactions to that. Let me talk it out with you. I understand the possible potential benefit of releasing him of that burden. However, if you have lived a life with a certain narrative, and you are perhaps a few months away from your death—let's hope he lives longer—and then all of a sudden someone comes to you and says, 'You've lived a lie,' that's pretty discombobulating. Especially since we agree that he really does experience these things as his reality, like all these events really happened. Think about a person who at age twenty-five is told, 'Oh by the way you were adopted.' Somehow, that just messes up things—as if their whole life has been a lie. I'm concerned about that, especially if he doesn't have enough time to come to terms with it. So that's my one reaction. I'm curious to know what he said when you told him he wasn't on Iwo Jima. How did he explain the fact that he had come up with that idea?"

"Well, at first he was angry at me. And then he was clearly distraught. Then the physician in me, the caring friend in me . . . well, quite honestly, I helped him with that explanation. I said, 'When you landed on the island, was there a big sign that said 'Welcome to Iwo Jima?'' And when I asked him how he knew he was on Iwo Jima, he told me that he found out later.

So, I tried to explain to him that this sort of confusion happens to all of us; that it happens to my wife and me. And he seemed to be able to accept that . . . sort of. But of course, this is a much bigger fish, the fact that he was never shot at."

"Yeah. That's incredible. When I think about you telling him that none of this really happened . . . I don't know. Does he have the capacity to digest that? I just thought of something . . . I want to look up something in his records. Aha! It says right here: 'Combat Vet Status: NOT ELIGIBLE.' So according to this record he is not a combat vet. That is pretty compelling evidence that what you have discovered is true."

At this point Gita was fully engaged. The time she had initially allotted for our interview had long since elapsed. She was obviously just as astonished by this strange turn of events as I was, in spite of her unflappable appearance. I tried to convince her that telling him the truth was the right thing to do: "The things he has told me he's done, which I believe he believes he has done, are horrifying to him. I believe that he is ashamed."

"Absolutely."

"So, I wonder if he is reaching out from his subconscious, questioning his own experience, trying perhaps to receive some measure of exoneration. I don't know. But I think it's a very powerful statement for him to have asked me to tell him if I find any more discrepancies in his story."

"Yes. That's right. And he is so guilt-ridden. But not just about the things he did in the war. He feels enormous guilt about how poorly he treated his wife. He talks about that all the time. And how bad of a father he was to his daughters. Although at the same time he thinks of himself as a good father. He is so very conflicted; this internal battle is ongoing all the time about many, many different issues. So what function might this fabrication have served for him? Maybe it was a way of explaining his behavior. Maybe it served as a way of explaining why he was such a bad dad or a bad husband. When I think about it in that context, he'll be even more shattered if you tell him the facts you have discovered. I don't know if he has the capacity to gain any benefit, accept it, integrate it, be fine with it. I don't know that he will be able to accept the fact that all of this—his entire life—has been a lie."

"You may be right. But that being said, does he deserve to know the truth? Doesn't he have the right to know the truth about his own life? Whether it's good for him or not. Sometimes the truth is painful."

"I don't know. When we talk with demented patients, there is something called validating therapy. Confronting them is not helpful. They say, 'It's Sunday; I must go to church,' when it's Thursday. You want to be with them in such a way that you don't keep shattering them. To say, 'No, it's not Sunday; we're not going to church' does not help them. And doing that over and over can be quite cruel. Everyone has the right to be cared for. The truth may appear to be logical, but there is also an ethical component. Murray's truth is not what the truth is. So, I would ask you a different question: Does he deserve for his truth—the truth he has lived with for who knows how many years—does he deserve for that truth to be shattered? Do you see what I mean? That question is from a different perspective. So how would you respond to that, as both a scientist and an ethical person?"

"To me the answer is not so clear-cut. I've thought about two possible endings to this story. He's never revealed any suicidal ideation to me; if he had I would certainly have shared that with you. But I can imagine somebody committing suicide over something like this."

"Well, he has expressed thoughts of suicide in the past."

"But on the other hand, I can also imagine this weight being lifted from him. Realizing that he was not the cold-blooded, heartless person that he thought he was."

"That is not going to happen. That's my opinion. But I could be wrong. First it would require that he could integrate the information."

"Well, that'd be your job."

"No; really, it's his job. Sure, I can help him with it. Look, you may provide him with data, but how he receives it, and digests it, and what he does with it . . . that's not a simple process, as you can imagine. Having the facts doesn't necessarily correct the situation. It may, or it may not. As I see it, you want him to know the truth. I'm not at all questioning your motives; I'm sure you want only what's best for him. I'm just not so sure it would simply lift this burden off his shoulders. In fact, I think a greater burden might be placed on him. Like: 'I've lived a lie. Why did I come up with these thoughts?' I think that will potentially be very disorienting. Of course, I don't know that for sure.

I do know, given his personality, that when he is presented with something that's hard for him to accept—you've seen him—he gets dis-integrated.

"You know, as I'm talking to you I keep thinking about what you've shared with me about his childhood. That is so interesting to me. It sounds like it wasn't really solid, so he comes into all this pathology in a very honest way."

"Do you think he is a narcissist?"

"Oh! Up the wazoo! Yeah. Absolutely. And why does someone become a narcissist? It's a woundedness to the core self. That's what I'm saying: There's something in his childhood that led to all this. And he's carried that with him through his military service and now into his nineties. Given that—if you confront him with, 'Hey buddy, you're wrong'—as his psychologist, I don't see the need to do that. I see the potential harm more than anything else. If you want me to be really direct, that would be my answer."

"I can appreciate that. I know that you have a very strong commitment to him and his family, and I would ask you not to share this information with his daughter."

"I will not discuss this with her. Quite frankly, I need to process this myself. I need to understand this better. For me, finding this out . . . I've been working with someone who was not in combat but has told me all these things. See what I mean . . . seriously? This is very disorienting! You know what I mean?"

"I know exactly what you mean. When I got his records in the mail, and I discovered all this . . . quite honestly, I didn't sleep at all that night. I couldn't stop thinking about the whole thing."

"And you're an intact person! So, if you and I, pretty intact people—maybe neurotic in some ways, but nevertheless intact—if we experience this like, 'Wow,' imagine what he will experience. This is heavy-duty stuff. I *love* my job. It's fascinating doing trauma work. The presentations are so varied. What the psyche can do and how it can fool you. I know people develop false memories. But to this extent, having worked with someone based on the understanding that he's seen combat . . . I don't know. I need to get a grasp of 'Now what?' I feel like my work with him will be affected by this. I'm thinking about certain things to ask him about. Like I wonder what would have happened if he had never joined the service."

"You know, he once made a statement to me that I've never heard from another World War II veteran. When I asked him what was the biggest mistake he ever made in his life, he said, 'Joining the military.' I've heard that said by veterans of more recent wars, but the so-called 'Greatest Generation'? I've never heard somebody from back then say something like that."

"I know. I was very surprised the first time he said it. And he has said it numerous times. It's like there is no sense of pride about what he's done, in spite of the fact that he did serve overseas. He was clearly ashamed of who he was—anxious, nervous, cheating on his wife. So, it would make sense that fabricating the combat experience was really about the avoidance of self. It's like he created this whole other person. But, of course that was never conscious on his part . . . or at least it isn't conscious now. Wow! This is the most fascinating thing! I can't wait to read your book."

CHAPTER 12

TOMORROW I'LL FORGET YOU

Gita escorted me out of her office and helped me find my way back to the hospital lobby. As we were walking down the stairs, she asked me about how this whole project got started in the first place. I recounted to her how when I first met Murray I simply saw him as a crotchety old man, then later as a mighty veteran of combat who had been robbed of his strength by the inevitable onslaught of time. As his story unfolded I began to see him as a man who had committed heinous acts in a time of war—acts that he would not have committed otherwise, and of which he was deeply ashamed. But now I found myself looking at him in an altogether different way—as that fragile, nervous thirteen-year-old boy who had nightmares and was afraid of the dark and struggled to earn the approval of a father who was distant and cold, and whose psychological torment has stayed with him, hidden beneath his crusty façade, for the entirety of his ninety-six years. And as I was talking to her I found myself rather unexpectedly overcome by emotion, and I could feel the tears welling up in my eyes. But I fought back those tears because for crying out loud you don't have to weep every time you have a conversation with a shrink.

Gita commented that it was remarkable to her how moved I appeared to be, and how deeply I had been affected by Murray, and by his story. And she made an interesting observation: that maybe my empathy for Murray relates back to my own childhood experience. I knew that she could probably see right through my strenuous effort to hold off those tears. As I returned to the sanctuary of my car, the tears flowed freely. I hadn't anticipated the depth of my feelings for Murray, now evoked by thinking about him as an innocent, wounded little boy. I also recognized what a talented psychologist Gita must be to have been able to get such an accurate handle on me after only a brief encounter. Of course, on the other hand, up until today she had been treating Murray for PTSD caused by a trauma that never happened, having been positively convinced that everything Murray had described to her was real.

After meeting with Gita, I was no better informed as to the etiology of Murray's fabricated memories. I absolutely, without a doubt, had to interview his sister. I went to visit Murray and asked him to talk to Evelyn once more on my behalf. Right in front of me he picked up the phone and called her, admonishing her to talk to me and answer my questions. When he hung up, he declared, "OK, she's agreed to talk to you. The next time you call she'll definitely talk to you."

I immediately went home and called her.

"Hello, Evelyn. This is Dr. Scott Zuckerman. Murray told me that he spoke to you and that you've agreed to share your memories with me."

"Well, what I can remember would just be a drop in the bucket."

"But won't you share that drop with me?"

"I'd sooner not."

Click.

What the fuck?! Was this old crow some sort of a sociopath, intentionally trying to torment me? I'd just heard her tell Murray she'd talk to me, not a half hour ago, and now she'd hung up on me again. For the third time! I called Murray and told him what had just happened.

"Well, I guess she really doesn't want to talk to you. There's nothing more I can do. She can be pretty stubborn once her mind is made up." Talk about the pot calling the kettle black.

I decided to take a different approach. I called Catherine and asked her to intervene, to see if she could convince her aunt to speak to me. About a week later Catherine called me with the result of her efforts: Evelyn did agree to an interview, but only on the condition that Murray be present throughout our conversation. I knew this wasn't optimal, because with Murray there I wouldn't necessarily be inclined to ask certain questions, and I might not be able to rely on Evelyn to give me candid answers. But it was better than nothing, and damned sure better than getting hung up on again. So, a couple of days later I loaded Murray into my car and we took the fifteen-minute drive to Evelyn's house, which essentially consisted of Murray criticizing every aspect of my driving for approximately fifteen minutes. He was even more like my own father than I had come to realize.

I brought Evelyn a box of milk chocolates from See's Candies in Salt Lake City, having been informed by Catherine that those were her favorite treat. After a cursory introduction, we settled into the living room, Murray on a sofa in front of the TV and Evelyn and I facing one another in a pair of armchairs on the other side of the room. I turned on every bit of charm I could muster.

"Evelyn, this is a very nice little house. How long have you been living in this house?"

"Since 1944."

"You've been living here in this same house since 1944? Wow, that's very special."

"I lost my husband four years ago. He and I moved in here together in 1944. And Murray and Phyllis lived right next door, on the corner. They had a house there, but it's since been torn down. My husband was a wonderful man. He absolutely adored me."

"I'm sorry for your loss. You know, Murray has told me that I could write his life story . . . his biography. He's told me everything that he could remember, and I've found out a lot of other stuff that he didn't tell me."

"You probably found out a lot of stuff that he didn't want you to find out."

"I don't know . . . maybe I did."

Murray appeared to be watching TV, but he was obviously listening to every word, and interrupted: "Yeah, well there's a lot of stuff that I didn't tell you."

Evelyn cackled a sadistic little laugh and repeated what Murray had just said: "Ha ha, see, there's a lot of stuff he didn't tell you."

I turned my attention to Murray.

"Is that true? That's the first time you're telling me that."

"Well, I'm being honest with you now."

"You weren't being honest with me before?"

"Yeah, well, we talked and I answered all your questions. But I didn't come forth with everything about my whole life."

Right at that critical moment, Evelyn's grandson abruptly entered the room. A wiry, scruffy man with a wisp of a mustache, he was wearing a t-shirt and shorts . . . and an ankle monitor. Evelyn proudly introduced him: "This is my grandson

Raymond. He lives with me. He takes care of his grandma. I took care of him when he was a baby, and now that he's an adult, he's taking care of me."

Raymond put his hand on Evelyn's shoulder and said, "Yeah, payback's a bitch. But I guess you must've done something right, now you've got somebody to watch after you."

I had immediately learned two things: that Raymond had inherited his grandmother's charming demeanor, and that whatever the reason was that he was under house arrest, I'd be best served to not do anything to irritate the old lady. After Raymond left the room I turned my attention back to Murray.

"Tell me what you're talking about. What sort of things didn't you tell me?"

"I didn't tell you I played hopscotch."

"See, now you're just pulling my leg."

Evelyn put in her two cents: "No, he's telling you the truth. We played hopscotch together."

I felt like after just five minutes my interview was deteriorating into some sort of a surrealistic nightmare. I half-expected Rod Serling to come out any minute and say, "Scott Zuckerman, a man on a journey into the twisted minds of two elderly lunatics . . . a journey that can only end . . . in the Twilight Zone." Actually, right about then Rod Serling would have been a welcome addition to the room.

I tried to redirect the dialogue: "So, let me ask you something, Evelyn. I called you on the phone a couple of times, maybe you don't remember."

"Oh yes, I remember."

"And you didn't want to talk to me."

"No, I didn't."

"Is that because you think Murray has some secrets that he doesn't want me to know about?"

"Yes, that's right."

Murray interjected again: "You can tell him anything you want, honey."

Evelyn chuckled that same little evil laugh and said, "I'm not going to tell him anything, 'cause I'm not talking to him. He's the one that's talking. I told him before he came here I wasn't going to say anything, and I'm not. Whatever you told him, he knows, and that's it."

It's hard to imagine, but the conversation was actually going downhill.

"Murray, what kind of secrets are you talking about? And don't give me any more nonsense about hopscotch. Are they secrets you've kept from your sister also?"

Evelyn answered, "No, I know all his secrets."

Murray responded, "I cheated on my wife."

"Well, that isn't a secret, because you've told me that."

Evelyn concurred: "And Phyllis knew it . . . she found out about it."

There was a brief but uncomfortable silence before Evelyn continued: "We all have secrets. Haven't you got a secret? We all had a little shady life somewhere in our past."

"Well, that's fair enough. But I actually don't have any secrets. I'm writing my own life story, my autobiography, but I've put that on hold to write about Murray."

"How did you find out about Murray?"

"I am Catherine's doctor, and I met Murray when he moved in with Catherine. And I'd like to think that Murray and I became friends. Wouldn't you say we're friends, Murray?"

"I would say so, yes."

"And when I found out that Murray served in the military overseas during World War II, I started talking to him about his experiences, and he agreed to let me write his story. And he's told me many things, but right now, I'm very curious to know what sort of secrets he's kept from me. Are they secrets from your service in the war, or secrets from before the war?"

Murray didn't look away from the TV, but he gave me a curt answer: "Before. During. After. Now if you'll excuse me, I'm watching this program."

At that particular moment, there was a commercial for dishwashing liquid on the TV. Evelyn cackled her wicked laugh again and I was getting annoyed.

"Murray, don't give me a hard time. We've been through a lot together, you and me."

"You came here to talk to her . . . so talk to her."

"But you're the one who just told me you've been keeping secrets from me, after all the time we've spent talking to each other. There's something else going on here, but I don't know what it is. I mean, do you guys have some secret together? Is that what it is? Something from your childhood?"

Murray answered, "No, not that I know of. We never played doctor, if that's what you're getting at."

Murray's comment prompted another acerbic snicker from his sister. The two of them were really testing my patience.

"That's not what I mean. You know that. Evelyn, do you feel like you guys had a happy childhood?"

This time the old battle-axe actually answered my question.

"Very happy. Yes. We had a very happy childhood, both of us."

"Murray told me that he didn't have a close relationship with your father. Did you have a close relationship with your dad?"

"Yes. We were very close."

"Do you agree with Murray's assessment that the two of them weren't that close?"

"I'm not answering you."

"I'm only asking your opinion. Do you feel that Murray and your dad were close to one another?"

"I thought they were."

"Murray, do you remember you told me about your relationship with your dad? Do you stand by what you told me before?"

"Yeah. Evelyn had a closer relationship with our father. Because she was the youngest."

Evelyn interjected, "Yes, I was the youngest, and I was spoiled." Somehow, I had no problem believing that. I went back to the task at hand.

"So, Evelyn, according to you, Murray has some secret. You said we all have secrets, and Murray has some secret."

"Yes."

"And you know what that secret is."

"Yes."

"But you ain't telling me."

"Yes."

I was truly perplexed as to how I could possibly proceed. I felt like I was back in medical school, at Kings County Hospital, doing my psychiatry rotation in the lockdown unit in Building G. The police would round up various miscreants they had found wandering the streets of Brooklyn, and drop them off for an evaluation. Some were drunks or drug addicts, some were schizophrenic, some were just homeless people down on their luck. I'd sit in a small, stark room with these individuals, just me and them and a wooden desk with a little button under it that you were supposed to push if you were in trouble. To this day I don't think those buttons were hooked up to anything; they were just there to give you something to do while you were being attacked by the patient. In any case, I had a very specific list of questions I was supposed to ask, and more often than not I'd get back a blank stare, a mumble, or at best a one-word response. Sitting there with Evelyn, staring at me with her beady little eyes and a smirk on her wrinkled face, I realized that after all my years as a doctor, I was no more adept at cracking these sorts of nuts now than I was then. After a lengthy silence, during which time I pondered whether Evelyn's coffee table might have had a little button under it, Murray finally spoke up.

"I don't know what it is either. I don't know what she's talking about."

"But you just said there are things that you haven't told me. I can't imagine what kind of secrets you would have kept from me, Murray, after all the things you've already told me. And you've told me those things in confidence—I'm not going to tell your sister the things you've told me. I haven't told anybody anything that you've told me."

"I asked my wife for a divorce one time. She became hysterical, and she fainted. This was while we were living in California. I've been sorry for that ever since."

Evelyn looked more serious, and she wasn't laughing anymore.

"She loved Murray. She'd have had to have loved him, to have put up with all his nonsense."

Murray agreed: "Yes, she would've. I was a no-good SOB to do all the stuff I did."

Evelyn seemed to be a little angry now.

"Why does he have to tell you his secrets, anyway?"

"He doesn't have to tell me anything. I'm trying to write his story, and I'm trying to be truthful about it. He never had to talk to me in the first place. I asked him, and he agreed. You understand? I'm not forcing anybody to do anything. I like Murray very much, and I'm not trying to do anything to harm him. Really, I just want to tell his story."

Murray interrupted: "And you're not going to tell it until after I've passed on."

"That is correct. And haven't I held true to my word so far?"

"Yeah."

I turned my attention back to Evelyn, and decided to be more direct: "Evelyn, I'll tell you I think we both know the same secret. That's my opinion."

Murray stopped looking at the TV and turned toward me: "What is it you think?"

"Well . . . I'm not really going to say right now."

Murray repeated himself: "What do you think the secret is?"

I repeated myself: "I'm not going to say right now."

Evelyn interjected and pointed at Murray.

"He wants *you* to say."

I turned toward Evelyn.

"Actually, I don't want Murray to say . . . I want *you* to say."

"Oh, well I told you before you came I wasn't going to tell you anything."

"I know. I know. And I think you're a very honest woman. You're true to your word." At this point I was smiling at her, resigned to the fact that the two of us were like an irresistible force meeting an immovable object. I actually felt a bit of admiration for the old bag. She was tenaciously guarding her brother's privacy, much as I would if he had been my brother. I decided to abandon, at least temporarily, this entire line of questioning in an effort to at least get some sort of a meaningful dialogue started.

"Evelyn, let's forget about Murray for a minute, and I'm just going to ask you about yourself and your own opinions. When Murray left and joined the Navy, you weren't a child at the time; you were a young woman. Do you remember how you felt back then? Were you worried about him, were you scared, were you proud of him?"

"I was mad at him."

Her answer took me by surprise.

"You were mad at him?"

"Well, yes. He didn't have to go . . . he volunteered. He had two children, and he didn't have to go. I didn't want him to go, and I was mad at him. He probably didn't know that."

Murray, still engaged in the conversation while pretending to watch the television, responded: "No, I didn't know that. At the time, I had no concern for anybody else but me. I didn't care about my wife nor my children."

"Do you think his wife was mad at him too?"

"No, I don't think she was ever mad at him, no matter what he did."

"You know, Evelyn, your response is very interesting to me. Nowadays we look back on World War II and we assume most people had this patriotic fervor, especially after the Japanese attacked Pearl Harbor. We hear about all the men joining the military, and everybody being patriotic, and here you are, an intelligent woman who was a young adult at the time, and you were not proud of your brother for enlisting, but you felt angry at him for doing so. Don't you think that people would find that to be interesting?"

"Probably. I never thought of it. I wasn't mad at him to the stage where I wouldn't talk to him or anything; I was just mad that he did it."

"Did you and Murray correspond while he was in the military?"

"No."

"You know, I have all the letters that Murray wrote back home to Phyllis. They're very interesting . . . kind of a snapshot of that moment in history."

Murray interrupted again: "Where did you get them from?"

"Remember Jason found them in the garage?"

"No, I don't remember that."

Evelyn said, almost apologetically, "We're both getting old and forgetful."

"I understand. Murray, do you remember that you gave me permission to get all your military records from the government?"

"I do remember that."

"You know, that was a long time ago that you gave me permission to get those records. But you never asked me if I ever got them."

"Well, because I didn't care whether you did or not."

"What do you think is in those records, Murray?"

"I have no idea. And I don't care. Because it isn't true. Military records are not accurate. Because they come from unreliable sources."

"Military records come from unreliable sources? Give me an example of what you mean by that."

"The officers that related certain incidents to the military hospital . . . their records were not accurate at all. They said what they wanted to say, and that's it. Not what it really was."

"So, you're saying that whatever is in your military records is false."

"Well I don't know what's in those records, so I can't say."

"And you don't care."

"No, I really don't care. What will be, will be. And what is, is."

Ah, there was the cryptic Murray Jacobs that I had come to know so well. I turned my attention back to his sister.

"Evelyn, you told me on the phone that when Murray came home from the military he was a 'nervous wreck.' Do you remember telling me that on the telephone?"

Evelyn looked annoyed that she had even revealed that tidbit of information, but she wasn't a liar so she had to confess.

"That's right, he was."

"Was he a kind of a nervous guy before he went into the military? Do you think he changed a lot while he was in the Navy?"

Evelyn gave me her Wicked Witch of the West stare for about a minute. I was waiting for her to threaten me with, "I'll get you, my pretty, and your little dog, too!" Instead she snarled, "If you want some answers about Murray you can ask him, don't ask me."

"But he can't answer me what he was like. If you said to me, 'What kind of a person are you?' I could give you an answer. But to get at the truth you'd have to ask my wife. I'm just trying to write a book. Quite honestly, you're the last living person who remembers him from before he went into the military."

Murray interjected: "When I got home I was like a fish out of water. I didn't know what I was doing or where I was going. I was no bargain before I went into the service, but I wasn't like that."

"Do you agree with that statement, Evelyn? Will you at least tell me that much?"

"I'd just as soon not say anything to you."

"I'm not sure what to make of that. He's telling me he was one way before he went into the Navy, and a very different way after. And you're not answering the question."

The old crow was starting to get riled up: "Because I already told you I'm not going to answer any of your questions. How many times do I have to tell you the same thing?"

"I understand. But I'm not really trying to get you to reveal any deep, dark secrets; I'm just trying to get your opinion of your brother. Like when you were a little girl, was he a good older brother to you? When you were five and he was eight, do you remember having fun together?"

I got the evil stare again, as the old woman begrudgingly mumbled "Uh-huh" under her breath.

"And when you were fifteen and he was eighteen did you still feel the same way about him?" This time she didn't say anything, but nodded affirmatively. She looked pissed off that I had somehow managed to squeeze an actual answer out of her. I was really starting to get irritated by how curmudgeonly the two of them were behaving. And I was disappointed in myself, for being unable to either charm or deceive a demented old woman into offering me the slightest bit of cooperation. My frustration led me to say something that I had not necessarily intended to say. But I was trying desperately to get some sort of a useful response from either of them.

"So, Murray, let me ask you a question. And maybe Evelyn will answer me and maybe she won't. There's something I found in your military record that you didn't tell me about. While you were overseas a lot of people back home were writing letters to get you discharged from the Navy. Do you remember that?"

"No, I don't. I do not remember that."

Evelyn chimed in immediately and for once gave me a definitive answer: "That never happened."

"I have those letters in my possession." After a half-hour of listening to Evelyn's stonewalling, it gave me pleasure to give her a piercing look of my own and confront her with the facts. At the very least I had gotten Murray's full attention. He asked, "Who were the letters from?"

"The letters were from your father, and his doctor, and the bishop of the local ward, and from a few other prominent citizens. They all said that your dad was very sick and was having a hard time running his shop."

Now Murray was pissed off.

"I don't know where you got all that crap from."

"I got it from the military; it's all in your service record."

"Well, that's what I'm talking about—the military does anything. I never seen the letters you're talking about at all. Not at all. That's a bunch of malarkey."

Evelyn attested to Murray's statement: "It isn't true."

"But I have those letters."

I had really gotten under Murray's skin. He barked at me, "Fine."

"So, are you saying that the military forged those documents?"

"Yes, I am. Yes, I am. I certainly am. Along with a lot of other stuff too. And there's nothing you nor I can do to change it, either."

"Do you have any idea why they would do something like that? Why would they care to forge letters from a bishop, or a barber, or from your father for that matter?"

"I have no idea."

"And why would all the letters say that your father was very sick and that he couldn't run his business and that you need to come home from the military to help him?"

"I don't know. I've never heard that."

Evelyn agreed: "This is the first time I've heard it, too."

"Well, I hope you don't think that I'm making it up."

"I don't know."

That comment from Murray stung.

"Really? Do you think that I would make something like that up, Murray? After all the time we've spent together?"

"Well, why would the military make up something like that?"

"I don't know."

"I don't know either."

"Well, why would I make it up?"

"You wouldn't."

"Right. I wouldn't. So as far as you're concerned, and as far as you remember, Evelyn, that never happened. Nobody back home ever wrote a letter to the military, and you don't remember your dad being sick with an ulcer while you were overseas."

Evelyn answered emphatically, "No."

And Murray agreed: "He wasn't sick."

I tried a bit of sarcasm.

"It's very fascinating to me that the military would create a whole scenario like that. I can't imagine why they would do that. Obviously, neither of you remembers it happening so it must never have happened."

Suddenly, Murray's position softened a bit.

"Well, if it did happen I don't remember it. I have no memory of that at all. I'm sure if they had written those letters then Evelyn would have heard something about it."

"Well she's already said she's not telling me, even if she had; but it seems to me that Evelyn doesn't remember any of this happening."

Murray addressed his sister: "Do you know anything about this, Evelyn?"

Evelyn spoke in a much more agreeable voice as she answered her brother.

"All I know is Daddy did have a bleeding ulcer when we lived in Copperton. But by the time we moved to Sandy he was well. And he wasn't bothered with ulcers when you went in the service. Daddy had his shoe and leather shop the whole time you were away."

"Evelyn, what were you doing during the war? Did you work at that shop with your dad?"

"I didn't work. I had a husband and two children."

"And was your husband in the service?"

"No, he worked up at the copper mine. And everybody who worked there had a job deferment. Including Murray. They couldn't have drafted him. But I don't know where those letters came from, because it's an untruth. Nobody tried to get Murray out of the service. He volunteered to go in, and he came out an honorable man." At this point Evelyn politely excused herself to go to the bathroom.

Although Murray denied knowing about the letters, he was clearly perseverating about their existence.

"I don't know why the military would give you that kind of information. I'm trying to fathom it. I'm trying to figure out why they would do that. But it wouldn't be the first time that the military made up false information. And I know what you're thinking."

"Tell me what I'm thinking."

"You're thinking the military couldn't be wrong."

"No. I'm not thinking that. But I am wondering where they would get that kind of information; like that your father did have a history of ulcers, the bishop's name, the barber's name, and all that kind of stuff. And I'm wondering why they would make the whole story up. I mean, that's quite a conspiracy theory."

"Don't you think my sister would have heard something about it?"

"Well, your sister is clearly not interested in revealing much information. But she seems in her response to be pretty vehement that the whole thing never happened. But, Murray, you're still being pretty vague about some secret. Your sister's not in the room right now. Murray, the things you've already told me, I can't imagine that you have some secret that you won't tell me now."

"Oh, I don't know. When I say secrets . . . little things. I'm not talking about anything big," Murray answered almost sheepishly, as if he were admitting that he had been breaking my balls.

Evelyn returned to the room and began speaking before she even sat down.

"You know, there's a lot of autobiographies out there. And I'm sure there's parts of each person's life that's not in there. They don't say, 'There's a part that I'm not going to tell.' But it just isn't there. And nobody knows it, and the book is written. That's all that matters. Murray has probably told you all that he wants you to know. And if it's enough to make a nice reading book, then write it. And if you think it's not flowery enough, tell Murray that you're not going to write it."

I said defiantly, "Oh, I'm going to write it."

In the meantime, Murray was still ruminating about what I had told him.

"It's bothering me that you gave me that information. Where did that story come from? Why would a bishop say something like that if it weren't true? And yet by the same token—as true as I'm sitting here—I have absolutely no knowledge of what you're saying at all. None whatsoever."

Again, Evelyn concurred: "I never have heard it."

I definitely believed that Murray was being sincere. I wasn't so sure about Evelyn. By the tone of her voice and by the look on her face, it did seem likely that she had no recollection of these letters ever having been sent. But she was being so evasive answering questions about Murray's military service—to the point of being defensive—that it appeared rather obvious that she was hiding something on behalf of her brother. One scenario I imagined was that Murray came home from the Navy and perhaps shared the true details of his experience with only one person—his closest confidant, Evelyn. Over the course of years, his memories were somehow replaced with all the vivid details that he shared with me; details that by now had become the basis of his reality. But maybe Evelyn still remembered exactly what Murray revealed to her back in 1945—a secret she vowed never to divulge and a promise she fully intended to keep.

Murray turned to me and said, rather solemnly, "So . . . you'll have to choose sides. And take one or the other."

"I'm not taking sides. You know whose side I'm on? I'm always on the side of the truth."

"Well, that's the best side to stay on."

"But I'm on your side too, Murray. I hope you believe that. You just said you're bothered by what I told you. I'm not trying to bother you. You believe that I'm your friend, don't you?"

"Yes . . . I do. But I can see your position, too. You're thinking, 'Well now let's see . . . the military said this and why would they say it if it weren't true?' I don't have an answer for that. I don't have an answer. If I did, I would say so. I really would say so. But I don't. I don't know. But it's very interesting."

The three of us sat quietly together for several minutes. Finally, I addressed Evelyn.

"You know, Evelyn, your thoughts about people's biographies are very wise. I understand what you're saying entirely, and your point is very well taken. A person writes their autobiography, and not everything is in there. There are parts that are just . . . private. Kept to themselves. I understand that. This project has taken me on a very interesting journey because Murray's life is intertwined with history. That's one reason why his story is interesting. It's not just a story of a person, but Murray was at a place and a time in history that was important, and therefore it's interesting. And as a physician, I have been taught to seek the truth. That's the cornerstone of the practice of medicine. The whole truth, whatever the truth is. You understand? I'm not being malicious; I'm not trying to be mean. I'm just trying to get at the truth. And maybe I'll find out and maybe I won't. I probably know more of the truth than you think. But then again maybe I don't. I wasn't there; I wasn't born yet."

Murray added another of his ambiguous comments.

"Well, you can always put two and two together and get four."

"What does that mean?"

"That means you gotta put everything together and analyze it. And it's either the truth or it's not the truth."

"Man, that's what I'm trying to do. Don't you believe that's what I'm trying to do?"

"Yeah, I do. I know that's what you're trying to do."

I turned my attention back to Evelyn.

"You know, Evelyn . . . I like you."

Evelyn said, very quietly, "Thank you."

"When we were talking on the phone, and you hung up on me, I thought I wasn't going to like you that much. But I do like you, and I'm going to tell you why. You're a very principled person, and you're a very loyal sister to your brother. I can see that. Because I know—I *know* that there's something you know and you're not telling me. And I'm being honest with you when I say that I really admire and respect that loyalty. I'm being very sincere, and I hope you take that at face value. Because I think loyalty is the most important thing. I don't think there's enough of it in the world. If I had a sister, I think I'd want her to be like you. There are too many people in the world who aren't trustworthy, who aren't dependable. You'd probably walk through fire for your brother, if he needed you to."

Murray interrupted: "I don't think she'd lie for me, though."

"She's not lying."

"Well, I don't think she would."

"And she's not. She's just not answering my questions. Which is preventing her from having to lie. Evelyn, was he a pretty loyal brother to you? Did he used to stick up for you when you were kids, protect you like a good big brother?"

"Yes."

"He was always there when you needed him?"

"I don't know that I ever needed him. But he was always by my side. We was together—we grew up together. We played together. Copperton was a little town that was secluded and away from the rest of the world. There wasn't any crime. We didn't hear any bad things about our neighbors. Everybody was peaceful and happy. That's where we lived, and that was our world. We made homemade candy and popcorn at night for entertainment. We might listen to a few programs on the radio. Those were the days I love to sit back and remember."

"Evelyn, may I ask you what you think of me? You spoke to me on the phone, now you're meeting me for the first time. I've been very honest in telling you my impression of you—tell me what you think of me. If you would be so kind."

"I think you're just a regular, ordinary man. I've met you today and tomorrow I'll forget you."

Of all the answers I might have anticipated, that wasn't one of them.

"Not many people say that about me. Most people find me to be fairly memorable. Most people would not consider me to be ordinary."

Evelyn gave me that sly little chuckle again.

"Well, I'm not most people."

"Obviously."

"Why you want to write a book, I still don't know."

"Why does anybody write a book? You've read a book. I'm sure you've read millions of books in your time. Somebody writes a book, somebody reads a book. A person writes a book because they think they have something interesting to say. I think your brother is a very interesting man. Do you believe me when I say that I like your brother?"

"I guess so . . . I really don't know. You probably like most people."

"There are a lot of people I don't like. And I'm pretty honest about it. If I don't like somebody, I don't like them. But I like your brother."

"That's good. I do too. If it makes him happy to talk to you, that's all that matters."

"Murray, let me ask you something. You never told anybody else your story; how come you agreed to talk to me?"

"Oh, I don't know, you just asked me. And I've told you more than I ever intended to."

"So, you would've just told anybody who asked you?"

"No, not necessarily."

"Right—so what I'm asking you is why you decided to talk to *me*."

"You just struck me as a guy that would tell the truth. Tell it like I told you. World War II is vanishing from the minds of the majority of people here in the United States. And I didn't want it to be lost. And the biggest reason was I thought that it might deter people from getting excited about ever getting into another war. I don't like war. I'd like to go back to the time when everything was peaceful, with no talk of war. But that'll never be again. There will always be something. Somebody's always threatening to bomb somebody else if they don't do something . . . or if they do something."

Murray closed his eyes.

"You're not falling asleep, are you?"

"No. I'm deep in thought. I really would not want to be a person that everything I said people would wonder whether it was the truth or not. I wouldn't want that. That would hurt me. To be thought of as a liar."

"There's no in-between there? There's either the truth or a lie? There's no room for error or forgetting?"

"I don't think there's any room for error between telling the truth and lying. It's either the truth or it's not the truth."

"So, if I said to you, for example, that the Mets won a baseball game yesterday, but it turns out that they lost . . . the only possibility is that I'm lying? There's not the possibility that I'm just mistaken?"

"Well, that's something else. There's lying, not lying, and guessing. In that case, you were just guessing. You didn't really know. So you wouldn't be classified as a liar."

"Do you think that I think you're lying?"

Murray just sat there looking at me, so I asked the question again, more deliberately.

"Do you think . . . that I think . . . that you're lying?"

"Well, to be honest with you, you've got those records, and I don't know what you're thinking. I'm trying to put myself in your place. Why would they have those letters in there if it wasn't the truth? And if it is the truth, then I'm lying when I say I don't know anything about what you're talking about."

"No, I'm going to have to disagree with you. It's quite possible that you never knew about everything that was happening here at home. Or it's possible that you knew once and you forgot. And that's not lying."

"Well, that's a possibility. I'll always say that it's a possibility that I just don't remember."

"I'm going to tell you that I don't believe that you're lying to me. I don't consider you to be a liar. I'm telling you that unequivocally, one hundred percent. Do you hear me? And do you believe me?"

"Yes, I do. I absolutely do."

"Do you remember we had that discrepancy about those dates and about Iwo Jima? And if you remember, after we had that discussion you said to me, 'If you find any more holes in this whole thing, I want to know about it.' Do you remember saying that?"

"Yes, I do. I certainly do. I remember telling you that."

"So, here's a difficult position that I'm in. You told me that, and I believe you. You told me that if there's anything I find, you want to know about it. It's your life, it ain't my life. But today I told you about a letter that some bishop wrote back in 1944, and you're telling me that you're disturbed by it."

"I am disturbed by it. It's bothering me."

"So, my choice is I can either be disturbing to you or I cannot fulfill your request to tell you anything that I discover. You see how that's a problem for me? What should I do?"

After sitting in silence for quite some time, Evelyn offered her opinion: "Leave that chapter out."

I found Evelyn's simplistic and concrete solution to be annoying.

"It's not just about a chapter—it's a question of what do I do about Murray. Because it's Murray's life. If a letter was written about me, and I didn't know about it or I didn't remember it—but it happened—I'd want to know about it. That's how I am. Now, Murray told me if I find anything he wants to know about it. But at the same time, I'm a very compassionate person, and I don't want to disturb the man."

Murray was still dwelling on the details of the letters.

"Well, I'll tell you—I don't know why something of that nature would be in there. Because my father and my mother would not have went to that length to try and get me out of the service. That's the fallacy. They wouldn't have done that. So I don't know. And anyway, it would have made much more sense if I were going to get out of the Navy to go back to working at the copper mine, rather than working at a damned shoe shop. The country needed every bit of metal we could get out of that mine to make bullets. I had a deferment. I didn't have to enlist in the first place. That was the biggest mistake I ever made."

"You're the only WWII vet I've ever heard say that. That's one of the things that makes your story so interesting, Murray. You are the only World War II veteran who I've ever heard utter those words. But the question remains: What do you think I ought to do now? I'm your friend, and now I feel a little sad that you're disturbed by what I've told you. Suppose I have some other fact that might upset you. Should I tell you about it?"

"I don't know. You probably know the answer to that better than I do."

"I don't, brother. Believe me I don't. Evelyn, what do you think I should do?"

"Just leave him alone; leave it be. Let sleeping dogs lie."

Murray agreed: "Amen."

"Well, now you're contradicting yourself. You told me that if I find any more inconsistencies that I should tell you."

"And I would like you to."

"But that's different than what Evelyn just said. Telling you would be the opposite of letting sleeping dogs lie. That's . . . that'd be like stirring up a hornet's nest. Evelyn's given me some advice. I don't know if I'm going to follow it or not, but I value her opinion. I said before that I like Evelyn and—"

Evelyn interrupted me: "Well I don't care, really, whether you do or don't."

"You don't care whether I like you? How come?"

"Because tomorrow I won't even remember you. I told you that already."

"Were you always like that, not caring whether people liked you or not?"

Murray offered an assessment of his sister: "Well, she was a very private girl. Quite introverted. She had her husband and her family consuming all of her time. And she was a very good wife. Good cook, kept the house clean, kept him in nice clothes. Her whole world revolved around her family."

Evelyn appreciated her brother's kind words.

"Thanks, bud. I still live in my own little world." Evelyn got up to go put on a sweater. It was about ninety-four degrees outside and probably the same in her house. Deep down inside, I still wanted to reveal everything I had discovered to Murray, even though now both his psychologist and his sister had dissuaded me from doing so.

"Murray, I want you to take a few days and sleep on this before you answer me. I want you to think about whether you want me to tell you any more of what's in your military records."

"Yeah, I do."

"You didn't sleep on it."

"I don't care. There might be something else in there that I'd want to know about."

"What if it's disturbing to you?"

"It'll just have to be disturbing . . . I don't know what else to tell you. Right now I've got to go to the bathroom." Murray got up, and using his walker, carefully made his way between Evelyn and me.

"I'll just sit here and visit with your sister, even though she probably won't talk to me about anything. You don't mind if I just sit here in this nice comfortable chair, right Evelyn?"

"No. Make yourself at home."

"This is a nice cozy house you have."

"We raised two children in this house. My husband was Italian, you know. Oh, here's my dog; his name is Lucky. My husband always wanted a little dog, but I never would agree to it. I told him, 'Dogs aren't for in the house, and I just don't want one, Dominic.' But then he got sick and I asked him if he still wanted a dog and he said, 'I sure do.' So I said, 'Let's go get one.' We went into the dog pound and got him, and on the way home I asked Dominic, 'What are we gonna name him?' and we both—right at the same time—said, 'Lucky.' So, he was my husband's dog till my husband went away. Then he became my dog. I miss my husband terribly."

As is usually the case, behind even the thickest veil of rancor, one can find at least some essence of humanity. At that moment, as Evelyn sat gently stroking her dog's chest, I didn't see her as a bitter old obstruction, but as a lonely widow whose beloved brother was the last surviving link to her idyllic past. I felt a genuine sense of compassion for her.

"I can only imagine . . . after so many years together."

"Seventy. We were married for seventy years." Evelyn must have recognized that I was sincerely sympathetic, and her demeanor became more subdued. "Thank you for the candy you brought me. I like chocolate, especially from See's. You know, I love my brother very much. We're very close. Always were."

I responded to Evelyn's tenderness with a softened attitude of my own.

"I care about Murray very much."

"OK. That's good. I'm glad."

"I'm really torn . . . I don't want to hurt him, but he tells me he wants the truth. I don't think he remembers the truth. I think he may have forgotten. And I really—genuinely—don't know what to do."

"Just leave it alone."

"Well, that is one option. Other people have told me that too."

"Murray and I both know that neither of us has too long to live. We're getting up there. We still have pretty good health. I still go see my son at his home in Montana. Somebody takes me to the airport, they put me on the plane, I get off the plane, and somebody meets me. I go to my son's house; he treats me like a queen until I leave again. My daughter is a registered nurse. She lives in Colorado and sometimes I go see her, too. But when I go see her somebody has to drive me; I don't fly. And Raymond is my son's boy. He takes care of me. He's very thoughtful. He never leaves the house without telling me where he's going and how long he'll be gone. Yes, I have a wonderful family. But I still miss my husband."

Murray made his way back to the sofa, and I could tell that I had already gotten everything I was going to get out of this encounter.

"Evelyn, it's been very nice to meet you, and I appreciate you allowing me to come into your home. And even though you won't remember me tomorrow, I'll remember you."

"It's OK whether you do or you don't . . . I really won't care."

CHAPTER 13

YOU WEREN'T THERE

I went back to see Murray the next week. He remained steadfast in his decision and insisted that I tell him more about the information contained within his military file.

"The last time we talked, at your sister's house, I told you that there were letters from back home, written on your behalf, in an effort to get you discharged from the Navy."

"Yes, I remember you telling me that."

"And you and your sister were very adamant that it never happened. I'm going to read one of those letters to you right now. This letter came from your military file. It's dated November 17, 1944. You were still overseas at that time. This was written by your father, Guy Jacobs. And it's signed by your father. And it was actually notarized, by a notary public." I proceeded to read the letter, word-for-word, as Murray listened attentively. When I finished, I asked Murray, "Do you have any comments? Do you believe this letter was real?"

"It may have been . . . my father might have needed some help and wanted to know if he could get me out to help him. But he didn't tell me about it. Have you got any letters in there from him to me?"

I took a deep breath, knowing I was about to be treading on very thin ice.

"What I've got here is a letter that you wrote."

"OK. Let's hear it."

"This was written on December 12, 1944. You were still overseas. I want to show you that you signed the letter. Does that look like your signature?"

"It could be, yeah."

"You understand I'm sharing this with you because you asked me to. I got your military records with your permission. And of course, as you would imagine, I read everything in those records. I've got these letters, and as I told you, I found it interesting that you never mentioned them. Your sister said that you had some secrets and that secrets should be left alone. And you were screwing around with me a little bit, telling me the secret was that the two of you played tiddlywinks when you were kids. I know you were just messing with me, and that's OK."

"We didn't play tiddlywinks; we played hopscotch. And I don't know what secrets she was talking about."

"I believe you when you say to me that you have no recollection of these letters. And you said to me, 'I'm either lying or I'm telling the truth.' And as I pointed out to you, there's a different possibility—that you just don't remember. You understand that not one piece of me thinks you're lying to me right now. I believe that everything you've told me, in your mind, is true. But I think your memory is . . . I think there's some holes in your memory."

"All right. If I'm telling you something, it's because I think it's the truth."

"I believe that's true. I believe you one hundred percent that that's true. And I'm telling you—I told you before when we were at your sister's house—I'm concerned that what I've found may upset you. Because it seems you get upset when you don't remember things correctly."

"OK."

"So this is a letter written by you, as best as I can tell."

"OK. Quit screwing around and read it!"

So, I went ahead and read him—verbatim—the letter that he, himself, had written nearly seventy years before.

"So, I'm wondering what you think about that."

"Let me tell you, my education that I had at that time would have never permitted me to have written a letter in the language that that is written. I must've had some very good help. I don't doubt that the letter was written. But I'm going to tell you something else along with it at the same time . . . I don't remember it." Murray was getting irritated and a little flustered. "I do not remember. Everything adds up to yes, I did write that letter. But I don't remember it if I did. And I'm not saying I didn't. Maybe I did. But maybe I didn't. I was an entirely—*entirely*—different person back then than I am now. Entirely different. I look at things different. I think of things different. In fact, I'm having a hard time thinking of anything right now. I feel like I'm in a fog. Things that happened yesterday seem like a long time ago.

I went to my sister's for breakfast yesterday. Her two grand-daughters came and got me and took me over there. One is from Colorado, one is from Michigan. I had breakfast, but don't ask me what I ate because I don't remember. It was only yesterday, but it doesn't seem like it. Everything seems so far away."

"Well, it's fair enough that your memory isn't what it used to be and that you honestly have no recollection of having written this letter. The fact is, that if I stopped twenty people on the street and asked them what they had for breakfast yesterday, probably half of them wouldn't know. But that being said, now that I've read the letter to you, do you have some opinion about it?"

"No. I don't have any opinion about it other than what I've already said. I'm not going to say 'Yes.' I'm not going to say 'No.' You've got it there; use it for whatever reason you think you need to use it. And let it fly. I don't know what to tell you. I really don't."

"When we were at your sister's house and I told you about these letters, you told me that the military was just making stuff up. Do you still believe that's true?"

"I think that the military put information into people's lives that was not true."

"But what about this?"

"I have no idea. I don't know whether it's true or not. If I had written that letter myself, it would be in a different sort of language than what it is. I just didn't have enough education to write a letter like that. That didn't come from an ordinary damned shovel operator."

"Fair enough. What about the letter from your dad?"

"I don't know about that. I believe that it could be true. Evelyn didn't know anything about it, either. I asked her after you were gone, and she still said that she didn't know anything about it. Yes, my father had been sick, but as far as I knew he wasn't sick during the war. Now, one thing you must understand: There were letters that we wrote back then that never reached their destinations. A lot of things happened that there seemed to be no explanation for."

"You know, your sister is an interesting person. I'm pretty good at reading people, but I can't figure out whether she was just being nasty to me and that she doesn't have anything to say or if she really knows some piece of information that she's kept secret all these years. So, what do you think? Do you think she was just being ornery? Or do you think she really has some secret and you don't even remember what it is?"

"I don't know what kind of a secret it would be. I'm being honest with you. Nothing that I know of."

"When I left, did you ask her?"

"Yeah."

"What did she say?"

"Nothing. Not a thing. I said, 'Why did you tell him you had a secret? And if you do, why didn't you tell him, so I would know too? Because I don't know what you're talking about.' And she just sat there looking at me. So, I still have no idea what she was talking about. One thing you must remember: She is having problems with her mind," said the pot about the kettle.

"Well, I suppose that's also a possibility; that she only thinks there's a secret. But she was sure acting like she was hiding something. I could be wrong, though. I could be wrong."

"Have you ever been wrong before?"

"Once I thought I was wrong, but I was mistaken."

"Ha ha! That was the reason you were wrong; you was wrong about thinking you were wrong!"

I don't think Murray had ever heard that old wisecrack before, and we both had a good laugh about it.

"I'm just joking with you. I've been wrong many times in my life. But I think Evelyn does have a secret. But I don't really know."

"Well, I wish she'd let us in on it."

"Really? You really want to know?"

"Yeah."

"But you asked her."

"I did."

"And she didn't tell you."

"No."

"What's up with that?"

"I don't know. But I'm going to ask her again. Yes, sir. Because the way she said it, she made it seem like she had some sinister secret that she was keeping, of something she and I both knew or did. And if there is something like that, I don't know what it would be. We didn't spend that much time together. We were close up until we got out of grade school. I led a pretty hectic life in my younger years, and I distanced myself from her and from the rest of my family. By the time we were in high school, we were not close at all. You know, I never did get my high school diploma. But I've gotten along all right. You know, I don't really understand why those letters would be of interest to you, anyway."

"Because it's a part of your story. And it's a part of your story that you don't remember."

"And I can understand what you're wondering. In your mind, you're thinking, 'How much more of the story don't he remember?' Sure . . . I can understand that. You're doing the uncovering though."

It seemed like an obvious statement, but I wasn't sure what Murray meant by that comment.

"I'm doing the uncovering?"

"Sure . . . you're doing the digging. And if you dig any more . . . bring it around."

"Is it wrong to do that? Do you think I'm wrong?"

"No, no, no. You're trying to write a book about my life and World War II. Primarily, I think you want to preserve the history of the war and my involvement in it. I've told you about as much as I can, and as good as I can. And that's all I can do. You've got the go-ahead from me to get whatever information you can, and whenever you find stuff like this, let's talk about it. Whether it's things I haven't told you, or something I told you that isn't so."

"So, anything I find . . . you want me to talk to you about it."

"If something is a fallacy, yes. If it disturbs you, yes."

"Well . . . 'disturb' isn't the right word." I had Murray sitting right in front of me, telling me what to do next. But I had Gita on one shoulder and Evelyn on the other, both telling me to do the exact opposite. "Disturbed" doesn't even begin to describe how I was feeling at that moment, but I tried to maintain a pretense of being calm and cool.

"I'm not disturbed. Well . . . maybe a little bit. Yeah, maybe a little bit."

"Wait a minute. You want this book to be as near accurate as possible, don't you?"

"Ideally."

"I don't mind you putting that in. I have no reason to object to you putting that business about the letters in there. Go ahead and put it in. It don't bother me."

I continued, but with considerable trepidation.

"This is tricky business for me. I've got to be honest with you; mostly, I care about you. You understand? I really care about you. But I'm also in search of the truth. Look, man . . . I found out that there was some discrepancy about whether you were on Iwo Jima or you were confused about which island you were on and you were very upset about that."

"I was upset with myself."

"So, I don't really want to upset you."

"I still feel like I was there."

"I understand. I understand that you feel like you were there. Did you ever talk to your psychologist about that?"

"No, but I'm going to. She's going to come here probably sometime in the next week. And I'm going to talk to her about it."

"I think that's a good idea. Because I think that you really remember being there. I'm not thinking—not one bit—'this guy's bullshitting me.' But I also know that you weren't there. I know that you weren't there, as best as I can know anything looking at documents that are seventy years old. So that's the difficulty for me. I really believe the truth is the important thing, and I also believe that I don't want to irritate you."

"There's things I've told you . . . that make me shudder when I think about them today. Things that still bother me. And I think in your mind, you're wondering, 'Well, is that true or not? Did that actually happen?' Because there's no way I can go back and authenticate it. Because the guys that were in on this . . . I have no idea where they're at. Or if they're even alive. I've never kept in contact with any of them. My best friend in the service, Yardbird, he was the only one I would have kept in contact with. But I lost him . . . right next to me. Part of him was splattered all over me."

Murray and I sat quietly; together, yet alone in our own thoughts. By the look on his face I could tell that Murray was thinking about the image of his good buddy being blown to bits right in front of him. I, on the other hand, was thinking about Doyle "Yardbird" Smith's obituary . . . in Texas . . . in 1981. I was at an impasse; I desperately wanted to tell Murray the truth about Yardbird, but I was terrified by the thought of how he might react. And anyway, I had more or less come to accept the fact that he wouldn't believe me. Several minutes went by with just the familiar ticking of the clock on the wall, until Murray finally spoke.

"You know . . . let's talk about something else, please. I don't want to talk about this. What we're talking about now—what happened to Yardbird—it's in my mind now. And I'm going to have a helluva time getting it out. It's adding fuel to the fire."

I happened to notice that right there on Murray's nightstand was the book in which he pointed out the photo of M. S. Blair, the officer who he had confessed to killing, but who I later found out had died in Florida in 1978. For some reason, I decided to see if a different line of inquiry might be more promising. I should have anticipated the response, but I went ahead, regardless.

"You told me about one particular officer that you had a bad interaction with. You remember that?"

Murray answered begrudgingly, "Yes."

"And you pointed him out to me in that book."

Murray became indignant and barked, "I don't want no more to do with that! You've got all you're gonna get about him. Please. Things happen. I don't want no more of that."

Murray was staring at me, obviously distraught. In his mind, there wasn't a shadow of a doubt that he had killed that man, but I knew that it never happened. And again, I was stuck between a burning desire to alleviate his guilt and the ultimately paralyzing fear that he would be incapable of accepting my words as the truth. So, I just sat there, staring back at him. He looked away from me and said quietly, "What do you think that I've been trying to live down my whole life, for God's sake?"

Disheartened, I mumbled, "I'm trying to find out. I'm just trying to find out." I'm not sure if I was speaking to Murray or to myself. "I'm going to let you go have your dinner in five minutes. Is that OK? I've got just one more question I want to ask you, then I'll leave you alone."

"All right."

"You don't remember sending that letter. But if you had been writing that letter—or if someone was writing that letter for you—if anybody was writing a letter like that, saying that they needed to go home to help their father, and that they had done their duty, etcetera, etcetera . . . don't you think it's odd that they would not have mentioned that they saw combat?"

"If I'd have mentioned that, it would have been cut out of the letter. We were told we were not to mention anything about combat, violence, the weather, nothing. Anything like that, they'd cut out every bit of it. All our letters were censored. And I don't know what you're getting at—I think I might know—but I'll tell you right now that you don't know what went on. Because you weren't there. I was there. So you don't really know. Now I'm going to go eat my supper. I'm sorry."

Murray got up abruptly, grabbed his walker, and actually was pushing his way past me to get out of the room.

"Why are you sorry?"

"I'm sorry that this ever happened."

"You're sorry you ever started talking to me?"

"No . . . I'm sorry these letters ever came up, and it's thrown a cloud over the whole thing. I'm sorry."

I put my arm around Murray's shoulder and said, "There's no reason to apologize to me."

Murray pulled away from me, as if he were repulsed, and he seemed to be in a kind of a frenzy to get out of the room.

"OK. Let's go. Will you open the door for me, please?"

I was hurt and surprised—although I shouldn't have been—by his unwillingness to accept my gesture of affection.

"I can't put my arm around you? I get the feeling you don't like me anymore. It's OK if you don't; your sister doesn't like me."

"No, I like you. I just don't want to talk anymore, that's all. As for Evelyn, she'll have to speak for herself."

As I drove home, my brain was overflowing with thoughts. Murray had become unhinged at just the slightest hint that I doubted the veracity of his stories. His reaction convinced me that Gita was probably right; confronting Murray with the facts of his military service would not serve to relieve his suffering, but rather to exacerbate it. As Evelyn had suggested, perhaps I should just let sleeping dogs lie. But within the tumult in my mind, something Murray had said was really bothering me: "You weren't there." Right . . . I wasn't there. The words kept reverberating in my head. I was having a hard time wrapping myself around the fact that while I thought I knew the truth— that damned elusive truth—I wasn't there to witness it. So who am I to say what really happened?

Sure, I have records and letters and dates and obituaries, and all sorts of so-called proof of the truth. But I'm listening to a guy telling me—not just telling me, but sincerely believing—that he saw combat in the Pacific in 1944, and what right do I have to tell him that he didn't? Any more than some idiot Holocaust-denier has the right to tell a survivor of Auschwitz that the whole thing didn't happen. Or some moron has the balls to look Neil Armstrong in the eye and tell him that the moon landing was a hoax. As I discovered earlier in the course of my research, eye-witness accounts aren't perfect—far from it. But they're damned sure better than most of the other evidence we have available, especially for events that happened seventy years ago.

Obviously, some of what I'd uncovered was irrefutable. Post-marks don't lie, so Murray couldn't have been on Iwo Jima, and obituaries are usually accurate, so Yardbird and Blair certainly survived the war. But those three words—"You weren't there"— were a revelation to me. I recognized that my investigation was far from over. I needed to talk to the guys that were there. I needed to seek out and interview any surviving members of the 100th Naval Construction Battalion that I could find and com-pare their experiences to those that Murray had described. In order to have any chance at all of determining what had hap-pened to Murray Jacobs, I was obligated to find out what had happened to the other thousand men who served alongside him.

Now, I'm not necessarily a proponent of the "infinite monkey theory," which suggests that a monkey randomly hitting a type-writer keyboard for an infinite amount of time could eventually produce the complete works of William Shakespeare. However, as metaphors go, when I'm trying to search for something on the Internet, I am essentially that monkey hitting those keys. I usually can get results, but the mechanism by which I get them is mysterious and irreproducible. Some combination of knowledge, intuition, and just plain luck. It was by that lengthy, haphazard process that I somehow came upon the contact in-formation for Captain A. N. Olsen, who authored *The King Bee*, a biography of Admiral Ben Moreell, the man who had come up with the idea for the Seabees in the first place. I nervously picked up the phone and cold-called him, and incredibly, Cap-tain Olsen himself answered the telephone. And he couldn't have been more cordial, supportive, and cooperative.

Captain Olsen advised me to check with the organization Navy Seabee Veterans of America, and gave me the contact in-formation for the national secretary of that group, Mel Ramige. Secretary Ramige was also extremely helpful, and he provided

me with the names and addresses of all the active members of
the Navy SVA whose records indicated that they had served in
the 100th NCB during World War II. Sadly, of over a thousand
men who had served in that battalion, the list consisted of only
twenty-three names. I sent each man a letter describing the
project, inquiring whether they had served in the Marshall Islands, and asking if they would be willing to share their memories of what they had experienced. Several letters were returned
unopened, marked "Return to Sender-Deceased." I received a
handful of responses, and while all were interesting, only a few
were helpful.

Rudolph Stallmann, of Kingston, New York, sent me a letter,
which I will excerpt here:

> Dr. Zuckerman
>> In answer to your letter.
>> I was in the 100 NCB and was transferred into a smaller
>> unit called a CB Maintenance Unit. My unit was 518. I was
>> sent to Guadalcanal, and was there when an ammunition ship
>> was torpedoed and all perished but one sailor. All were buried
>> on Guadalcanal but eventually buried in Arlington National
>> Cemetery in Washington D.C.
>> On September 14 I will be 93 years old. I was not in the
>> Marshall Islands. Unfortunately I have not been in contact with
>> anyone in my original outfit. I'm sorry I can't be more helpful.
>> Sincerely
>> Rudolph Stallmann

Stallmann's experience was not relevant to my task at hand,
but I found it nonetheless intriguing. A construction battalion
maintenance unit (CBMU) was usually about one-quarter the
size of a regular construction battalion, and its purpose was to
take over the maintenance of a base after the initial construction
had been completed. The 518th CBMU served on Guadalcanal
in the Solomon Islands from April 1944 through August 1945.[15]
A bit of further investigation revealed that on January 29, 1945,
the USS *Serpens*, a Coast Guard-manned ammunition ship, exploded while anchored just offshore at Guadalcanal. Most of
the ship disintegrated, killing 198 Coast Guard crewmen, fifty-
seven Army stevedores, and a physician. The explosion was so
powerful that a soldier who was ashore at the time was killed

by shrapnel. Incredibly, two members of the crew who were in the boatswain's locker were injured but survived. The incident was initially attributed to enemy action, but a court of inquiry determined that the cause of the explosion could not be established, and in 1949, the Navy attributed the loss to "an accident intrinsic to the process of loading depth charges." This disaster represents the largest single loss of life ever suffered by the US Coast Guard.[13] And as more and more eyewitnesses to the tragedy die, this incredible event fades further and further into the category of ancient history.

A few days later I got a phone call from Don French, an eighty-five-year-old Seabee veteran currently living in Mesa, Arizona. French grew up in Michigan, and by age eleven he was working at a filling station pumping gas. At age sixteen he was working on manhole covers for the city of Flint, and at age seventeen he worked for General Motors. He remembers very clearly that on December 7, 1941, he was with his family in their 1938 Buick, listening to President Roosevelt as he addressed the nation. French enlisted in 1944, at the age of eighteen, was assigned to the Seabees, and was sent to the Great Lakes Training Center in Illinois. He was about to ship out of New York Harbor on VE Day, but was immediately put on a train to California instead. He was assigned to the 100th NCB and was en route to the Philippines on the day that Japan surrendered.

While on Samar Island in the Philippines, French spent time in the 99th and 61st NCBs, as well as the 100th, eventually achieving the rank of carpenter's mate, 3rd class. French told me, "Our unit bonded like a brotherhood. Although we worked in adverse conditions the men I worked with were as close to me as my brothers." He went on to tell me about a friend of his who was killed by a Japanese sniper after the war had been officially declared over: "The guy's name was Gates; I don't remember his first name. He was in the cab of a truck that was pulling a trailer. The driver's seat was open—uncovered—and he got shot right in the head." Don French was discharged from the Navy in June 1946.

"All I wanted was *out*," he said. "On our way back home I threw my .45 into the ocean, somewhere around the Aleutian Islands."

After the war, he worked as a lineman for Michigan Bell Telephone.

To this day he remains proud of his service. "Without the military defending our shores, our country would be in jeopardy."

And I think he appreciated my efforts to get the facts straight.

"We didn't talk about it for so many years . . . so many of the pieces of history are lost forever. Even my military records are wrong—one of the battalions I served in is missing. You'd think they'd be able to get something as simple as that right."

I enjoyed speaking with Don, and I appreciated his willingness to share his memories. His service didn't coincide with Murray's, and he was never on Majuro, so our discussion unfortunately didn't shed any light on the situation at hand. Perhaps the most pertinent thing Don said was that remark about his military records. It definitely piqued my curiosity. If his records could be inaccurate, so could Murray's.

The next day I got an email from Eileen Avitable, whose father, Charles Bodie, was one of the Seabee veterans on my list.

My father was indeed part of the 100th Naval Construction Battalion, having enlisted in 1943. I know he spoke of the Marshall Islands, but did not see combat at all. More than likely, he could provide you with some additional information; however, due to a stroke in 2009 he is unable to form the words his mind thinks. With advancing age his intelligibility has become almost nil. He lives with my husband and I, and while his memory for current events is poor, he would love to regale anyone with his memories of his wartime experiences. It would all be gibberish unfortunately.

I remember my father saying that he and a buddy signed up with the Seabees as it sounded more interesting than the other options. My husband remembers him saying that he was on the Sacajawea *troop ship heading to the Marshall Islands and they used to call it the 'Sack of Shit' (Only my husband would remember this fact!). I remember Dad telling me that sometimes pilots who would come to the Marshalls would exchange liquor for extra rations.*

Dad's job as a Seabee, as best as we can tell, was as part of a demolition crew. On June 9, 1945 he was wounded when an explosion went off prematurely as they were blasting coral for a runway in Hawaii. He returned home on the hospital ship USS Refuge, *and his service ended in 1946. On the hospital ship after he was wounded, he refused to sleep below and always found some type of accommodations on deck, as he was claustrophobic.*

I know that my father returned home with some background in construction skills that he never possessed before the war. He became quite a good cabinet and furniture maker as a hobby. As I indicated before, it is too bad his memories, while numerous and keen, are unintelligible. I wish we could be more helpful. We do wish you the best of luck in your investigations.

Eileen Avitable

I contacted Eileen and requested that she ask her father if he knew Murray Jacobs. She informed me that he did not, and that as far as she knew, he never continued a relationship with any of his buddies from the Seabees. So, Charles Bodie was a man whose service did coincide with Murray's, but while he might have known him back then, he doesn't remember him now. And even if he did, his inability to communicate his thoughts has robbed us of whatever details he might have otherwise been able to share.

Three men, and only one who followed a path that could have possibly intersected with Murray's. And the ravages of age and illness have now forever sealed his knowledge of the truth within the recesses of his mind, inaccessible to the rest of us. But each man's journey is still a tiny piece in the much larger puzzle that is the history of World War II itself. That's why every person's experience has value, and why every story is worth hearing—before it's too late.

One man was an observer of the worst catastrophe in the history of the Coast Guard. Another had witnessed a friend senselessly and ironically murdered after the hostilities had ended. And a third was wounded while doing construction for the war effort on what was ostensibly the safety of US soil. While none of these men might have fired a shot at the enemy or been fired upon themselves, they each served our country admirably in its time of greatest need. And they each spent months, even years, away from their homes and families on an adventure that would undoubtedly impact them deeply for the rest of their lives. And each, in his own way, could bear witness to history. Unfortunately for me, though, none could bear witness to the specific history of Murray Jacobs.

Then I got a phone call from Robert G. Arthurs, from Lacombe, Louisiana. "Bobby" Arthurs was the youngest man in
the 100th Naval Construction Battalion, having forged his birth
certificate at the age of fifteen to enlist in the Navy. Bobby was
born in New Orleans, and he spoke with a charming Cajun
drawl. He had been with the 100th from its very inception, and
he stayed with the battalion for the duration of the war. His
memory was razor sharp, and he regaled me with stories about
Majuro and the Philippines. He didn't know Murray, but the two
of them served at the same time, and presumably in the same
place—at least until Murray was sent home. I spoke to Bobby
for nearly an hour and came to realize that he was my strongest
link to the history of Murray Jacobs. Talking to Bobby would
give me a real chance of uncovering the truth. Because he was
there. So, I did the only rational thing I could think of: I planned
a trip to Louisiana.

CHAPTER 14

WE LUCKED OUT

Julie and I flew to New Orleans, rented a car, and drove forty-five minutes east on Interstate 10 to the community of La-combe, located on the northern shore of Lake Pontchartrain. It was the first time I could remember landing in New Orleans and not going directly from the airport to Mother's for one of those debris po'boys. But this was going to be a short trip, and I want-ed to spend as much time with Bobby as possible, so sacrifices had to be made. As we pulled up to their house, Bobby and his wife were on the porch—along with their three dogs—waiting to greet us. Bobby appeared much more youthful than I'd imag-ined, and his warm smile immediately made us feel welcome. He shook my hand as he introduced his wife: "This is my wife, Patrice—we call her Pat." An elegant, polite, and most definitely southern woman, Pat welcomed us into their home and seemed both surprised and honored that two doctors from Utah would travel all the way to Louisiana just to hear her husband's war stories.

Bobby was obviously thrilled to have the opportunity to share the details of his experience in the military, and as soon as we were done with the introductions, he was anxious to get down to business. While Julie and Pat chatted in the living room, Bobby took me into the dining room, where he had already spread out a map of the Pacific Ocean to show me precisely where he had been. But before we got to his time in the Navy, I asked him to start from the beginning.

"I grew up here in Louisiana, never had been out of New Orleans, actually. My mother died when I was seven, so my dad raised us. She died in childbirth, while giving birth to my youngest brother. I went to a Catholic school, and you had to go to church every morning; my dad made us go. I never did do homework or anything in school; in fact, I never did bring a book home. I was fourteen when I graduated, or they just let me pass—I don't know which—out of the seventh grade. And I started working at a grocery store, cleaning chickens, cutting them and feathering them, getting a dollar a day. I wasn't getting anywhere, so I went to the New Orleans Port of Embarkation where the Merchant Marines were. They were signing me up and everything to be a cabin boy, but when I told them I was fourteen, they ran me out of the damned building.

"So, when I just turned fifteen I answered an ad and started selling magazines, traveling with a man and his wife in a car. There was three of us kids and the two of them, and we went through Mississippi and Alabama selling *McCall's*, *Redbook*, and *Better Homes & Gardens*. It was the first time I'd been out of New Orleans. When we got to Pensacola, Florida, there was a group of women who was also selling magazines, and I think we were doing better than them—I didn't know all the details. But anyway, I got arrested, and I don't mean easily. This other guy and I were standing in front of a theater on a Sunday morning, looking to see what was playing, and the cop threw us onto the ground backwards and into the car. Nobody ever told me anything, but it appeared that those women made charges against us. We were just a couple of kids, and I didn't know any of them women. I didn't know nothing . . . I didn't know which way was up. But they fingerprinted me and photos and all the rest, and put us in jail. And I was in there with *men*. Lucky for me, the only thing they was worried about was whether I was going to eat all the beans and rice they were serving. They were all real happy when I told them to go ahead and take them, and after that, they pretty much just left me alone. Finally, the head of the magazine company bailed us out and the charges were dropped. You know, that jail in Pensacola—today it's an art museum."

"When was that, about 1942?"

"Well, I was born in December of '27, and I had just barely turned fifteen when I was arrested, so it must've been January of 1943."

"I know times were different back then, but what did your father think of all this?"

"I never did tell him. I don't know to this day if he ever found out. My father . . . he was not there. He was Irish; my mother was German. This'll tell you something: My aunt—my mother's sister—when I was an adult she told me that the day my mother moved out of their family house to go with my daddy, their mother said she wished she was dead rather than to go live with that drunk. He was very hard on the drinking. And he was a little fellow; I mean he was nowhere near my size. And he'd pick fights all the time—and he'd lose. Heh, heh . . . you'd think he would've learned something somewhere along the way.

"Anyway, I wound up in Montgomery, Alabama, and we was hardly selling anything. We had to pay rent in hotels and eat in restaurants and we were starving. One of the other kids with me says, 'Why don't we join the Navy?' And I said, 'OK.' So, I went into the recruiting station in Montgomery, and I knew enough by now to change that date. I've still got the birth certificate where I'd erased the date, and you can see it, but they weren't worried too much about it back then. I did have to send some papers to my dad, who signed and mailed them back to me. And they put me in the Seabees. I didn't know what the hell the Seabees was. I didn't know what I was doing in the first place."

"December 7, 1941 . . . tell me about that day, and how you felt afterwards."

"It was a Sunday, of course. I was just about fourteen, working at the grocery store, making a dollar a day, killing chickens all day long. On Sundays, I just did cleanup work there. In the afternoon, I'd always go to Canal Street and I went to the movies. I went to almost every movie in town, one after the other. And in between movies I'd stop at Woolworth's and get a bowl of ice cream. I remember coming out of the last movie, sometime around seven o'clock at night, and where I caught the streetcar to go home there was a radio broadcast on, and that's when I found out about Pearl Harbor.

"I never did give any thought to the war; I was just a kid at that time. I certainly had never thought about going in the Navy. Especially after I got rejected by the Merchant Marines. And after I did sign up I was always afraid they were going to catch me for lying about my age and send me home. I remember when we first got to the receiving center, they'd take your old clothes, and my shoes had holes in the bottom and I had put cardboard in them. And the sailors who were issuing our clothes said, 'Boy, you must come from a rough place!' Ha ha! When it'd rain you had to change the cardboard more often. But then they gave me a second-class seamen's rating. Don't ask me

Bobby Arthurs, circa 1945.

why, because most went in as an apprentice, which is two or three grades lower.

"So, I wound up on a train going to Campy Peary, Virginia. And I had rank—when I was fifteen years old! Anybody could've seen I was just a kid. Every place I went the officers would say, 'How old are you?' But nobody ever sent me home. I was lucky. As soon as we got off the train at Camp Peary, somebody says, 'Arthurs . . . boiler watch!' I'll never forget thinking, 'What the hell is boiler watch?' They put you in a big room where there's a big boiler that heats water for the whole barracks. And you'd just sit in this room where this boiler's boiling water. I guess you were supposed to do something if something went wrong, but I didn't know nothing. I wouldn't have knew if it was wrong or right! Every place I went I was always called for this extra duty—trash things, in other words. You see, in the Seabees, most of the guys was in their forties and fifties; they were much older. One of them older guys told me, 'Why don't you go with the surveyors?' So, I went and they took me. And I was holding rods and driving stakes. And I'd go up to the bulldozer operators and the graders and tell them what the crew boss said to do. So actually, I did talk to the dragline people, but I don't remember them, because, you know, I wasn't associated with them or anything. But I know I talked to your guy, because there was only three of them there.

"You told me your guy was in Company C, which was more or less the heavy equipment operators. I was in Headquarters Company, which ran the whole battalion, and included the censors, police, draftsmen, and surveyors. You see, Majuro was made up of all these little islands, and we connected them with causeways. The draglines pulled up coral and the bulldozers smoothed it into roads connecting all the islands. All of this went on at the same time we were building the airstrip; there were close to 1,100 men working, and that's a lot of men. They'd put a group of us on each little island in the morning with sandwiches, and we'd traverse the island making a map. And they'd come in the evening and pick us up in an LCI [Landing Craft Infantry] and take us home. One day, they didn't come get us. They left us there, and it was night. So, the crew chief lit a fire. The next thing you know, the Marines came, with guns loaded. Heh, heh . . . they didn't know who the hell we were, and they made us walk out into the water with our hands up. There was nobody supposed to be on those islands. They had their machine guns on us and we were hollering, 'We're Americans, can't you tell we're Americans?'"

I had brought along several of the photographs from Murray's album—including some pictures of Murray—and I showed them to Bobby to see if they looked familiar.

"Oh yes, that's the Marshalls, all right. But I don't recognize any of the men in the pictures; they must have been in a different company. And even though I'm sure I must have seen your guy on more than one occasion, I sure don't remember him now. You see, mostly you just kept in a tight little circle of friends that you had."

Then I showed Bobby the photos from Murray's envelope—the graphic ones that I later found out were most likely taken on Peleliu.

"That's definitely some combat, I'll tell you that. These were taken at some major battle. This is heavy, heavy fighting. How did he get all of these pictures?"

"I don't know. That's part of the mystery that I'm trying to solve."

"Look at this place . . . I wonder if that could've been Kwajalein in the Marshalls. Because I believe some of our people went to Kwajalein and that was a major battle. And it happened at around the same time we were landing on Majuro. But there's no doubt these are not from Majuro. Majuro never looked anything like this. This is all major stuff. I don't know how you'd get . . . I could never have gotten ahold of anything like this. This was nowheres where I was. To get these kind of pictures, you'd have to know somebody that was there."

"These clearly look to me like original photographs, don't you think?"

"Most definitely. Somebody took these with their personal camera. And sold them. Like I have some that I bought for twenty cents apiece from a guy in our outfit who was a photographer.

"Here . . . wait just a minute. Let me show you something. This is the official book of our battalion."

Bobby had the same book that Murray had shown me: *Century . . . 100th U.S. Naval Construction Battalion.* He opened it up to the pages that showed photographs of all the men. I pointed to the photograph of M. S. Blair and asked Bobby if he knew him.

"I remember him, yeah. He was up high in rank. But I don't remember anything personal about him. My company commander was this guy right here, Robert Blake. I always did whatever they told me, so I never had any problems with him, or anybody else for that matter. That's probably why I kept getting promoted."

We came upon a photo of one of the large water tanks on Majuro.

"Murray told me that the water that came out of those desalinators did not taste very good."

"Hoo-boy. It was terrible. And hot. And Lord, those machines were noisy. I mean, you don't know what noise is until you hear one of those things. We learned quick that the water from the coconuts tasted better. The ones that you drank were the green ones that fell fresh off the trees. The ones that you ate were the ones that were down for a while, because they had more meat in them."

Bobby also had some of his own photos from Majuro.

"Look at this . . . here's a picture of one of the draglines. For all I know, your guy could've been the one operating it."

I noticed there were some photos taken from someplace called "Island X," and I asked Bobby to explain.

"Everyplace you went was 'Island X.' They never gave you a name."

"So, when did you find out that the place you were was Majuro?"

"Probably afterwards. They never told you nothing. You got on a boat and you went someplace."

"So, did you even know you were in the Marshall Islands?"

"I doubt that, seriously. You didn't know where you were going. Nobody told you anything."

"So, you're fifteen years old; maybe by now you've just turned sixteen. You've been through basic training, shipped out to Pearl Harbor, now it's January 1944, and you're on a boat headed to who knows where. Were you scared?"

"No. I loved it. I thought it was an adventure, personally."

"But by then—1944—you must have heard stories about what had happened on other islands."

"Not really. We didn't know anything. I didn't know much about the war until after I came home. It took us like two weeks to get from one place to the other—I remember that. And we always had a destroyer escort. We did take fire from a Japanese Zero while we were en route to Majuro, but when they called general quarters most everybody in our outfit had to go below, so I missed out on all the excitement. Of course, I would have rather stayed on deck.

[Author's note: A general quarters alarm is an announcement made aboard a naval vessel indicating that all available personnel are to report to their battle stations immediately.]

"We landed in four LSTs, and each of them had like two hundred fifty, three hundred men, and all our equipment. We could see people running on the beaches, and we all went ashore with our rifles ready. But it wound up being natives. There was a couple of Japanese civilians—a man and a woman—that was captured on Majuro. I saw them. But the rest of the Japanese had already left and went to Kwajalein. They abandoned Majuro. I saw all the equipment they had left. We also found a Japanese bomber that had been shot down. The pilot had been decapitated. Back when we was going through Montgomery, Alabama, all the women and men was hollering, 'Bring home a Jap's tooth.' So, I went and took his head, put it in a bucket of water to keep the smell down, and brought it back to the tent. And I was trying to get a tooth out of it, but one of the older guys told me I shouldn't do that. I actually did have a little piece of the airplane, but I lost track of it."

"You told me on the telephone that while you were doing the construction, occasionally a Japanese plane would come nearby."

"We had already established air control, so they couldn't get too close. We were never bombed or anything like that. You see, after we were there just a few days, they took all our rifles and ammunition away from us. Then, I don't know if it was maybe a month or two months later, we got an alert that Japan was moving forces from one of the nearby places—I think it was Truk Island—and we didn't know where they were going. So they reissued all our ammunition and rifles and made us dig foxholes. Nothing ever came of it, but then a lot of the guys didn't want to give back their rifles, but they had to—eventually."

"But you were on the island with the Marines, right?"

"The Marines were like our armed guards. We did the construction, and the Marines manned anti-aircraft batteries all around Majuro."

"When you were on Majuro, did you know of any men from the 100th who went on detachments to other islands?"

"Yes, there were detachments taken. I know that happened. Specialists were sent elsewhere, and some of them never came back. I don't know where they went or what ever happened to them—it was secret stuff. I know some of them went to dangerous places, and your guy could have been one of them. But I don't know too much about that; it wasn't anyone in my associations, so I wouldn't have been interested in that back then. I was aware that they were sending people elsewhere, but I didn't know who, why, or where. Actually, if you'd have asked me where I was, I wouldn't have been able to tell you. But if somebody was sent out on a detachment, it would've been to do construction work, not primarily to fight. We were more valuable than a soldier, really. Because a soldier could shoot, but if you were an equipment operator you were definitely more valuable."

"My friend, Murray . . . he tells me that he saw quite a bit of violent combat, and in his mind, it was on Majuro. But based on what you're telling me, which confirms everything I've read about Majuro, it doesn't seem like there was any combat there at all. But he just might've been confused as to where he was."

"That's easy to do. Every island looks about the same. I just recently learned that they had individual names for all the little islands in Majuro. You know, there's a dozen of them, or so. And they all have their own individual names; you can see it on those maps. I didn't know that.

"You saw his discharge papers, right? He should have 'Asiatic Pacific With One Star.' That's for the invasion of the Marshall Islands. Does he have that?"

I couldn't recall seeing those words anywhere in Murray's file.

"Well, I'm not sure. But I know he was on Majuro. It says so in his records."

"Well, if he was on Majuro his papers have got to say what mine says. Let me get mine, so you know what to look for. I'll be right back."

Bobby left the room to retrieve his military documents, and Julie seized the opportunity to tell me a bit of what she had learned from her conversation with Pat: "So they had a pet cougar for thirteen years, who lived in the house and played in a big swimming pool outside."

"A pet cougar?! You mean, like a mountain lion?"

Pat answered, in a perfectly matter-of-fact fashion, "Yes, that's right."

As I was trying to process that strange morsel of information, Bobby returned and sat down.

"See right here under 'Remarks'? It says, 'Asiatic Pacific, One Star.' That was for the Marshall Islands. Then here it says, 'Philippine Liberation.' Because I went with the outfit to the Philippines, but he didn't; you told me he had gone home by then. The one star was for participating in one major battle. The invasion of the Marshall Islands was significant enough to earn one star. We didn't get one for the Philippines because we weren't near any combat. In the Marshall Islands, we actually was in it, you know, we waded ashore—and we lucked out, that's the way I look at it. But in the Philippine Islands there was nothing around where we were."

For as many times as I had examined Murray's records, I couldn't for the life of me remember what was printed under 'Remarks.'

Bobby continued: "See, it lists all your ratings. I started out as a seaman, second class, and I came out a carpenter's mate, second class. But see, mine should also say 'World War II Victory Medal' where it says that other stuff. But it doesn't. Because when I got discharged, at the end of 1945, there was like a million guys coming home. And the people typing didn't care about nothing. And I definitely earned it, 'cause I was over there."

"So no bullets were fired on Majuro."

"Not that I know of. I wouldn't swear to it, because things could've happened that I didn't know about."

"Sure. But it seems like you have quite a good memory. It seems like you would remember if you were being shot at."

"Yeah. Heh, heh—I remember when we got put off that damned boat we was like waist-high; we had an old-fashioned Enfield rifle that was made in World War I, with a hundred rounds of ammunition and a bayonet about a foot long. We had a full pack, a gas mask, canteen, and we walked ashore in water that was waist-deep. And you could see people running, but you couldn't tell who they were—they were just little specks—but nobody was shooting at us. Definitely nobody shot at us. I've always felt like we were the ones who lucked out because we never came under fire. But you see, the Army was supposed to have gone through Majuro before we got there. But their story don't add up, because they said there was nobody left, but obviously there was those few Japanese that were still there. Sometimes in a war things don't add up."

"Yes, that's right. Do you feel that the military kept information about combat secret back then? If a man was in combat was there some secrecy about it?"

"I wouldn't put anything past them. They could just lose records."

"Murray is very convinced that there was very heavy resistance at Majuro. Now, he's not bragging to me; I'll tell you that for sure. He has never told anybody all these stories, and some of the things he told me he participated in—like the torture of prisoners—these aren't things he's proud of. In fact, these are things that he's haunted by."

Bobby squinted and looked at me quizzically.

"What prisoners?"

"Well, that's what I'm trying to find out. According to him, on some island they came upon Japanese prisoners and they tortured them and killed them."

"You know, I'm very active with the VFW [Veterans of Foreign Wars]. And I know a lot of Marines. And the Marines did execute Japanese soldiers. They hated them. Because they would booby-trap themselves and commit suicide when they surrendered and kill the Marines. And I know Marines that told me flat out, 'We threw them over the back of the boat when nobody was looking.'"

"Right. Nowadays we look at what soldiers do and we judge it pretty harshly. I'm not condoning throwing a prisoner off the back of a boat, but I think it's unfair to judge a man who does that, while you're sitting at home in your living room."

"That's right. You're in an outfit, and you've got friends you make, and one of them gets killed by underhanded stuff like that—you don't take that easy. Japan did terrible stuff. In China, they butchered people in all the big cities. Women, children, babies . . . they'd beat them with hammers and all kinds of brutal things. They were terrible, mean people. That's what gets me about when that submarine accidentally sunk that Japanese fishing boat off of Hawaii a few years ago. You knew about that?"

"No . . . tell me. When was this?"

"In the last couple of years. It was a pretty good-sized fishing boat that had some high-school students on it. And this atomic submarine from the United States had civilian passengers aboard, and the captain let them in the control room. And when the submarine surfaced, it came up under that boat and sank it in about a thousand feet of water. Half of the crew and several of those students were killed. And the Navy went and picked that ship up off the bottom and got the bodies out. And we apologized and paid like ten million dollars to the Japanese government. But they sank the *Arizona*; they didn't come pick that sucker up. And to this day I don't believe they ever apologized properly for doing it. But . . . that's what happens.

[Author's note: The incident to which Bobby is referring was a collision between *Ehime Maru*, a Japanese fishing trawler, and the USS *Greeneville*, a US Navy nuclear-powered submarine, in February 2001.[14]]

"But anyway, I'll tell you, in my experience with the VFW, I've met a lot of people that think things happened to them that didn't. Or they embellish. I know one guy who said he was a colonel in the Marine Corps, and it turned out he was a private in the Army. Another guy said he earned the Congressional Medal of Honor, but he had nothing. I've seen a whole bunch of them like that. You can see it on the news, too."

"Absolutely. There was recently a case like that in Utah. A Korean War veteran—an eighty-six-year-old guy who was in the Air Force—contacted his congressman, Jason Chaffetz, and convinced him to present medals to him that he claimed he had earned. So, in a public ceremony, Chaffetz gives this guy the Distinguished Service Cross, a Silver Star, and a Purple Heart. But it turns out when the Pentagon investigated the man's records, he hadn't actually earned any of them. He did serve in the military, but the documents he presented to Chaffetz were fraudulent. I'm aware that there are cases like this. And if my friend Murray had said things like, 'I was a hero and I saved my buddy's life,' then I would agree that he could just be exaggerating or embellishing his story. But when he tells me things that he's never told anybody, things that he's ashamed of—and I believe that he really is ashamed—and he tells me that I can't publish this book until after he dies . . . why would somebody make that up? Have you ever heard of somebody making up stories like that?"

"You know, I told you I went to the seventh grade. When I came home from the service, I went to a high school for veterans and I graduated. Then I went to LSU and I studied psychology a little bit before I went into law enforcement. And what I learned is, people do things just to make themselves feel better. They lie. They just flat-out lie."

I knew what Bobby was saying was true, but I tried to convince him that it wasn't applicable to Murray: "Well, I worked in an emergency room for thirteen years, and I had to have a pretty good sense of when somebody was lying to me. I've got pretty good radar about who's telling me the truth and who isn't. And I am firmly convinced that Murray believes that he experienced all these things."

"Well, it could be. You know, it seems to me you must be pretty good friends with this guy to have flown all the way to Louisiana just to talk to me."

"Well, the truth is, you've also got a very interesting story. Youngest man in the whole battalion . . . a fifteen-year-old boy who enlisted in the military. And it sounds like your motivation may not have been entirely patriotic."

"My motive was hunger! Ha ha! Joining the Navy was the best thing I ever did. Because . . . I left something out . . . something that's not flattering. Before I went in the Navy, nobody was buying any magazines. So, I got so desperate—I don't know what the rest of them did—but I went into a bank and got some blank common checks. And I don't know how I learned this, but I started writing checks for subscriptions with kids' names that I had known in school. When I turned in the checks, I'd get my commission, and I was able to survive. I don't know how many I wrote . . . it could've been three, it could've been a dozen. But then the checks started bouncing. And I already had signed up with the Navy, so when the crew boss confronted me about all this, I told him, 'Yeah . . . I'm starving . . . what else can I do?' He dropped the whole thing. Of course he couldn't have done anything about it anyway. I was in the Navy. But if that had continued I would have wound up in jail again, most definitely. I can honestly say that being in the Navy saved my life."

That sentiment was a stark contrast to Murray's opinion of his military service. As I contemplated that paradox, I realized that it was almost time for the four of us to go to dinner. I asked Bobby about his time in the Navy after leaving the Marshall Islands.

"After we left Majuro, we went back to Pearl Harbor. We stayed there for two or three months, then we went to Samar Island, in the Philippines. That wasn't an amphibious landing— we didn't have to wade ashore—the LSTs dropped us off right on the beach. In fact, there was a whole bunch of Filipino people just standing there watching us. And by then they had issued us carbines, which was a nice light rifle. Of course, once we landed they took those rifles away from us. Most of the time we were in the Philippines we were building schools and hospitals.

"Now, at that time I had never been on a date in my life. By the time we got to the Philippines, I was probably seventeen then. The people who lived there did laundry for our outfit, and I met this young lady. She couldn't speak English, and I had learned a few words, but not much. But I started following her when she went home in the evening. It was a narrow path through the jungle and up a little hill. I went up there and met her family; they lived in a bamboo hut with a thatch roof. Near the end of the war things got more relaxed, and when we'd get off duty, I used to go up there at night. Her daddy built a little hut for us, and I'd stay up there and I'd come back in the morning. This one evening I was going up that little path, on my merry way, and I run right into a Japanese soldier. The jungle was so thick I didn't see him until I was as close to him as I am to you. He had a red bandana, a loincloth, a rifle slung on his shoulder, and a little pack. And he had a machete in his hand. And when I run into him all I did was smile, wave, and say 'Hi' and kept on going the way I was going. If I would've turned around I'm sure he would've killed me with that machete. I was unarmed; like I told you before, they took our guns away from us immediately. But I startled him, he startled me, and we each just kept walking in our own direction.

"It turns out there were lots of these stragglers in the Philippines. In fact, the last Japanese soldier surrendered in 1974. He had been hiding in the Philippines for almost thirty years! When I got to my girlfriend's house, the whole family was scared out of their minds. That Japanese soldier had just come from there, and he had stolen some of their rice. Some people might doubt that story is true. I wish I could take a lie-detector test, because I can still see that fellow as clear as day.

"I got discharged in January of '46. I went back to where I lived as a child, the Ninth Ward. Right across the street was the Lone Star Cement Company, on the Industrial Canal, which connects Lake Pontchartrain to the Mississippi River. I was eighteen, and I went over there with my discharge papers, but the guy in charge just took them and threw them down on the desk in front of me. He didn't think they were worth anything. He had never been in the service; he was home making big money. However, I got hired. How do you figure out people? You see, what was in my favor was I looked innocent and quiet. And I was—I didn't drink or smoke. And you know what job I got? They call it 'Process Control Chemist.' I had to give written orders to the crane operators to put this many buckets of mud in a hopper, and so much water to add to it, and it'd come out a slurry. Then they'd transfer it to a big basin, and I'd run tests on it and add the calcium carbonate and chemicals. Then it'd come out of this long kiln—almost three thousand degrees heat—and then you'd add gypsum to it, which would control the cement settling time. You had to be careful of how much gypsum went in there; you didn't want it to be too fast or slow."

"How did you know anything about that?"

"I didn't! Ha ha! But it must've been simple, because I did it . . . with a seventh-grade education. And I worked there about twelve years. At first when I came home I was living in my uncle's house—three of us in one room. My dad swept streets in New Orleans for a living, and he got paid twice a month. Twenty-two dollars every two weeks. He was supposed to give half to my uncle for groceries, but most of the time he just drank it up. I can still hear my uncle hollering at him, saying he was gonna kick us all out. My dad was terrible, just terrible. I still can't see how he could do those things. I had six hundred dollars saved up, which in those days was some money. Eventually I wanted to get out of the city, so I came over here. Just by luck I found this place. I didn't know Lacombe from the moon. I designed and built this house; I put the forms down for the concrete slab; I did the plumbing, electrical, the roof. The only thing I didn't do was lay the bricks."

As we gathered our wives and prepared to leave for dinner, Bobby had one more thing to say: "You know, I organize the

Seabee reunions, and I have spoken to a lot of Seabees. I have never spoken to a Seabee, from my outfit or any other, who saw extensive combat. That's never come up. We wouldn't have been sent someplace specifically for combat . . . we would've been sent to build something. There was guys in our outfit that died on Majuro. They drowned. The undertow dragged them out to sea. But we were never fired upon. Never really in harm's way, so to speak. We served our country, did our jobs, and were able to learn a trade in the process. I never felt like our lives were in danger. We were the lucky ones."

CHAPTER 15

THERE AIN'T NO SENSE EVEN TALKING TO YOU

Julie and I insisted on treating Bobby and Pat to dinner at their favorite restaurant, as a way of thanking them for their hospitality. The place they chose was Sal & Judy's; an Italian/Creole restaurant right in the heart of Lacombe, which basically means it's in the middle of nowhere.

The place was packed, surprisingly elegant, and Bobby was treated like royalty from the moment we walked in. We ordered our dinner, and while we were waiting for our food to arrive I took the opportunity to ask Bobby and Pat about their personal life.

"You guys have been married forty-five years, is that right?"

Pat corrected me, ever so politely: "No, it's been forty-seven years."

"Bobby told me forty-five on the phone."

Julie, thinking quickly, said, "Well you must have talked to him two years ago!"

Bobby laughed, and I responded, "Oh yeah . . . that's right. I don't want to get him in any trouble." Pat chuckled as well. She was probably used to Bobby forgetting how long they had been married, even though he could recall every detail of the things he experienced back in 1944.

"How did you guys meet?"

Bobby answered, "We both worked at the newspaper in New Orleans, the *Times-Picayune*. I was an electrician, and Patsy was doing payroll for all the drivers. I had quit the cement plant. It was around 1958, and I started out as a carpenter making seventy-five dollars a week—big money. When the newspaper went into automation, I took a course in electronics so I could fix all the machines, and by the time I quit, I was making a hundred twenty-five dollars a week.

"It was a six-story building, and it was full of girls. And I asked every girl in that building for a date. Some said yes, some said no. I dated one girl who was a ballet dancer. She was eighteen, and built like a clock, you know? All the men in the building were always ogling her, and somehow or another—don't ask me how—I wound up dating her. But she was engaged to a sailor . . . all the time I was with her. She didn't want to be alone, let me put it to you that way. She wanted company, if you know what I mean. He was off wherever, but when he came home that was the end of that. And then, along came Pat."

Pat added, "He asked me out for a year and a half."

Bobby responded, "Well, she was dating an Air Force man at the time. And I had strikes against me because of my age; I'm sixteen years older than Pat. But I'm still hanging around, and I do all the work around here."

I decided to get the female perspective: "Pat, what made you finally say yes?"

"The first date I agreed to go on was a wedding. I liked him. I had seen him around the building and—"

Bobby interrupted: "I made a good impression. She didn't know me then—didn't know my true colors. Heh, heh."

Pat laughed.

"No. Everybody was horrified, even my boss. My boss said, 'What are you going to do when he turns forty?' So I said, 'I'll trade him in for two twenties.'"

We all got a good laugh out of that comment.

Pat continued, "Plus he was married before. That was another strike against him."

Bobby elaborated: "I got married to a girl named Beverly when I first came home. We were married about twelve years. We had no children. She left me when I moved here. I told her, if you just want to take some time and figure some stuff out, I understand. But she started dating, and I said, 'It's over.' That's the way I am. I'm one way."

"And how many children do you two have?"

Bobby answered, "We've got a boy and a girl."

"Tell me about them. How old are they, where do they live?"

This time Bobby deferred to Pat: "How old are they?" He chuckled even as he said it, amused by the selective lapses in his otherwise stellar memory. Pat gave a definitive answer.

"Our daughter is forty-seven, and our son is forty-two. They live in North Carolina. Both of them lived right here in Lacombe, but they worked in New Orleans, and their company was wiped out when Katrina hit, so that's why they moved to North Carolina. We just went up to North Carolina because our son got married. Our son's first wife got murdered. She and him broke up, and she went crazy . . . got into all kinds of stuff. She wound up with some undesirables, and it was a murder-suicide. She had two kids from before she met our son, and we accept them as our grandchildren. The boy is in the Air Force, and the girl is in college. Basically, we just get to see our kids on the holidays. One's coming for Thanksgiving; the other one's coming for Christmas."

"How was it for you guys during Katrina? Did you have to evacuate?"

Bobby responded, "No, I've never evacuated. I've been here sixty years, and the most water I ever saw was Katrina. I have a fence in my backyard that's about four feet high, and the water was up to the top of that fence. But luckily, the backyard slopes downward, so it never did get up to the house. You see, from my house, you go about three hundred feet and the road ends. Then there's woods for about five hundred feet, then there's a swamp that's about a mile. Then you come to a beach and that's Lake Pontchartrain, right there. All that water came up and came this way. The house didn't take any damage, but the electricity went out. We've got a pretty good-sized generator here, but I ran out of gas after a week. I can only keep so much gas here. I've been through a whole bunch of hurricanes—New Orleans has flooded so many times just in my lifetime. In fact, one of the worst floods in history happened in 1927, the year I was born."

I added my perspective on the Crescent City: "New Orleans is a very unique city, maybe one of the most unusual cities in the United States. It's almost like a different country altogether. Pat, are you from New Orleans, originally?"

"Yes, born and raised. And I never wanted to stay there. When I got old enough, I wanted out. In fact, I wanted to be an airline stewardess, but I was too young. I was nineteen or twenty years old, and you had to be twenty-one."

Bobby interjected, "I can't even remember that far back."

"Well, I didn't even know you then."

Bobby smiled and said, "You didn't? Well, how did you survive?"

Pat snapped back, "Better!"

Julie and I had a good laugh listening to their snappy exchange. Our food arrived just in the nick of time, before Bobby could get himself into any more trouble. Of course, since we were in Louisiana, we had to try the gumbo. It was fabulous: thick, rich, and incredibly flavorful.

Pat elaborated on her feelings toward the Big Easy: "I hate New Orleans. It's a city that's filled with crime. Where we live here, St. Tammany Parish, it's like a whole different world."

I responded, "I understand what you mean. We've certainly noticed that New Orleans is a little dirtier than the average city. And there's more public drunkenness, which we don't really appreciate. But New Orleans has also got some wonderful food and music, and great museums. I'm sure you've been to the National World War II Museum."

Bobby answered succinctly, "Nope."

I was shocked. "You haven't? Why on earth would you have not gone there?"

"Well, it doesn't interest me, really."

"But that museum is phenomenal. Julie and I have been there several times. You know, when they first built it, it was the National D-Day Museum, and—"

Bobby interrupted me rather abruptly: "Right. And I didn't like that. That's what turned me off. Because that was one battle, really. And it was important—a great battle—but there was nothing about the Pacific. And that's where I served. And anyway, I have VCR tapes of all my favorite movies and programs about the war. And not only World War II, but Korea and Vietnam, Desert Storm, everything. Like, did you ever see the movie *The Man Who Would Be King*?"

"Yeah."

"That's the kind of stuff I like."

"I know why you like that movie. You must be a Freemason."

"That's right. I'm a 32nd degree Freemason and past master of the local lodge here in Lacombe. I've been in that organization about sixty years. You get out of that what you put into it . . . like a lot of things. But like in every organization, there's people who go into it to get what they think they're going to get, and they're disappointed. I've seen guys who get expelled from the Freemasons. You do something wrong, you don't want to go before a board of Freemasons, because they won't show you any mercy."

"Yes, I know. My father was expelled from the Masons."

"He was expelled? What did he do?"

"He committed a felony . . . theft."

"Yeah . . . well, that'll do it. But there's a lot of worse things he could've done."

"Quite honestly—and I'm not a member of that organization—but my father was a life-long member. He was master of his lodge, he was the grand lecturer, he was very devoted to it. I've always felt like he was judged by society—he did his time in prison—and if that organization really is a fraternity, they should have accepted him back."

"It's not that kind of an organization. They don't forgive. When you go in, you take an oath. And they specify in this oath—which is not short, and you've got to memorize it and be examined on it—you can't violate any of the rules. And they don't care who you are. But you know, there's something I wanted to talk to you about. This thing with Israel and the Palestinians. They don't look like they're ever going to get together. You talk about a war."

Bobby's abrupt redirection of the conversation caught me off guard, but I offered my opinion: "The problem is, you've got people who are very dogmatic in their belief that they have the right to a particular piece of land. And if you said to them, 'We'll give you ten times that piece of land, but it's over here' . . . they don't want it. And there's no solution. There's a lot of hatred there, and I don't believe it's ever going to end. And you've got one group of people who wants the other group of people wiped off the face of the Earth."

Bobby responded: "There's a lot of people in all those places, who don't want all this stupid stuff . . . but they have no voice. To me, there's only one way to stop it. You have to counter force with force, otherwise they take it as a weakness. But as far as sending all these young guys to Afghanistan, Iraq, and all them places, and their guys are shooting our guys, and our guys are getting killed . . . they shouldn't do that. They ought to use these drones. Now . . . every now and then they kill a baby, or a dog, or a cat . . . but that's the price you pay."

"Well . . . that's an interesting point of view. War today is different than it was back when you were in the service though.

In World War II, the civilian casualties were enormous. Today that wouldn't be acceptable."

"Look at Dresden. They bombed that place until there was nothing left. And it was all civilians."

I was impressed with Bobby's knowledge of history, and added, "Or people talk about the use of the atomic bomb. There's been a lot of criticism of Truman—revisionist history—for his decision to use nuclear weapons. But we were firebombing Japan incessantly when that bomb was dropped, and thousands of civilians were killed in the process."

"Japan would never have surrendered. We would have lost hundreds of thousands of our men. And the Japanese would have fought with their children. So those atomic bombs saved their country. And the proof of the pudding is that they're our great allies today."

I decided to share a story that had made a strong impression on me and influenced how I feel about our country's use of the atomic bomb. "When Julie and I went to Hawaii, we visited Pearl Harbor, and we took a tour of the USS *Missouri*, the battleship on which Japan formally surrendered. And we had a very unique tour guide: an older gentleman who grew up in Korea during World War II. As you may already know, Korea had been colonized by Japan back in 1910. And this man told us that as the war was winding down, Japanese soldiers came through his town and gave every person a wooden spear, anticipating an invasion by Allied forces. And he distinctly remembers that his family was told that when the Americans came, they should use the spear to kill as many soldiers as they could before they were killed themselves. So, I think you're right . . . Japan was prepared to fight until the bitter end. How do you feel towards Japanese people? How did you feel back then, and how do you feel about them now?"

"I'm fine with them. I accept them like I accept you. Back then, during the war . . . I didn't know what was happening. I wasn't interested in history in those days. Mostly, I found out about things after the war. Everything was a secret, to start with. We didn't have radios or newspapers or anything. We rarely ever heard anything. I know I sent letters home, and when I got home, they were all cut up."

Our conversation was interrupted by the arrival of our entrees. Pat had the crabmeat au gratin, Julie had speckled trout, and I followed Bobby's lead and tried the redfish Nicholas: broiled to perfection then topped with shrimp, crabmeat, and mushrooms. Absolutely delicious. You could tell the food was fantastic, because as soon as the plates arrived a deafening silence fell over our table. All you could hear was the gentle clinking of our forks.

As we finished eating, Pat returned the dialogue to something a bit more lighthearted.

"So, Scott, you know where he took me on our second date? To a cemetery!"

Bobby started laughing before Pat could even finish her sentence.

"Ha ha ha! Chalmette National Cemetery . . . dates back to the Civil War. And it was also a battleground: the Battle of New Orleans in 1815."

I liked Bobby more with each passing minute.

"Now that's my kind of guy! I would've married him, too, if I were you, Pat. I mean, taking you to a cemetery . . . what a romantic!" I thought back to something Julie had mentioned while we were at the house. "And how did you wind up with a mountain lion as a pet?"

Bobby answered, "We bought it. Pat saw an ad in *USA Today*. It said, 'Come to Oklahoma, Hunt a Cougar.' Or you could buy one. She buys it. She sent fifteen hundred dollars off, and I said, 'We'll never see that again.' Then we got a call from the airport; the guy says, 'We've got a bird for you.' Turns out, it wasn't a bird, but a baby cougar in a crate, and it was making all these squealing sounds."

Pat had some photos of the cougar in her purse. There was one picture of the animal jumping six feet straight up in the air to procure a carton of milk, and a photo of their son, Jason, lying in bed cuddling the giant feline. Pat pointed to one photo and explained, "See, here he is playing with our dog, Duke. Duke was bigger than him at the time, but then when he got older he'd just play too rough."

Bobby added, "Well he'd drive you nuts biting on you. Just playing, of course. He wasn't vicious . . . he just played rough. But I used to be all cut up. He'd stand up on his hind legs and put his paws on my shoulders and I'd be looking up at him. He weighed about two hundred pounds."

I found the whole thing astonishing.

"Well, look at the size of the paw on that animal! That paw is the size of my head!"

Pat got a good laugh out of that observation and said, "Yeah, but he was a sweetie. He lived with us for thirteen years. In the wild they only live to be about seven. We used to have the veterinarian from Audubon Park Zoo in New Orleans come over and handle things. It was expensive."

Bobby shared another interesting story: "You think that's bad? When I left the newspaper, I joined the sheriff's department as a deputy right here in Lacombe. And there was this one lady; she had a full-grown male African lion. And all she had was some chicken wire around trees to keep him in. And he would get out and they'd call me, because it was my area. And I'd go and have to get that scoundrel back to where he belonged. And he would come—I might have to pull on him a little—but whenever he licked you, it was like getting slapped with a file! Believe me, it'd take your skin right off. But what happened was, one day he got out and knocked over an elderly person who was getting his mail. Anyway, I charged her with something—I believe it was permitting a dangerous animal to run loose—and she wanted to give me the lion."

Pat added, "Oh, and I would've taken it, too."

But Bobby was the voice of reason: "He was just too big. Those animals weigh four or five hundred pounds."

I was still trying to process Bobby's story.

"You know, what I find interesting . . . you're a police officer and you get a call and you've got to go corral up a lion. I think that if I was in your position, I'm not letting that lion get close enough to lick me. So, the fact that you know what his tongue felt like, I find that very interesting."

Bobby gave a very serious answer.

"Well, you see, the thing is, if you've got a job, you've got to handle your job. I've handled murders, rapes, burglaries, armed robberies, suicides. I've gone into muddy water, feeling around to find a body. I've done all that. But that's the job. There was only one policeman here in Lacombe . . . me. And there was twenty-three barrooms in my area. And there was always fights, but I've never had to shoot anybody. There was one black guy that was very dangerous; he'd murdered a couple of people. He was standing outside one of those bars one night, and I had a warrant for his arrest. I walked into the bar right past him, and when I came out he figured I wasn't worried about him. But then I walked right up to him, pulled my pistol, and I said, 'You're under arrest. I know you've got a gun on you . . . if you run I'm gonna shoot you.' Some of the other colored guys, they all knew me and they knew I was an expert shot. The rest of the guys who were standing there grabbed him and threw him in my car. Most of the time that's the way I made arrests . . . the people arrested them for me. There's more police in town now. They've got them crawling all over each other. And actually, there's only one barroom now; back then I had twenty-three.

"I've been associated with black people all my life. There was segregation, don't get me wrong. Like in the streetcars: the blacks sat in the back, the whites sat in the front. And when the black kids went to a white school . . . God, you'd think the world came to an end. You've seen all that, in Arkansas, and it happened in New Orleans, too. You know, how can people do those kind of things? How could the people in Germany have burned all those people? But then, if you really look at history— going back to the Romans, and the Huns—everybody murdered everybody. It's human nature. But most of the white people I knew here in Louisiana thought that whole segregation business was stupid stuff.

"To this day I can walk around anywhere in Lacombe and everybody—black or white—comes up to me and shakes my hand. Because I treated everybody decent. If I went to a house and said, 'I have a warrant for your husband or your son' and then they'd say, 'He's not here, Mr. Arthurs.' I'd say, 'OK, when he comes home, tell him I'm looking for him.' I didn't break in doors or kick in houses and all that stuff. I never beat anybody. There are policemen out there that are . . . hell, I've had more trouble with policemen than I had with criminals.

"So many policemen, in my estimate, want to be the judge, jury, and executioner. And they think they're above the law. There was one guy who was doing electrical work, on duty, in uniform. One time he was doing some work at somebody's house, and he got a terrible cut on his head. So, he gets on the highway and calls it in like he got injured in the line of duty. Well, he did that in my town, and I caught him at it. And he got fired. The police hated me for that."

"I would think a lot of police wouldn't like a guy like you. That reminds me of another good old movie . . . "

"*Serpico.*" Bobby finished the sentence for me.

"That's exactly right! You're like Frank Serpico!"

Julie made an observation: "You guys remind me of each other! You only just met and you're finishing each other's sentences!"

I couldn't argue the point. I definitely felt a strong connection with Bobby.

"Did you find corruption during your time in the Navy?"

"Well, I know there was a lieutenant in our outfit—actually this happened on Majuro. They found out he had faked his college papers. And they put him on garbage detail . . . heh, heh. He was in a lieutenant's uniform picking up garbage. I'll never forget that guy! That was a big scandal on Majuro."

As our coffee arrived Bobby returned to telling us about his time as a police officer: "People live in all kinds of houses around here . . . from shacks all the way up to big mansions. I have found that the people who are the most comfortable think they are above everybody else. Thirty years ago, there was this local guy who got a ticket from a state trooper and he gave it to a politician to get it fixed . . . because they do that around here. But the politician didn't fix it, and when they called the guy's name out in court, he wasn't there to pay it, so the judge issued a warrant for his arrest. So, I drove up to his house in my police car—and I was in uniform—and his wife answered the door and I told her I was here to talk to her husband about this ticket. And she turned her German Shepherd on me while I was standing outside her door! I got back in my car and I said, 'Lady, if it had been any other policeman they would've shot and killed your dog and it'd be your fault.' Some people are just stupid. Eventually the guy came home, and he starts criticizing me, giving me a hard time about how I was supposedly harassing his wife and threatening his dog. Now this happened thirty years ago, and you know I ran into him in the post office about two weeks ago. I didn't really recognize him at first, but he comes up to me and he starts some talk about how I was illegally parked or something. I said, 'I know you . . . you're Anderson. You're going to be stupid all your life, so there ain't no sense even talking to you.'"

I laughed so hard at that comment I think some coffee sprayed out of my nose.

"I finally retired from the sheriff's office in 1985, after twenty-three years. Then I went to work as a patrolman on the

Causeway Bridge. You can't believe the stuff I saw people doing while they were driving over that causeway . . . reading a book, eating a three-course meal, fixing their hair. One day I was in my car, patrolling the bridge in broad daylight. There was a vehicle in front of me, a small van, and all of a sudden, I saw glass break out the side. Just as I was thinking to myself, 'I wonder what happened?' I saw a big behind sticking out that broken window. So, I turned on my lights and the vehicle pulled over and this big, fat black woman fell out of that window onto the bridge. Well, I had all the traffic stopped, so I got out of the car and I ran up there, and it turns out it was an attendant transporting this woman from Charity Hospital in New Orleans over to Southeast Psychiatric Hospital in Mandeville—that's just the next town over from here. Well, she didn't want to go. So she's on the railing of the bridge, straddling it, and I said, 'That's dangerous; you might fall in that water.' And she says, 'I'm not going over there . . . I'll drown first!' And I said, 'Well, you might not be going there, but before you drown those sharks are gonna eat you.' She says, 'What sharks?!' And there's no sharks in that water, but I said, 'Those sharks that's right under you . . . you might want to get off of there.' Well that changed her mind.

"You know, everyplace I go I wind up running things, and it's not like I volunteer for it. We have a museum in Lacombe. It's a 1912 schoolhouse, and it's on the National Register of Historic Places. It's packed to the walls with antiques, going back to the nineteenth century. I'm the curator now for about eighteen years. In fact, if you'd like, after we finish up here we can go over to the museum and I can open it up for you . . . I've got the keys."

"Julie and I would really like that. Let me ask you something, Bobby . . . are you proud of your service?"

"Oh yeah. But I had put it out of my mind for many years. Only after I turned sixty-five, and I went to the VA—and I may not have been aware of anything, like you asked me before if I was scared, and I wasn't—but they said I had Post-Traumatic Stress Disorder. You know, I was not always an outgoing, friendly person. My whole life I've always had a deep feeling that I was inferior. I had problems, but I've overcome them. I am a more friendly person today. I smile at people."

"But do you think your problems were a result of your military service?"

"I have no idea. My youngest brother, who's dead, was in the Marine Corps in Korea. He was a tank commander. When he came home, he got married, but that fell apart and he went back in the Marines. Then he became a terrible alcoholic, and he was discharged for being drunk on guard duty. A short while after, he committed suicide. A lot of people in my family had terrible lives. Really."

"It seems to me—and I don't want to overstep my bounds—but it sounds like you had a pretty rugged childhood. Did your dad ever hit you?"

"Oh . . . many times. And not just with his hands. He had a blackjack and he'd hit all of us with it. And in the head. My dad lived to be seventy-eight, and I never did have a good relationship with him . . . I hated him. Well, I don't know if I hated him. I talked to him, I visited him, I showed him respect. If he was in the hospital for something I'd go there to see him. I didn't like him though. I'll give you a good example: when I got married the first time, he bought us a television as a present. A month or so later, the constable came and repossessed it. That was his history. He would buy stuff and not pay for it."

"Your childhood doesn't sound like it was happy. And plus, you were growing up during the Great Depression."

"I'll tell you what we ate for breakfast. I never saw milk in my childhood. You either drank coffee or water, and toast. Like a prison meal . . . heh, heh. For lunch, we usually had a peanut butter and jelly sandwich. For supper, we'd have something like meatballs and spaghetti. On Sunday, we each got two donuts and a roll—that was a treat. We had an icebox, but there was never anything in it. Growing up under those circumstances, I think you could understand why I really appreciate a good meal like the one we just had."

We left Sal & Judy's and took a short drive over to the Bayou Lacombe Rural Museum. A quaint, wooden building, it was jam-packed with all sorts of antiques and artifacts. I could tell how much hard work Bobby had put into the museum, although our nephew Pete, the professional archivist, might have cringed at how some of the items were being displayed. Bobby and Pat proudly gave Julie and me a private tour.

"When I took over as curator, most of the stuff wasn't displayed. It was just in storage. The building itself is an old schoolhouse constructed in 1912, mostly out of heartwood pine. The whole roof came off in Katrina. There's people still living that went to school here as children, and we've got their pictures right over here, along with their class photos from when they were kids. There's a piano that came out of the red-light district in New Orleans."

We spent well over an hour at the museum. There were dozens of Native American artifacts, mostly from the Choctaw tribe. There were relics from the Civil War and both World Wars. I easily could have spent several hours examining the various exhibits more carefully. But it was getting late, everybody was getting tired, and it was time for us to go. Julie and I drove Bobby and Pat back to their home, thanked them for spending the day with us, and we made our way back to the hotel. I reflected upon everything Bobby Arthurs had told me about his time in the Navy, and I recalled Murray's description of his own experience. Two men, in the same place, at the same time, yet their experiences guided their lives in diametrically opposite directions. To paraphrase Dickens: for one it was the best of times, for the other it was the worst of times. In one it cultivated wisdom, in the other it fostered foolishness. It led one to a lifetime of light, the other to a lifetime of darkness. Ironically, as different as the two men were from one another, they shared at least one substantial trait: neither had a good relationship with his father. And coincidentally or not, neither did I.

CHAPTER 16

YOU CAN BELIEVE WHAT YOU WANT

During the course of our visit, Bobby gave me the contact information for two members of the 100th NCB with whom he had kept in touch. The first was Larry Duncan, who served with Bobby in Headquarters Company. I called him at his home in Clackamas, Oregon. I introduced myself and asked him to tell me about his time in the service.

"I volunteered when I was seventeen in 1943. At the time I went in they had just started this Construction Battalion business, and when I enlisted here in downtown Portland, that's where I went. They sent me right to Williamsburg, Virginia, for boot camp, and then they sent us down to Gulfport, Mississippi, for advanced training. Finally, they sent us out to Port Hueneme, and from there we shipped out to Hawaii. In Hawaii, our first job was repairing the runways on Ford Island. I was on the blacktop crew, which is hot and tiresome, but I was young and it didn't make any difference to me.

"Then we went over to Majuro and I was a surveyor. As I recall, there were about six of us, and I spent a lot of time holding rods and levels, and I also had some driving duties. Most of the guys in the battalion were five or ten years older than I was at the time."

"How would you describe the landing on Majuro? Was there any resistance?"

"We went in on an LST, they dropped the ramp, and we strolled ashore. There wasn't any combat that I know of. We had a couple of scares from Japanese planes coming over, but they never bothered us or dropped any bombs or whatever. We were scared, of course—green, and young, and scared—but nothing ever happened. We didn't know what was going on; we didn't have a clue. We'd understood that there were some Marines that were going to go in on the first wave and we were going to be the second wave. From then on, we never knew what was going to happen. But there weren't any Japanese to speak of on the island. Just a doctor and his wife, I think, and maybe a few guards . . . not enough to worry about. So, all of our fears were in vain."

"Did you know of any men in your unit who went off with detachments to other islands where there was combat?"

"I can't answer that question . . . I just don't know. I was too low on the totem pole and too green to ask questions."

"I've read that there were seventeen men from the 100th that were sent with the Marines over to an island called Angaur, near Peleliu. You don't know anybody personally who went on that detachment?"

"No. I do recall there was some sort of a conversation about Peleliu, but my memory just doesn't drag up any specifics about it at all."

"You know, I'm faced with a difficult task . . . I want to get history right, and—"

Larry interrupted me, "That is a difficult thing to do. Heh, heh. I appreciate your effort. History is oftentimes a point of view. The atrocities that we blamed the Japanese for was heroism when we did it. And you do realize that the men you're interviewing are getting a little long in the tooth. But I would've remembered if I had been in combat, I'm sure of that.

"After we left Majuro, we went back to Hawaii, then we went to the Philippines, and we stayed there until the end of the war. And we came back on the *Ticonderoga*, which was a state-of-the-art aircraft carrier. So, the trip back to San Francisco was pretty quick. When we went out to Hawaii originally, we went on the USS *Sacajawea*, which was a Liberty Ship, and it was not a pleasant voyage. I remember it was Thanksgiving and they served us creamed turkey, and that was not a good deal. There was guys getting sick all over the place."

"You don't happen to remember a man who ran one of the draglines, by the name of Murray Jacobs, do you?"

"No, I really don't. I know about the draglines and all the heavy equipment; as far as that goes, as an engineer, I spent quite a bit of time standing around and watching them. But I never got involved in any of the operation, other than showing them where to go. Mostly we just stayed with the guys in our own company. Our officers were all nice guys, and they treated us OK, and we were able to talk to them without any problems.

The people in Headquarters Company were the engineers, the cooks, some of the security details. About all we got out of that was some goodies from the cooks."

"Larry, how would you sum up your military experience? How do you feel about it when you look back on it today?"

"It was great. I've always thought it was a great adventure. I was raised here in the Pacific Northwest, in logging camps, bouncing from town to town, and I didn't know a thing. So the experience was great. Of course, the aftermath, in terms of recognition for service, and developing friendships with people like Bobby Arthurs, that I'd been with for three and a half years . . . that's been a great experience as well."

"So, have you lived in Oregon your whole life?"

"No, I was born in Spirit Lake, Idaho." Larry began to speak with a bit more hesitation. "When I was about four years old . . . my dad . . . my father left me then. He just left us. So we moved over to Spokane, where my mother met a fellow that was an itinerant worker. So every couple of months we'd move from one town to another. We went through a lot of small towns on our way to Hoquiam, Washington. And then from there we went south to Portland, Oregon. That was in 1940. So, since 1940, my home—except for my time in the service—has been in Oregon. There isn't any place I'd rather be."

"My wife and I . . . our nephew lives in Portland, and we've really come to enjoy Oregon. One of our favorite places to visit is Crater Lake National Park. We find it to be absolutely stunning—spiritual, really.

"I couldn't agree with you more. Isn't that just beautiful?"

"Larry, what did you do for a living after you left the service?"

"I used the GI Bill and got a couple of degrees; one in forest management and one in civil engineering. So, my career was with the federal government, in the Bureau of Land Management. I worked as a forester, then as a civil engineer, and as a manager. I loved my career. It was fascinating to me."

"Is there anything else about your time in the service that you would be interested in sharing with me?"

"Well . . . I remember being pretty gratified when a plane came in all shot up. That was on Majuro. I think it was a B-25, and the pilot and co-pilot stepped out with their pistols drawn. Ha ha . . . they didn't know where they were. It must've been only a week or two after we landed on the island ourselves."

"Larry, I really appreciate your service to our country, both during your time in the military and in all the years you spent with the Bureau of Land Management. And I want to thank you for taking the time to talk to me. As you correctly observed, documenting history, particularly seventy years after the fact . . . it is not that easy. I'm trying to get the facts straight, so I've been doing a lot of research, and it's taken me quite a bit of time. I'm hoping within a couple of years to have this book published."

"Good luck on that. I hope I'm around in a couple of years to enjoy reading it."

Larry Duncan: extremely nice guy, very humble, clearly made the most of his experience in the Navy. Never saw combat, didn't know anybody in his outfit that saw combat.

The other man whose contact information Bobby had given me was George Schlangen, from Colton, California. He was in C Company, the same as Murray, so I hoped he could provide me with a few more details. I called him, introduced myself, and asked him how he got involved in the Seabees.

"Well, I was seventeen years old and in high school. The Navy had a program called the V-12 program for kids to become officers while they were going to college. I passed all the tests, and I thought I was all set, and I went to Los Angeles to see if I was physically all right, and they told me I was color-blind. So they kicked me out of that program, and they told me that even though I couldn't get into the regular Navy, the Seabees would take me. They didn't care whether you were color-blind or not. That's how I got into the Seabees, when I was seventeen years old. That was in 1943. We went to boot camp first, and after about six weeks, we formed the 100th Battalion."

"So, did you stay with the 100th until the war ended?"

"Yes."

"So you landed with them on Majuro, in the Marshall Islands?"

"Yes, I did."

"Tell me what that experience was like."

"It was very good. We were very lucky. The Japs had left there to go to Eniwetok and Kwajalein. They left all their equipment, everything that they had . . . they just left it. And it was just a case of luck. If we'd have went to Eniwetok or Kwajalein, both of which are in the Marshall Islands, it might've been a different story. At Majuro, the Marines went in the first day, we went in the second day, and there was no Japs there, so we were very lucky."

"Do you know of anybody in your battalion who did go on to Kwajalein?"

"No. We had a group a few months later that went to Peleliu to build a facility for storing ammunition and fuel for the ships and for the airplanes. There were about twenty of them, mostly welders, and they were there probably for a month or two and then they came back. That was the only detachment that we had."

"Was that detachment from C Company?"

"Yes, at least one of them was. They were from all the companies, but one guy was in my own tent. His name was Jack Holland. He was from New Orleans. He was one of the fellows that went; I don't know the rest of them. But I do know that he went, because there was six men in a tent in those days, and he was one of the fellows that left for about two months."

"This guy Jack Holland . . . was he a friend of yours?"

"Well, we lived together in the same tent for about five or six months, so I guess you could say that."

"Ha ha! I suppose if you're living with somebody in a tent for six months, by the time you're done you're either friends or enemies."

"Yeah . . . we used to read each other's mail, so if you didn't get any mail you could read your buddy's mail. It was all right. There was no secrets amongst us; everybody was just a good friend."

"Do you know if he saw combat when he went to Peleliu or did he go in after the fighting was over?"

"The combat was over, I'm almost sure. And that's about all I know about that. We were just very fortunate. You know, just the luck of the draw. We could've went to a different island and it would've been a different story."

"What was your job in C Company?"

"I was with what they called the materiel crew. We went in on LSTs and they dropped the front ramp down, and all the materiel was unloaded in a hurry and dumped into one great big pile. Our job was then to sort it all out and get it to wherever it was needed. I was just a seaman at the time, and I was the only seaman on the crew. Everybody else had a rating but me. And there was about twenty-five or thirty of us."

"Did you ever come across any of the heavy equipment operators while you were there? Particularly any of the dragline operators?"

"Well, yes, one of the guys in my tent was . . . Jasper Shields. He was a seaman, like myself, but he became a dragline operator. A fellow name of Ray Proper took him under his wing and taught him everything he knew. Then also he became a heavy equipment operator for the state of Arkansas when he got out of the service."

"Did you happen to know a man by the name of Murray Jacobs? He was in C Company."

"The name is familiar . . . but I don't think I knew him that well. I think there was around two hundred and forty men to a company."

"Do you know if Jasper Shields is still alive?"

"No, he died about two or three years ago. We were very good friends for a very long time."

"I'm sorry for your loss. You know, one of the reasons that I've made this project a priority is that you guys are getting older and I want to get this historical information down, because you guys know stuff that nobody else knows . . . because you were there."

"Well, that's true, but . . . heh, heh . . . our memory gets a little old too, sometimes."

"I understand, I understand. I wish I had done this project ten years ago."

"That would've been good. You know, we started having reunions in about 1992, and we had close to a hundred people there that time, and now we're down to just a handful. There was eleven hundred and forty-seven men in our outfit, and I don't think there's very many left anymore. I was seventeen when I went in, I'm eighty-seven now . . . so you do the math. And the average age in our outfit was thirty years old."

"So, after you left Majuro, you went back to Pearl Harbor, and you were still with the 100th when they went to the Philippines . . . is that correct?"

"That's right. We were building a hospital there, and when the war ended, we just stopped work, and that was the end of it. We got shipped back home. I was a carpenter's mate, second class by that time."

"What did you do for a living after the war?"

"I became a plumber."

"Did you learn that trade in the Seabees?"

"No, I was a carpenter, did a lot of carpentry work, built a lot of quonset huts, but there was no demand for that when I got out. So, eventually I became a plumber, and I worked at Kaiser Steel over in Fontana for seventeen years as a pipefitter."

"Have you lived in California your whole life?"

"Yeah, I was born here, same town I'm in right now . . . Colton."

"When you look back on it, what's your overall opinion of your time in the military?"

"It was a necessary thing, I do believe. And I think the Seabees were necessary, too. They could've probably used Army Engineers just as well, but I think the Seabees served a very specific purpose. They had to build a base everywhere they went, as stepping-stones all the way across the Pacific. Because in those days, you know, planes couldn't travel as far as they do now—they'd run out of fuel. There was no way that they could have gone all the way from Hawaii to Japan. And Doolittle's raid was, I think, a joke because it didn't accomplish a helluva lot." [George is referring to the air raid by US B-25 bombers on Tokyo in April 1942, led by Lieutenant Colonel James Doolittle.]

"Well, it was really a public relations mission, to boost morale . . . don't you think?"

"It was . . . but was it worth it? Who knows? It was a one-way trip; they knew those bombers couldn't make it back to the carrier. They were sighted by a Japanese patrol boat before they had wanted to launch, so they took off farther from Japan than they should've. It was a sad situation. A lot of men got killed or captured."

"But some of the crews made it out, through China."

"Yes. I don't know the percentages. But the ones that wound up in Japanese hands had a rough time of it, to say the least. What we have always said is, 'If it wasn't for the Seabees, you'd be eating raw fish and rice instead of hamburgers and french fries.'"

"Ha ha! Yes . . . I think that's true, and I want to thank you for your service. It's because of men like you that men like me are free to do whatever it is that we choose to do. But I want to ask you that same question again, because you answered it in very general terms, about the war and about the Seabees. But what I really want to know is your opinion of your own personal experience in the Navy. Do you feel like it was a good experience for you? Did it enrich your life?"

"Oh, yes, yes, yes, yes, yes. I've met people from all over the country. So it was good. And it was necessary."

"So, you feel your life benefitted from being in the Seabees?"

"Well . . . in a way yes, and in a way no. I was all set to go to college and I lost interest in it after I got back home. So in a way it was good, but in a way it wasn't. Being in high school when the war started, and knowing that you were going to go in the service—not a good time for a young kid, I would say that."

"Were you nervous or scared when you were approaching the Marshall Islands? You didn't know what you were going to face when you landed on Majuro."

"We were too dumb to be scared. We were naive. I carried a BAR [Browning Automatic Rifle], which I felt was a pretty good weapon. If we'd have gotten into any combat, I would have felt very comfortable with that weapon. It weighed about twenty pounds fully loaded, you know. Each clip held about twenty rounds, and it had a tripod on the front if you had to lay it down."

"But you never saw combat; you never had to fire that weapon in anger at anybody."

"Nope. We were lucky. Just the luck of the draw."

"And your friend Jack Holland, who you said went over to Peleliu . . . it sounds like you remained friends with him after the war. He never shared with you that he saw any combat when he was on Peleliu?"

"I'm almost positive that he didn't."

"And is he also deceased?"

"Yes. He was older than I was. Jasper and I were the same age, but Holland was probably twenty-four or twenty-five at the time. So, yeah . . . he's gone."

"Is there anything else you'd like to share with me about your military experience?"

"Not really. I can't think of a thing. It was a necessary thing that happened, that's all I can say. We were attacked by Japan, and we had to do something."

"This book that I'm writing, it's taking quite a bit of time to get the research done properly. I want to portray history as accurately as possible. It has not been an easy task by any stretch of the imagination."

"Well . . . it's a little late, isn't it?"

"Yes, well . . . but I can only do what I can do. I wasn't born until 1961, so I'm doing the best I can. I came to know Murray Jacobs only a few years ago, and now I'm trying to tell his story. I want to thank you for your participation in this project, and I'd like to thank you once again for your service to our country. What you guys did all those years ago has made it possible for us to live our lives today. To me, the men of your generation built our country and allowed us to remain free, and I want you to know how much I appreciate you. Thank you very much, George."

"Well, OK. It's been a pleasure talking to you."

George Schlangen: sharp memory, straightforward, perhaps a bit curt. He knew two men who might have been extremely helpful: one, a dragline operator who would have definitely known Murray; the other, one of the seventeen men in the detachment to Peleliu who could have provided me with the details of that mission. But now they're both dead. Schlangen stated the obvious when he said I was too late getting into the game, but there's not a damned thing I can do about that now. All I can do is play the hand I've been dealt. Every person I've interviewed, every bit of evidence I've been able to gather, and there isn't anything to suggest that anyone in the 100th Naval Construction Battalion was involved in any violent conflict with the Japanese throughout the duration of the war.

I went back to see Murray about a week later, almost exactly a year after our first real interview. When I arrived, he was asleep in his chair by the front door. It took some doing, but I managed to awaken him. There was nobody else at home, so we sat in the living room. As soon as I sat down on the sofa, Tony, the Jack Russell terrier, made himself comfortable on my lap. Murray had the TV on in the background tuned to a station that was playing some light instrumental music. The house was eerily peaceful, especially compared to the usual chaos.

"Murray, when we first started talking about your life and about your past, you said to me, 'I think you might hate me by the time we're all done.' Do you remember telling me that?"

"Well . . . I should have reworded that. I thought that you would hate the man that I was—the man that we've been talking about. Because I hate that man. But I don't feel I'm that man anymore. I feel like I'm a different man. I don't think I'd be capable of doing the things I did back then. I don't mean physically—that's obvious—I mean morally I couldn't behave that way today. I did what had to be done, more or less. I mean, it wasn't only me—there was lots of guys that did the same like I did."

"I don't hate you—the man you were then nor the man you are today. But here's the thing . . . I'm going to say those same words back to you right now. Because I'm going to tell you something, and I hope you don't hate me when we're done."

"OK."

"We've spent a lot of time together, and I've enjoyed talking to you. And—I'm going to be very blunt about this—I've done a lot of research about everything you've told me. And to be perfectly honest, as far as I can tell, you were never in a combat situation at all. And all those things you told me that you did . . . you didn't do."

Murray stared at me, almost as if he were looking right through me.

"They were figments of my imagination."

I answered quietly, succinctly, "Yes." The word almost got stuck in my throat.

"OK. Let it go at that. Fine. No, I don't hate you for saying it. That's good. Because I don't like it anyhow." Murray looked away, and even after all the hours I had spent with him, I couldn't tell whether he was being genuine or sarcastic, whether he was angry or sad.

"I know you don't like it. And I can't figure out why it would be a figment of your imagination. Because I'll tell you one thing I know for a fact: I know you're not making it up or lying to me. I know that one hundred percent."

A silence fell between us. The mood had become somber; rays of sunlight were filtering in through the front windows, and soft music was emanating from the television. The room had suddenly taken on the aura of a funeral parlor. Although I had anticipated this conversation for months, I was at a loss for words. Finally, Murray spoke.

"I went on three different invasions. It was kill or be killed, and I killed at any opportunity I had." Murray grunted and looked at the floor. "I swore I wasn't going to go back and talk about this again. I'm not going to talk about it no more. I don't want to talk about it. I don't want to get riled up today."

"You know, I've debated for a long time whether to tell you this. But it's your life, and I feel that you have the right to know what I found out. I respect you, and that's why I've told you. Personally, I think that what I just told you is the secret that your sister's been keeping all these years. And she's not telling me, and she's not telling you either. That's what I think."

"Oh yeah? Well I talked to her just yesterday. I said, 'Why did you tell him we had a secret?' She says, 'I don't know.' And I said, 'Well if we have a secret, tell me what it is.' And she says, 'I don't know what it is.' So I don't think she's playing with a full deck."

"Well . . . that's possible, too." There was no way I could refute that statement. "Just so you know, as we talked about right at the beginning, I haven't talked to your family about any of this. It's between you and me."

"Yeah . . . everything is between you and me. But I've told you one thing, too. I told you that the military did not divulge everything that went on."

"But, just as an example, you told me about an officer you killed. I researched that guy, and I found out that he died in 1978. He didn't die during the war. I have his obituary."

"He died in '78? Good. Very good." This time the sarcasm was obvious.

"Doesn't it make you feel any better, knowing that you didn't do those terrible things that you told me about?"

"Not a bit. It don't make me feel a bit better. Nor worse. Neither one. I'm not going to let it bother me. You can believe what you want. You can throw the whole damned thing in the garbage can. That's fine with me."

"Well, I'm not doing that either."

Murray spoke haltingly, and his voice became muffled.

"I know one thing . . . I would've never agreed to this kind of a situation at all. I would never have put myself through all this."

"You regret doing it?"

"To a certain degree . . . yes."

That hurt me. My voice trembled as I muttered, "I'm sorry for that. I'm sorry for any pain I've caused you."

"Well . . . it's brought a lot of things to light that I hoped were over with, buried and dead. You've brought them to the forefront now, and I don't like that. I didn't realize, in the beginning, what this was going to entail. Had I realized it, I would have said no. And that's what I should have said."

"Well, for what it's worth, it's turned out quite differently than I thought it was going to turn out, too. I don't regret it though, because I feel that I've gotten to know you better, and I feel we've become friends."

"Yes, well, it's been very painful for me. When we first started, I said to you, 'There is no one that I know of who can substantiate what I'm going to say.' I told you about experiences I had during World War II. And I told you the truth. If you want to believe them . . . believe them. If you don't . . . don't. I can do nothing about it—not a thing. I didn't dream up a bedtime story for you. All I can say is, you take what I've said, sort the wheat from the chaff, and do what you want with it."

"There's a fallacy in what you just said to me. You said that if I want to believe it, I can, and if I don't want to believe it, I shouldn't. Quite honestly, I think that's not the right statement. Because I want to believe everything you've told me. But if I look at a body of evidence, and there are facts . . . "

"So, everything I've told you is just a big lie."

"I didn't say it was a lie."

"Yes, you did!" Murray was clearly angry now.

I was getting frustrated myself, and responded, "I said it didn't happen. There's a difference between a lie, and something that's incorrect. A lie is willful. I was hoping that by telling you this, somewhere in your mind it would alleviate some of the pain and guilt you've experienced over things that you think you did."

"I'll tell you . . . this is something that really hurts me. Because I went through hell. Why do you think I've been fighting PTSD? What do you think caused that? You don't think I have PTSD?"

"I do think you have PTSD."

"For ten years I woke up every night, sweat pouring down my face, my heart racing. What do you think I was having nightmares about? I fought this when I got out of the service, and them dirty, stinking bastards in the military didn't help me at all. They didn't know what was the matter with me. They said it was battle fatigue. I suffered. And I put my family through hell. My wonderful wife . . . why she stayed with me, I don't know. I put her through hell. Finally, I got hold of an old psychiatrist here at the VA—Dr. Schmidt. He had been in the war, and he knew exactly what was wrong with me. At first, I saw him twice a week, then once a week, and eventually, when I got to where I was feeling a little better, he cut it down to once a month. And I was very sorry when he died."

"You like your doctor at the VA now, right?"

"Yeah . . . she isn't bad. She's coming tonight at five o'clock. She comes here to the house; she don't make me go all the way there."

"Anyway, it might just be semantics, but there are two things that I want to make very clear to you. This is very important to me, because I care about you, and I have a lot of respect for you. The first thing is that I do not believe that you're lying. Number two, I want to believe every word you're telling me, with my heart and soul. Do you understand?"

"Yeah. But all your research says it's bullshit."

"The research says that your memory . . . your memories are incorrect."

"Why would I make this up?"

"Well, you're not making it up. I think your mind is playing tricks on you. That's my belief. I can't understand why your mind would concoct the things that you told me. I could understand making yourself out to be some kind of a hero. But I can't imagine why your mind would create some of the things that you feel so badly about. You told me things that you hate yourself for, and I don't believe that they actually took place. All the research I've done—I've talked to every living person in your battalion that I could find—and all the evidence I could gather convinces me that the things you told me did not happen. I don't know what else to say. Like that officer. You pointed to a picture of an officer. You said, 'That's the son-of-a-bitch, he looks exactly like the way he was.' Those are your words . . . you pointed right at him and you told me you killed him."

"I didn't exactly say I killed him."

"Well . . . there's nobody else here but you, me, and the dog. Let's call it what it was. And I thought about that, and I wrapped myself around it, and I didn't think less of you for it, because I felt like that was a part of where you were back then. And I could imagine myself in that same position—you're in a different world, not in the world here in Utah, but you're over there—seeing all kinds of shit and doing all kinds of shit that you wouldn't do otherwise. And I believed every word you said. And I still believe that you really think that happened, and you hate yourself for it. But I did research on that guy, and I found his obituary . . . in 1978 . . . in Indiana. So how could you have killed him? Unless you went to his house in Indiana in 1978."

"I don't want to talk about this anymore."

The two of us sat together for about thirty minutes. Mostly we were just quiet, listening to the music. I was petting the dog. Every now and then Murray would initiate some small talk about the weather or some local politics. Then, out of the blue, he said, "Somewhere on my discharge papers it says I was in combat."

"I thought you didn't want to talk about this anymore."

"I don't."

"Because if you want to talk about it . . . I'll talk about it. I have all your discharge papers. I'll tell you everything that's in there if you want."

"I don't."

I sat with Murray for another fifteen or twenty minutes, then I left. And that was it. We never spoke about the war again. In the months that followed, I'd visit him occasionally, bring him a root beer or some chocolate-covered almonds, and we'd chat about football or golf or food or about his health. But never about World War II. Our friendship devolved into something that was cordial but superficial. The elephant in the room was there, and we tried to ignore it, but it definitely had its effect on each of us, and on our relationship. I had so much that I wanted to tell him—about Yardbird and Bobby Arthurs and all the other men to whom I'd spoken, and about everything I had learned from the medical reports in his military file. But I never told him anything else.

Catherine informed me that her father passed away quietly on May 8, 2013, almost seventy years to the day after he boarded that Union Pacific Railroad train headed for basic training. I found myself sadder than I thought I'd be, although his death was hardly unexpected. The preceding month had seen him become increasingly weak, to the point of being completely bedridden and devoid of basic human functions. Perhaps I was sad because of his ultimate frailty and vulnerability, the same fate that awaits us all. Or perhaps I was mourning the death of a man with whom I had suddenly and unexpectedly developed an intense emotional connection, only to have that bond severed almost as abruptly as it was formed.

And in the end, what did I accomplish? About a month after Murray died, I happened to bump into Gita at a local market. Naturally, our conversation turned to the subject of Murray, and Gita shared with me something he had said to her in their final meeting—the session that took place only a few hours after my last interview with him. She said that he seemed rather serene and told her, "The war has left me now." What exactly had he meant by that? She was as puzzled by that statement as I was. Did I actually succeed in offering some tranquility to his otherwise troubled mind? Unlikely. He was probably just worn out by my lack of faith and tired of dredging up all the old memories, regardless of whether they were real or imagined. Or maybe it was just another of those vague, nebulous things he'd sometimes say. In any event, I'm left not knowing if I did more harm than good, just as I'll never know exactly what Murray did or didn't experience on those islands all those years ago. At least one thing is certain . . . now that he's dead, his dreams will stop, and his nightmare is finally over.

CHAPTER 17

I'D RATHER YOU DIDN'T

Murray's death brought my odyssey to what I thought was its natural conclusion. I had transcribed the audio from my last few interviews and was putting the finishing touches on the manuscript. But then, what I thought would be a routine encounter with another of my patients unexpectedly changed my perspective entirely.

I first met John Parnell in 2007, when he contacted me about treating his low back pain with acupuncture. John was born in North Carolina in 1930, and he grew up on a farm. A short, sturdy man with a full head of white hair and Coke-bottle glasses, John spoke with a pronounced Appalachian twang. In the course of taking his medical history, I learned that John had served in Army Logistics from 1948 until 1970, ultimately achieving the rank of master sergeant. He was part of the US occupation forces in Okinawa, and then served in both Korea and Vietnam. He was married for fifty-five years, but his wife died two years before I met him.

John's back pain responded very well to acupuncture, and I continued seeing him regularly about every six weeks. Naturally, I'd ask him about his military service, and he was always willing to share his recollections with me. He saw a fair amount of combat, but his only injury was a fracture of his left orbit [eye socket] that he suffered—while playing baseball—in Korea. It didn't earn him a Purple Heart, but he did require surgery, and it left him with a prominent nasal quality to his speech. John had a great memory, a sharp wit, and when he laughed his whole body shook as he cackled and grinned.

"There was this one time in Vietnam, around 1968, we were in support of the 1st Air Cavalry. We had to bring in some supplies, so I went with one other guy and the pilot in a Huey [Bell UH-1 helicopter]. Me and the other guy drew straws to see which one would stay in the chopper and man the fifty [.50 caliber machine gun] and which one would help unload the supplies. I lost, so I had to get out and start unloading, and the next thing I knew we was taking fire from the North Vietnamese. I turned around to get back in the chopper, and you know that sucker started taking off without me! I motioned for him to come back down, but he just kept on going, so I lowered my M79 [grenade launcher] and laid one right across his bow. I loaded up another round, and then he came back down to get me . . . hee, hee, hee. When I got back in the chopper the pilot says, 'You weren't really going to shoot me were you?' And I said, 'Well, let me put it to you this way . . . we was all going to go, or we was all going to stay.'"

I asked John about his time on Okinawa.

"Well, we were mostly on the south end of the island, around Naha, which is the capital. We didn't get up north too often. There was still a few Japanese soldiers hiding up there, and every now and then they'd come out of a cave and start shooting at us. But it didn't really amount to much, especially compared to what the Marines went through when they took the island in the first place. Probably the worst thing I experienced on Okinawa was a typhoon that must've lasted a week—worst storm I've ever seen. The wind was so bad it just tore some of our quonset huts to pieces. There were big sheets of corrugated steel flying all over the place . . . it's a miracle none of us were killed."

During one visit, I inquired whether John had ever witnessed any war crimes perpetrated by either United States or enemy troops. John told me the following story.

"When I was in Vietnam, there was always some local kids who would come around, do your laundry, polish up your boots, and that kind of thing. One time, these kids—who we had known for quite some time—came into the mess tent with their shoeshine box. I had just finished eating, and was a little ways from the tent, and the next thing I knew the whole tent blew up. Those kids had brought a bomb, or some grenades, in that box. I don't know how many of our guys were killed or wounded. Well, we saw those kids running away, and we shot every one of them. That's the thing . . . when you're in a war, you never can tell who's your friend and who's your enemy."

I asked John specifically if he had witnessed any misconduct by our servicemen while he was on Okinawa. He replied very hesitantly.

"Well . . . let's just say . . . we're not as clean as we appear to be. This one time, I was on a security detail, and I saw a guy raping a girl right there on the beach. I felt like shooting him right on the spot. But we grabbed him and turned him over to the military police. The thing is, after a while you'd get used to it, so a lot of times you just don't get involved."

Even after everything I'd learned, I still found that sort of incident to be disconcerting, and I struggled to understand the aberrant mentality that leads to such abhorrent behavior. I asked John whether he thought such men were inherently evil, their depravity simply enabled by their circumstances, or if these were decent men of otherwise moral character, corrupted by an absurd, violent situation.

"I think it's a little of both . . . probably fifty-fifty. You don't always have reliable, Christian souls there. And some of the younger guys would be bullied into doing certain things by the older guys. There was prostitution, too. There must've been a half-dozen brothels in downtown Naha. But that's everywhere; I saw it in Korea and Vietnam too. I wasn't brought up that way. I was taught to treat a lady with respect."

About two weeks after Murray died, I showed up at John's home for one of our regular sessions. John had just returned from seeing a doctor at the VA hospital, and he told me something that I found very interesting.

"You know, I saw a surgeon at the VA today, and I had never met him before, and he was being real thorough. He was looking through my file, and he says to me, 'How come it says here you were in the military from 1948 until 1970, but there's no record of where you were in 1963? According to your records, in 1963 you ceased to exist.' And I told him, 'That's because in 1963 I was in Laos . . . except we were never in Laos.' You see, we were never supposed to be in Laos, even though we were there. So, the military just eliminated me from existence for that year . . . no record of where I was, what I was doing, no medical records, nothing."

I found that to be very intriguing indeed. The Army had deliberately erased all evidence of a man's service for an entire year. So, was it possible—even remotely imaginable—that Murray was also involved in some sort of illicit mission, perhaps something that had gone so terribly awry that the Navy had redacted all proof that it had ever taken place? My curiosity was rekindled. Adding fuel to the fire, when I asked John for permission to use his name in this book, he thought about it for a moment and replied, "I'd rather you didn't. I think there's some things I've done, some places I've been, that the military would just as soon nobody knew about." Fascinating! After all these years—decades, really—John had been so indoctrinated with the idea that his actions were to be kept secret, that he still did not want his identity to be made public. So, in maintaining his anonymity, John Parnell is not his actual name.

I decided to scrutinize Murray's records yet again, this time with a fine-tooth comb, searching not only for any clues I might have previously overlooked, but also checking for any omissions, discrepancies, or mistakes that might have been made. Thinking back on several of the other men I'd interviewed, a recurrent theme was that their records were inaccurate. There was Don French, whose records didn't include one of the battalions in which he served. And Bobby Arthurs' records failed to indicate that he'd earned the World War II Victory Medal.

You'd think that a manila envelope would contain a finite number of pages and a fixed amount of data. But it seemed like every time I opened up Murray's file, I found something new. The first thing I took note of was the 'Remarks' section on Murray's "Notice of Separation from the U.S. Naval Service." It was blank. Where it should have said "Asiatic Pacific, One Star" just like Bobby Arthurs' did—because I know for a fact Murray was in the Marshall Islands—it said nothing. So, for certain, this document was inaccurate. This was confirmed by another piece of evidence: Murray's written transfer to the Naval Hospital in Aiea Heights (Hawaii) dated February 2, 1945, which specifically states, "Participated in the capture and occupation of Majuro Atoll, Marshall Islands, Feb. 1, 1944 to June 28, 1944."

The next item I came across, something I had somehow missed, was a single entry in his medical record, dated August 1, 1944. It simply states:

Examined this date and found to be physically qualified for temporary additional duty.

Now, what makes that entry particularly interesting is that the official itinerary of the 100th NCB, dated June 19, 1945, includes the following:

July 25, 1944 - One officer and seventeen men on temporary duty with pontoon detachment serving at Anguar [*sic*], Peleliu Islands.

Those dates are awfully close. It doesn't require a leap of faith to assume that the physical exam that Murray underwent was to clear him to participate in the detachment that went to Angaur and Peleliu. Additionally, I found a notation indicating that Murray was given a tetanus toxoid booster on July 31, 1944—perhaps also in preparation for the detachment to Angaur. But then again, there is a record of a dental examination having been done on September 16, and the invasion of Peleliu took place on September 15, and the invasion of Angaur on September 17, 1944. So, the only way Murray could've set foot on Angaur or Peleliu is if the date of that dental treatment is wrong—an error that is certainly plausible.

The next item was the "Summary of Service," which I have previously described, but will reprint here:

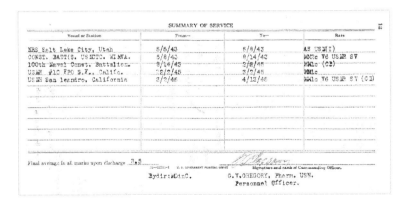

This is the next page, which I obviously did not examine closely enough before:

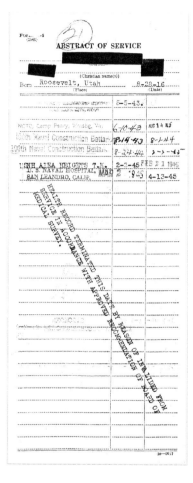

The "Summary of Service" has Murray with the 100th NCB from August 14, 1943, until February 2, 1945. The "Abstract of Service" has him with the 100th NCB from August 14, 1943, until August 1, 1944, then again from August 24, 1944, until February 2, 1945. Why don't the two forms correspond? Was it simply an oversight, or was he someplace the Navy didn't want documented in his records?

The mystery heightens: The next page I came across was a "Standard Transfer Order." I'd guess that the reason I didn't pay close enough attention to it before was that it is a very poor photocopy, barely legible. But it was dated August 23, 1944, and under the heading, "Ultimate Destination and Nature of Duty," it clearly states:

> Proceed, as your transportation may direct, and report [to]: Commanding Officer, 100th NCB, for duty. (Temporary detached duty completed this date).

So, I had an order directing him to return to the 100th after "Temporary detached duty," but from where? I went through his file several more times and couldn't find any evidence of any order sending him to any detached duty. Again . . . was this just an oversight? I had forms in triplicate indicating he returned some damned overcoat, half-a-dozen pages devoted to his life insurance, copies of every letter sent from every *schmendrick* in his neighborhood trying to get him discharged, but this one particular order, indicating where in the hell he was for three weeks in August of 1944, this piece of paper just happened to disappear.

I suppose it's possible that this particularly important document was lost, just by an unfortunate confluence of coincidence and incompetence. After all, I am a believer in Hanlon's Razor, which states, "Never attribute to malice that which is adequately explained by stupidity." But given everything I know about military cover-ups—not just from what John Parnell told me, but from stories like that of the USS *Indianapolis* or of Pat Tillman— I certainly didn't have a hard time convincing myself that from August 1, 1944 to August 23, 1944, Murray was someplace, doing something, that the Navy would just as soon nobody knew about.

[I am not going to elaborate on the events surrounding the sinking of the *Indianapolis* in 1945, nor on the death of Pat Tillman in 2004. Both were tragic, and involved egregious deception by the United States military. I would encourage the reader to explore these episodes in greater depth, and especially to read the outstanding book *Abandon Ship!* by Richard Newcomb.]

One possibility is that he did go with the detachment that was headed to Angaur, but for some unknown reason he was returned to the battalion after just three weeks, before the invasion took place. What could have been the reason? His medical records seem very thorough, so I have to believe that if it had been a health-related issue, there would have been some notation to that effect. Throughout his service, all of his conduct marks are excellent, so it seems unlikely to have been some sort of a disciplinary issue. So why would he have returned from the Angaur detachment prematurely?

A different scenario is that there was another detachment, right around the same time—one that was not only redacted from Murray's records, but that never made it into the official itinerary of the 100th. In August of 1944, the 100th NCB had already returned to Pearl Harbor, so where might such a detachment have gone? Could they have been sent to Guam or Tinian? The battles for those islands were in their latter stages by early August 1944. Both are about 3,800 miles from Hawaii, a journey of seven or eight days in an LST, shorter in a faster vessel. Either of those islands are a distinct possibility, although a very short turnaround would have been required, since Murray was back with the 100th after just twenty-two days.

Consider the Battle of Tinian, for example. On July 28, 1944, four days after the Marines landed on Tinian, and three days before Murray was cleared for "temporary additional duty," severe weather conditions resulted in damage to pontoon causeways, disrupting the unloading of supplies.[16] Theoretically, a detachment of Seabees might have been called upon to repair those causeways. Moreover, after the island was secured, fifteen thousand Seabees were needed to build a massive airfield on Tinian, from which B-29 Superfortress bombers would take off for attacks on the Japanese mainland (including the atomic bombs that were dropped on Hiroshima and Nagasaki). So, let's say that a detachment from the 100th was deemed necessary, and on July 31, Murray was administered his tetanus toxoid vaccine, and the next day he underwent the medical exam that cleared him for "temporary additional duty." The group departs from Pearl Harbor on August 1 and arrives on Tinian a week later on August 8. Or . . . could they have possibly arrived by August 3, as hostilities were ending and a flag-raising ceremony was being conducted? Was it a flag being raised on Tinian that Murray witnessed, only later to have the reality of what he saw supplanted in his jumbled memory by the more famous image from Iwo Jima?

One thing's for sure: If the Navy did try to redact all evidence of an entire detachment, something must have gotten really fucked up somewhere along the way. By August 10, four

Tinian Flag Raising Ceremony, 3 August 1944. From left to right: Vice Admiral Harry W. Hill, USN; Major General Harry Schmidt, USMC; Admiral Raymond A. Spruance, USN; Lieutenant General Holland M. Smith, USMC; Vice Admiral Richmond K. Turner, USN; Major General Thomas E. Watson, USMC; Major General Clifton B. Cates, USMC. (Official US Navy photograph, National Archives.)

thousand Japanese civilians had been killed on Tinian, and thirteen thousand were being held prisoner. So, could the Seabees in this hypothetical detachment from the 100th—including Murray—have participated in some of the criminal activities that we know were perpetrated by our servicemen in the Pacific? Execution of prisoners? Rape of local women? Killing of civilians? If not participants, could they have been witnesses? In either case, perhaps they were quickly whisked off the island and brought back to Pearl Harbor, to avoid any further embarrassment to the Navy. If this seems like a far-fetched and unrealistically cynical scenario, I would strongly suggest reading the excellent book, *Bringing Mulligan Home* by Dale Maharidge. It will eradicate any lingering fantasies you might have about World War II being somehow more sanitary than other conflicts, our soldiers innocent and virtuous.

Obviously, the situation I've created is entirely conjecture on my part, speculation at best and perhaps even hallucinatory. But Murray went *somewhere* for three weeks in August of 1944. A picture like the one I've painted—however outland-ish it may seem—would certainly explain Murray's lifelong nightmares and feelings of guilt. It would even explain how his records could have accurately described him as having never experienced combat, although he would have nonetheless been exposed to the horrors of war. Maybe he hated Blair because he was the officer who sent him on that detachment. Maybe he *wished* he had killed him. And it's also interesting to recall that Murray's frantic efforts to get himself discharged from the Navy began only a couple of months after he returned to the 100th in November 1944. Of course, the seeds for that debacle were planted long before, as evidenced within the letters he wrote to his wife in 1943. But maybe his sister Evelyn, who died just a few months after Murray, was the only person he ever told about what really happened on that detachment. And maybe that truth was the secret that Evelyn guarded so stringently.

It's perhaps equally likely that during those three weeks in August Murray was sent on some routine temporary detail over to the other side of Oahu, for a job as mundane as repairing a latrine or building a new officer's club. And he could have gotten his photos of Peleliu from one of the men who actually did go on the detachment to that island; maybe from George Schlangen's buddy, Jack Holland. And maybe Murray heard stories about Peleliu from the men who were there, and he in-corporated those stories into his own experience as a means of avoiding the shame that must have accompanied his discharge due to "Psychoneurosis, Anxiety Neurosis." And maybe after seventy years of having the same stories cluttering his mind, he became absolutely, subconsciously convinced that it had all re-ally happened, right down to the sordid details. And maybe the only person he ever told the truth—that he never experienced combat—was his sister, who took *that* secret with her to the grave. And maybe . . . well, just maybe. "Maybe" is all I've got. I couldn't get at the truth before Murray died, so how the hell am I ever going to get at it?

I did come upon one more interesting discrepancy in the final pages of Murray's medical file. Upon Murray's discharge from the US Naval Hospital in Aiea Heights (Hawaii) on Febru-ary 21, 1945, Captain Howard K. Gray, chief of surgery, clearly noted that Murray's condition did NOT exist prior to enlistment (DNEPTE). This is reiterated upon his admission to the US Naval

Dr. Howard Kramer Gray, with President Franklin D. Roosevelt, 1938.

Hospital in San Leandro, California on March 2, 1945. However, on April 2, 1945, Commander James Humbert, senior member of the Board of Medical Survey, specifically states that Murray's condition DID exist prior to enlistment, and that it was NOT aggravated by military service. Now, what are we to make of that? Just another little mix-up? I seriously doubt that. A careless rubber-stamp by the doctor in Hawaii? Highly unlikely. Captain Howard Kramer Gray was no miscellaneous quack— he was a highly decorated physician, who operated on James Roosevelt (FDR's son) in 1938; had served in the Navy since December 1941; saw action at Eniwetok, Kwajalein, Saipan, and Guam; and who, after the war, proceeded to become the chief of surgery at the Mayo Clinic.[17] Not the sort of doctor who'd be prone to mistakes. One may presume that this abrupt and unexplained reversal of diagnosis was a purposeful attempt by the Board of Medical Survey to limit the Navy's responsibility to take care of whatever medical or psychiatric problems Murray might develop subsequent to his discharge. One might wonder how many other records were similarly falsified, resulting in countless veterans of that era being abandoned by the military, left to deal with their "battle fatigue" on their own. After the war, the Bowery was probably full of such veterans, all trying to find the answers to their "existed prior to enlistment" problems at the bottom of a bottle.

Let's just think about this for a minute. If Murray was so screwed up in April 1945 that he was deemed unfit for service—at a time when the military had such a desperate need for manpower that they had recently lowered the standards for being draft-eligible—and he was really just as screwed up in 1943, and his service didn't make him any worse, then how could the Navy have accepted him in the first place? So even if his anxiety, or neurosis, or whatever you want to call it, did predate his induction into the military—which I definitely believe to be true—then certainly it must have been exacerbated by his experience in the Navy. At a minimum, the Board of Medical Survey was wrong. More likely, they were intentionally trying to attenuate their liability, and thereby reduce the benefits to which Murray might have otherwise been entitled. And it does not require much imagination to believe that this was one more brick in a wall of denial—a further attempt to completely obliterate whatever it was that Murray experienced overseas from the annals of history. Perhaps the Navy didn't want you to know what Murray experienced during the war. No . . . they'd rather you didn't.

CHAPTER 18

I WASN'T THERE

Sometimes you have a "lightbulb moment." An instant of great mental clarity and insight, and you can pinpoint exactly when it happened.

This is not one of those times.

I spent weeks, even months, ruminating about what Murray did or didn't experience, wondering how I could possibly gather any more information. At some point—I have no idea how or exactly when—I came to the realization that I did, indeed, have one piece of physical evidence at my disposal that could potentially provide me with one more clue. The knife.

Murray told me that he had given his knife to his grandson, Jason. The knife that was handcrafted in Utah in 1943. The knife that Murray took with him when he went overseas. The same knife with which Murray claimed to have gutted a Japanese soldier. I knew it was a long shot, after seventy years, but if there was evidence of human blood on that knife, then perhaps I would have one more link to the past, another glimpse at the ever-elusive truth.

I contacted Jason, who still had the knife in his possession. He gave it to Catherine, who brought it to me. As I contemplated how I could get the knife tested, Julie reminded me that our friend, Tom Fuller, had been the director of the Histocompatibility and Immunogenetics Laboratory at the University of Utah. Tom had recently retired, but I asked him if he would be willing to help. Sure enough, Tom was both willing and able. He sent the knife to one of his former colleagues, Kevin T. Williams, senior technologist at the H & I Lab.

To the naked eye, the knife looked clean. Both Tom and Kevin, in their experience with forensic analysis, suggested that if there were any blood that could be tested on the knife, the best place to find a hidden specimen would be in the crotch between the handle and the blade. The first procedure Kevin performed used a commercial kit, manufactured by Qiagen, and it failed to isolate any detectable DNA. This was disappointing, but not an unexpected result. Persevering, Kevin subsequently tried a different DNA isolation kit, from Promega Corp., and that did yield a DNA isolate. When I asked Tom why the tests produced different results, he explained, "The reason for the differences in success will never be clarified, as the kits marketed by these companies are proprietary with regard to the exact reagents and formulations used to isolate DNA. One kit is not necessarily better than the other, rather it may possibly be related to the source material; very old, non-preserved, desiccated material as opposed to fresh, liquid blood."

This was very exciting news—evidence of human DNA on the knife. Of course, the DNA could belong to either Murray or Jason, the only two people, as far as I know, to have had the knife in their possession. This is an important possibility to rule out, although the fact of the matter is that I own dozens of knives, and I'm pretty sure none of them have my DNA (or anyone else's, for that matter) on the blade. Anyway, if any conclusions were to be drawn about the specimen on the knife, it would be essential to make certain that it wasn't blood from Murray or Jason. Murray was no longer around to provide me with a DNA sample for comparison, so I used the next best source: Catherine. If her DNA did not correspond to the DNA isolated from the knife, it would eliminate both Jason and Murray as a potential source.

[I acknowledge that this conclusion requires one to accept as fact that Murray is Catherine's biological father. In the course of my decade-long relationship with this family, and throughout my extensive interviews with Murray, Catherine, and even Evelyn, there has never been the slightest hint of infidelity on the part of Catherine's mother, Phyllis, or any question of the veracity of Murray's paternity. Therefore, I am comfortable with this assumption, although I recognize that it falls a bit short of incontrovertible.]

This next level of testing involved a procedure called HLA typing. Human Leukocyte Antigens (HLA) are proteins found on white blood cells. They are inherited from each parent, and allow the immune system to distinguish the body's own proteins from the proteins of foreign invaders such as viruses and bacteria. There are over 7,000 subtypes of HLA proteins in humans, divided into groups that include A, B, DRB, and DQB. Each parent contributes a specific, intact sequence of these proteins (called a haplotype) to their offspring, resulting in a combination that is unique to every person. Because of the extraordinary diversity that has evolved in humans, the chance of two unrelated individuals having an identical sequence of HLA proteins is unlikely, although possible. Since the proteins are inherited, there are differences observed between different ethnic groups, and between people from different geographic locations.

The test that Kevin performed was a solid-phase, high-resolution, reverse sequence-specific oligonucleotide hybridization DNA typing procedure, using a commercial kit manufactured by One Lambda, Inc., a branch of Thermo Fisher Scientific. (Don't worry, there will not be a quiz at the end of this chapter.)

The specific HLA typing of the specimen on the knife was:

Haplo-type	A	B	DRB	DQB
1	3	14	4	03:02
2	30	35	14	06:09

The fact that only one group of HLA proteins was found means that only one person's blood contaminated this knife.

Catherine's HLA typing is as follows:

Haplo-type	A	B	DRB	DQB
1	68	7	04:04/23	03:02
2	68	44	13:01	06:03

Since neither of Catherine's haplotypes is identical to one of the haplotypes found on the knife, and since she would, by definition, have to share one haplotype with her father and one with her son, this result indicates that the blood found on the knife does not belong to either Murray or Jason.

The next question is whether we might be able to determine more details about the person whose blood is on the knife. To answer this question, I enlisted the assistance of two of Julie's colleagues, LaDee Dangerfield and Linda Meaux. When someone needs a bone marrow transplant to treat cancer or certain other life-threatening diseases, a donor needs to be located who has the same HLA type as the patient, in order to prevent the patient's body from rejecting the donor bone marrow, and to protect the patient from being harmed by the donor bone marrow. The National Marrow Donor Program (NMDP) is a database of 12.5 million volunteers who have undergone HLA typing to see if they could be a potential match for someone with an illness that might be cured with a bone marrow transplant. [If the reader is interested in learning more about the NMDP, and possibly registering as a life-saving donor, please visit the website www.bethematch.org. The NMDP has facilitated over 50,000 unrelated transplants worldwide over the past twenty-five years.]

LaDee and Linda conducted a "world book search" of the NMDP registry in an attempt to find other people with the precise HLA typing found on the knife. Potential donors are only partially typed due to the expense, and once a potential donor is identified, the complete HLA typing is done to determine if there is an exact match. In a database consisting of 12.5 million individuals, the person whose blood is on the knife had ZERO exact matches, and only two donors who were even close: a fifty-one-year-old black female who registered in 1994, and a thirty-two-year-old white female who registered in 2006. Each of these individuals had only a two percent chance of even being a seven-eighths match for the blood on the knife. According to Julie, "Each protein on the knife is not uncommon in and of itself, but the rarity is the combination of the proteins. These are never seen together in one person. This combination is so rare that if the person whose blood is on the knife were alive today, and came to me with a life-threatening disease that required a bone marrow transplant, I would have to tell them that there is no donor available anywhere in the world to save their life."

One final question is whether there is anything about this combination of proteins that might give us a clue as to the ethnic or geographic ancestry of the individual from whom the blood originated. A careful analysis of the global database of HLA typing revealed that the ethnic descent of the person whose blood is on the knife could not be determined. There was no statistical correlation between the blood on the knife and any one population of people, such as Japanese, Pacific Islands, Caucasian, etc. However, it is unlikely that the person was from

Utah, as Julie tells me that amongst her patients here, where the population is fairly homogeneous, there is generally a thirty percent probability of identifying a match in the NMDP.

To summarize this unavoidably scientific, rather technical report, Murray's knife had concrete evidence of blood on it. The blood was of human origin, and there had to have been enough of a specimen initially that after who knows how many years, there was still an adequate amount of blood present to provide a usable sample. The blood came from just one person. That person is neither Murray nor Jason, the only two people known to have had the knife in their possession. The person's ethnicity can't be determined, but they were almost certainly not from Utah. And their blood is so rare that not a single match could be found from a search of millions of people around the world. To whom did the blood once belong? And how did it come to be on a knife that belonged to Murray Jacobs? Did this blood once flow through the veins of a Japanese soldier, whose unique genetic line was forever terminated when he was killed on the island of Tinian? Pure speculation, of course. The fact of the matter is that by analyzing the knife I did not clarify the truth—I made it far more complicated.

So, in the end, what story is this? It could be the story of a troubled, nervous young man, who enlisted in the Navy even though he had a deferment, in order to escape the unwanted rigors of family life, who then became increasingly anxious while overseas even though he was never in harm's way, ultimately being declared unfit for duty, and who, while in the psychiatric ward of a Naval hospital, was exposed to the vivid stories of other men who had actually been in combat in the Pacific, and later adopted those stories, and maybe even someone else's photographs, as his own, in an attempt to hide from the embarrassment of having been mustered out of the Navy, and perhaps as an excuse for his otherwise immoral behavior, gradually and subconsciously incorporating those vicarious experiences into his own memory, weaving his comrades' nightmares into the fabric of his own dreams, to the point of developing all the classic symptoms of PTSD, as diagnosed and treated by an expert psychologist, living the remainder of his life absolutely convinced he had seen things that he did not actually see and done things that he did not actually do.

Or . . . perhaps it is the story of a narcissistic man who enlisted in the Navy because he didn't care about anyone but himself, who sought out the freedom the Navy might offer, at least relative to the burden of having a wife and two daughters, allowing him the opportunity to pursue his relentless philandering, and who, in the course of his otherwise mundane service, found himself unexpectedly on a mission during which a Japanese prisoner was tortured, or a civilian was murdered, or a woman was raped, or some combination of the above, or some equally abhorrent transgression that may have involved a knife that was manufactured in Utah, an event whose very existence was deliberately redacted in its entirety by the United States Navy; an incident which he vowed to keep veiled in secrecy but which haunted him, resulting in his discharge due to "Anxiety Neurosis" and eventually evolved to become PTSD, his mind creating all sorts of imaginary details that served to disguise the sordid reality of what actually happened, constructing nightmares designed to camouflage the abomination of what he and his comrades experienced, until the line between real and imagined memories became so blurred that even he couldn't tell the difference.

I believe now that I will never know the truth. I will forever wonder what took place on those islands seventy years ago. Because when it's all said and done, I wasn't there. And the man who was there is dead. And he didn't know the truth either—he only thought he did.

MM1C Murray Jacobs.

NOTES

1. Olsen, Capt. A.N., USN (Ret.) CEC. "The King Bee: A Biography of Admiral Ben Moreell." Trafford Publishing, 2007.

2. www.ibiblio.org (Building the Navy's Bases Online: Majuro, in the Marshall Islands).

3. The Pacific War Online Encyclopedia: www.pwencycl.kgbudge .com.

4. Digital Micronesia-An Electronic Library and Archive (marshall.csu.edu.au).

5. Harris, Sheldon. "Factories of Death: Japanese Biological Warfare 1932-1945 and the American Cover-up." Routledge, 2002.

6. Erickson, George E. "U.S. Navy War Crimes Trials 1945-1949." Washburn Law Journal (1965).

7. Bergerud, Eric. "Touched With Fire : The Land War in the South Pacific." Viking Penguin 1996.

8. Harrison, Simon. "Skull Trophies of the Pacific War." 2006 Journal of the Royal Anthropological Institute.

9. Fussell, Paul. "Thank God for the Atom Bomb, and an After-word on Japanese Skulls." (1988).

10. Nevada Daily Mail June 13, 1944.

11. New York Times, "Roosevelt Rejects Gift Made of Japanese Bone" 8/10/1944 Page 30.

12. Harvard Gazette : www.harvard.edu ("The Frank Knox Memorial Fellowships: Who was Frank Knox?").

13. www.uscg.mil/history/. The US Coast Guard Historian's Office Official Website.

14. www.abcnews.go.com February 10, 2001.

15. www.history.navy.mil National Museum of the U.S. Navy (100th Naval Construction Battalion).

16. Rottman, Gordon L. and Gerrard, Howard (2004) "Saipan and Tinian 1944: Piercing the Japanese Empire." Oxford: Osprey Publishing.

17. findagrave.com.

18. www.history.army.mil U.S. Army Center of Military History.

ACKNOWLEDGMENTS

This project would not have been possible without the unwavering support of my beautiful wife, Dr. Julie Asch. She has been my biggest fan, my muse, and the light at the end of my tunnel. She has also been my primary source of income for the duration of this endeavor.

I am eternally grateful to my three beloved nephews: Peter Asch, Ben Asch, and Saul Levy. They are special young men, each with a unique perspective and a particular set of skills that I find to be perpetually helpful.

I am indebted to Bridget Shears for providing me the technical means with which I conducted all of my interviews. Which basically means I borrowed her tape recorder and never returned it. Now I'm using it for the next book.

I would like to recognize the contribution of my "CSI" team of Tom Fuller, Kevin Williams, Linda Meaux, and LaDee Dangerfield. You all know a lot of cool stuff that the rest of us don't know, and you provided one final piece to a puzzle that remains unfinished.

Special thanks to Dr. Joseph Helms for teaching me acupuncture, Dr. Richard Kravath for teaching me about electrolytes, and Dr. Joe Perno for teaching me about Utah. You all played a role in this project, and perhaps you will find yourselves amongst the deleted scenes on the DVD.

A special word of thanks to Dr. Ruth Zimmer, for her encouragement, sound advice, and uncompromising positivity. A pessimist like me can always benefit from an optimist's bright (albeit disturbing) outlook.

Thanks to Lawrence Knorr at Sunbury Press, for giving a fledgling author a chance. Thanks to Terry Kennedy for his beautiful design of the cover, and Crystal Devine for her wonderful design of the book. Thanks to my editor, Kate Matson, for making me think, keeping me honest, and teaching me a thing or two (or three) along the way.

Finally, I am forever beholden to Murray's family, especially "Catherine" and "Jason." Their trust in me was limitless, and it allowed me to bring to fruition an accomplishment that would have been otherwise impossible. Thank you for welcoming me into your home and ultimately into your family. I hope I have created a work of which you can all be proud.

ABOUT THE AUTHOR

Dr. Scott Zuckerman was born in Brooklyn, New York, and attended Stuyvesant High School in lower Manhattan. His high school English teacher, Frank McCourt—who would later win a Pulitzer Prize for his memoir, *Angela's Ashes*—inscribed in his yearbook, "You have displayed the writer's gift. Cultivate it." Forty years later, after a successful career as a physician, Zuckerman has heeded McCourt's advice. *Dreams of My Comrades* was awarded first place in the nonfiction category of the 2015 Utah Original Writing Competition.

Photo by Jake Shane, courtesy of the *Park Record*.